ISBN 978-1-331-59018-7
PIBN 10209813

1 MONTH OF
FREE
READING

at
www.ForgottenBooks.com

By purchasing this book you are
eligible for one month membership to
ForgottenBooks.com, giving you
unlimited access to our entire
collection of over 1,000,000 titles via
our web site and mobile apps.

To claim your free month visit:
www.forgottenbooks.com/free209813

English
Français
Deutsche
Italiano
Español
Português

www.forgottenbooks.com

Mythology Photography **Fiction**
Fishing Christianity **Art** Cooking
Essays Buddhism Freemasonry
Medicine **Biology** Music **Ancient**
Egypt Evolution Carpentry Physics
Dance Geology **Mathematics** Fitness
Shakespeare **Folklore** Yoga Marketing
Confidence Immortality Biographies
Poetry **Psychology** Witchcraft
Electronics Chemistry History **Law**
Accounting **Philosophy** Anthropology
Alchemy Drama Quantum Mechanics
Atheism Sexual Health **Ancient History**
Entrepreneurship Languages Sport
Paleontology Needlework Islam
Metaphysics Investment Archaeology
Parenting Statistics Criminology
Motivational

JOHN CHINAMAN AT HOME

SKETCHES OF MEN, MANNERS AND THINGS IN CHINA

BY

THE REV. E. J. HARDY, M.A. *Think*

CHAPLAIN TO H.B.M. FORCES *you write*

AUTHOR OF " HOW TO BE HAPPY THOUGH MARRIED "

ILLUSTRATED

SECOND IMPRESSION

LONDON: T. FISHER UNWIN
1 ADELPHI TERRACE. MCMVI

First Impression, 1905.
Second Impression, 1906.

To

SIR HENRY BLAKE, G.C.M.G.,

A FORMER JUST AND ENLIGHTENED GOVERNOR OF HONG KONG

FROM WHOM AND FROM LADY BLAKE I RECEIVED

MUCH INFORMATION AND KINDNESS,

THIS BOOK IS DEDICATED.

Preface

—◦◊◦—

WHEN I went to China I had a great ambition. It was to gain the distinction of not writing a book on that country. I failed to do this because of the fascination of the subject, and my only excuse is that things Chinese are so many and so complicated that there is room for every independent inquirer and observer.

Many Europeans live in China for years without learning anything of the habits and customs of the people. They tell you that these are "beastly," and that they take no interest in them. As for the ordinary globe-trotter, to him it may be said, in the words of the prophet Isaiah, "Thou seest many things but thou observest them not." To take no interest, however, in a nation that was contemporary with ancient Egypt, Babylon, Nineveh, Greece and Rome, and that has staying power in it still, is stupid. Though stupid in other respects, I was not in this, for I heard, read, and observed everything I could about a people who are always peculiar though not always zealous of good works during the three years and a half when I was Chaplain to the Forces at Hong Kong, and when I was from time to time on leave of absence in China proper. The villages in the New Territory, where I often went on military manœuvres and field-days, taught me much.

It was not necessary to solve the problem of China or to give advice to the Foreign Office, as that has been done by every writer who has spent two days in Hong Kong and one in Canton. Only the everyday Celestial things that interested and puzzled me when I first came out have been described. It is a book for unlearned visitors to China. I have not spoken of my work as Chaplain to the Forces, as this has been done in a former book—"Mr. Thomas Atkins."

Whatever is said of China—a country which is a hundred and four times larger than England—will probably be true only of some parts. "Customs differ every tenth li," and it would be impossible that a population as great as that of the whole of Europe should all act alike.

To master the Chinese language thoroughly would require "a head of oak, lungs of brass, nerves of steel, a constitution of iron, the patience of Job, and the lifetime of Methuselah." How clever of the Chinese to be able to speak to each other! I felt that unless Chinese were spoken in the other world it would be no good in my trying to learn it.

But even those who know his language cannot get a Chinaman to explain. Ask him why a thing is so and so. He answers that it always has been that way, and if you are not satisfied he thinks that it is you and not he who is unreasonable. Then the Chinese delight to astonish foreigners, and freely lie in order to do so. An inhabitant of Canton being told that the King of Great Britain was, on certain occasions, drawn in a carriage by eight cream-coloured horses, answered without a moment's hesitation, "China Emperor twenty-four!"

Contents

11

List of Illustrations

KOWLOON.

To face page 23.

CHAPTER I

HONG KONG

Meaning of the word and description—Population—No useless restrictions—
The furthest sentry-box of the British Empire—A cosmopolitan Clapham
Junction—"Green hills with sea scattered amongst them"—The
Botanical Gardens—Birds and insects—Varied human beings—"Heard
in the tram"—Climate—Cost of living—"Distended with food"—
Bathing parties—Some civilians nicer than others—Bachelor messes—
Games—The races.

HONG KONG, the meaning of which is either "Good
Harbour," or "Fragrant Streams," is one of a group
of islands off the south-east coast of China. It is ten miles
long, with a mean breadth of about three miles; it is rugged
and mountainous, and there is but little of it that can be
cultivated. The colony embraces the peninsula of Kowloon,
some four miles in extent off the mainland, and, in addition,
the neighbouring territory, including, with islands, about 370
square miles, which has recently been leased (that is, given
through fear) to Great Britain.

The population of Victoria, the capital of the island and
of Kowloon opposite it, is 325,631 Chinese and 18,581 non-
Chinese. Most of the Chinese are males; they leave their
wives at Canton, from whence they come, because they do
not trust European morals or because these ladies can live
cheaper there. Do the grass widowers want their clothes
mended? There are women wearing owlish spectacles who
sit at street-corners and earn a living with their needles.

The worst of the Chinese is that there are so many of them. They get on your nerves. No matter what you are doing, you feel that you are being overlooked. The celestial part of Hong Kong is more crowded than any place except a herring-barrel, and there are always more people wanting to come into it. In Hong Kong there is no "squeezing," a fact which, in the opinion of the Chinese, compensates even for the necessity of acquiring cleaner habits. It was a pathetic sight during a water famine to see the orderly way in which thousands of Chinese, each having empty buckets, were marshalled in long lines by British European soldiers to get water that was brought from a distance in water-boats. This paternal care of Government is not appreciated, however, when it forcibly cleanses a house in which a person has had plague. To prevent such sanitary nonsense, as the Chinese think it, they will conceal a dead person as long as possible in a house if unable to dump the corpse down in the street.

In things indifferent, however, there is in Hong Kong an amount of liberty that agreeably surprises foreign visitors. They are not worried about passports or asked what they are going to do or how much money they have. There are none of the useless restrictions which the meddlesome officialism of French and German colonies invent. Approximate to decent behaviour in our Hong Kong shop for all nations, and you can do what you like.

An Irish soldier, when ordered to Hong Kong, remarked that they could not send him further from home without sending him nearer. Hong Kong is the furthest sentry-box of the British Empire, and is nearly as important to us as Malta and Gibraltar. China is likely to be the cockpit where European nations will fight. It certainly is the problem of the twentieth century, and we must keep a strong fleet in her waters to watch the solution of the problem. For this fleet Hong Kong is the coaling-station. As for foreign ships of war, they come to Hong Kong in such numbers and so often that no fewer than 240 guns were fired in salutes in the harbour in one day.

But in addition to being a most important outpost of empire, Hong Kong is a sort of cosmopolitan Clapham Junction, where passengers change and goods are transhipped for everywhere. If we British cannot take pride in the way we came by the place, we may in what we have done with it. When we took Hong Kong, sixty-four years ago, there were only a few fishermen's or pirates' huts upon it; now it is, if not the first or second, at least the third port in the world. The harbour, which looks like a lake, is ten miles long and from one to five wide. It is surrounded by many-coloured hills of trap and granite. Words cannot depict the cloud-effects over these hills or the beauty of the sun setting behind them.

There is not the tropical vegetation of Ceylon and Penang, but Hong Kong has a weird beauty of its own. The view at night from the sea, when the lights of the ships and of the houses on the hillsides seem to mingle with the stars, is unsurpassed. "Well, at all events," I said to a grumbler who was looking with me at one of the views, "you cannot deny Hong Kong beauty." "What is it, after all," she answered, "but green hills with sea scattered amongst them?" To this kind of women, the sigh of a lover, a drop of dew, and a primrose on a river brink are only wind, water, and vegetable. Another lady remarked in my hearing: "Hong Kong is a place to see, but not to live in." May she never be in a worse place!

The Botanical Gardens are beautifully laid out, and contain so many large, thick-leaved indiarubber trees that you can always get a shaded walk. There is generally some new flowering tree to be seen. Most tropical trees have leaves all the year, the old ones not falling off until the young ones appear; and the buds that will mature into green leaves are red when they first come out, blushing like *débutantes*. The trees in spring have the tints of autumn in Western lands, and the azaleas flower with a glory that would have made Solomon look foolish. In the New Territory, rice, fruit, sugar, and vegetables grow, and so plentiful are pineapples that they sell for two cents each, wholesale.

It is worth coming to Hong Kong to see the moths, beetles, butterflies, and spiders. From the tip of one wing of an Atlas moth to the tip of another is sometimes as much as eleven inches. One butterfly looks as if it were dressed in a swallow-tailed coat of black and blue velvet. On warm days *cicada* make a whizzing sound by the vibration of two flaps under the abdomen.

So many beautiful birds labelled to belong to Hong Kong are in the museum and so few outside that it would almost seem as if they had nearly all obtained the immortality of stuffing. However, I have seen a few very beautiful ones outside, generally near Stanley, the place where the British tried first to live in.

And the specimens of human beings seen in the streets of Victoria are not less varied—Chinese, Cingalese, Japanese, Koreans, Malays, Parsees, Portuguese. Like a statue a Sikh policeman stands at a street-corner, and Indian soldiers wearing brilliant turbans stride by on pipe-stem legs inserted into very long shoes.

The sanitary arrangement of Victoria falls between two stools, being a mixture of the no-drainage or carrying-away system that best suits Chinese cities and the European plan. The almost entire absence of dust and mud in Hong Kong in all seasons is agreeable and healthy.

Hong Kong is built as it were in three layers or storeys. Business is done on the ground floor, on the second storey are dwelling-houses and gardens, and to top-side, as the Peak is called, come in summer Europeans who can afford to be cool. The Peak includes the hills, eighteen hundred and twenty-five feet high, south of Victoria. It is connected with the town by a cable tramway. The journey occupies only seven minutes, but in less time than this a reputation may be slain, and "Heard in the tram" is the authority for many a lie. Those who travel up and down in the tram two or three or four times a day get very tired of each other. One can meet a person twice a day with breezy enthusiasm, but the third time the smile of recognition is sickly, and the fourth time there is an incipient scowl. To those not accustomed to the tram the houses on either side look as if they were toppling over. New-comers hold on to their seats and murmur, "Oh my!" It is a funny experience being carried in a chair on the Peak. You only want a feeding-bottle and a rattle to be a baby once more, and when those who bear you talk you are reminded of Balaam's ass.

From November to April the climate of Hong Kong is usually delightful. Practically, no rain falls during this period, which is that of the north-east monsoon; day after day brings a clear blue sky, a warm sun, and a cool, dry, northerly wind. In the evening fires are often required. The remainder of the year is the hot and rainy season, and when it does rain in Hong Kong it knows how to do it. The rainfall in twenty-four hours has been as much as in a whole year in England. Even on the lower levels the thermometer rarely goes above 90° F., but this is much more trying than the same temperature in places with a drier atmosphere. Walk a hundred yards, and when in motion you may not feel very warm, but when you stop you are bathed in perspiration. Then the Peak of Hong Kong, which saves those who live on it, destroys those who do not, for it prevents the wind that prevails in summer from ventilating the city of Victoria. At the Peak the thermometer is from six to eight degrees lower than at Victoria. There are fewer Chinese, and the nights are noiseless. There is, however, one great drawback to the Peak. Every now and then in spring and summer it is shrouded in a fog that suggests suicide, and mildews gowns, hats, and other vanities.   This last is not altogether a disadvantage, as the airing of their clothes gives ladies something to do during the hot part of the day, when they cannot go out.   If you live on the Peak your clothes rot ; if you live below, you rot.   True, some escape with their lives, but they will probably have lost first their teeth, then their hearing, and then their minds.

Very often it is their own fault, for people in Kong Kong take liberties with their health such as they would not take at home.   They should avoid chills, keep out of the sun and club bars, and remember that the man who eats little eats much, because he lives longer to eat.   If only grown-up people were as wise as children !   Children thrive on the Peak, and sealed bottles of very good milk can be bought for them.

The worst evils in life are those that do not come, and this is often the case with those awful storms called typhoons. They are signalled, our houses are shut up, and we swelter in darkness.   Mr. Typhoon is afraid of the scandal and other disagreeables of Hong Kong, and goes elsewhere.   When he does come, however, he destroys houses, shipping, and sometimes human life.   If you venture out, you have to go on your knees to avoid being blown away.

There are nice houses on the Peak, with concrete courts for playing tennis, but with no better gardens than that which consists of a few pots containing flowers.   Houses, servants, and food cost about double what they did a dozen years ago. The allowances of officers have not increased as much as they should.   We get chair allowance, but we ought to get dentists' allowance, so tough is the food in Hong Kong and so expensive the dentists.

Spirits, tobacco, and wine are cheap—perhaps too cheap —and reach-me-down clothes do not cost much more than they are worth.   Some of the Chinese shops have a great deal of carving and gilding upon their fronts, but they make the many globe-trotters that pass through pay well for this. One must be careful what one buys in these shops. A lady observed a man reading Chinese characters on the front of a silver belt which she was wearing. " You understand the language," she said, "so do tell me the literal meaning of these characters. I am told they stand for happiness." With shy hesitation the Chinese scholar answered, " They may mean that indirectly, but the literal translation of what is on the clasp of your belt is, ' Distended with food.' "

In the winter Hong Kong is gay. Those " in the swim " may dine or dance out every evening. In summer people are in the swim in a more literal sense, for that is the time for bathing parties, a form of amusement so healthy and rational that one wonders how society took to it. Between four and five o'clock a party steam in a launch to where the sea is clean and there is a sandy beach upon which tents or mat sheds have been put up to serve as dressing-rooms for the ladies. The men don bathing kit on the now curtained launch and swim to join the diving-*belles* as several Hong Kong ladies may be called, so proficient are they in aquatic exercises. When tired of throwing about a football in the water, the bathers retire, the men to the launch and the ladies to the tents. Here they are given cherry brandy, and the sexes clothe and reunite. Tea is then served, either on land or on the launch during the return journey. Sometimes people dine on the launches, and, being in no hurry to burn and dissolve in Hong Kong, stay out pretty late in the moonlight. The Governor, the two Admirals, the General, and the Chief Justice lead society, and the Bishop blesses their doings as far as he conscientiously can. Of the civilians in Hong Kong, all that we shall say is that some are nicer than others. The number ones, twos, and even threes of the great commercial firms are sometimes social successes. There are distinctions, however, that are not easy to understand. Why should pig-iron turn up its nose at tenpenny nails? To this distant land people come with double names that sound formidable until it is discovered that the double-barrelled ones discharge very small shot at home. The Service people call the civilians dollar-snatchers, and the latter think of the former as dollar-lackers. Dancing days and nights begin with the three practice dances that precede the ball which is given by Scotch residents on each St. Andrew's night. The great difficulty men have is to get partners, so few unmarried girls are in the colony. Here it is men and not women who are wall-flowers.

If men cannot get partners for a dance unless they bespeak them days before, it is even more difficult to get them for life. Owing to this scarcity of wife material, as well as to impe-cuniosity, young European men, instead of marrying, form themselves into bachelor messes. Just before leaving Hong Kong, I dined at one of these establishments. It was monstrous. There were six mere men daring to have as nice a drawing-room, as well arranged a table, and as good servants as any house I have seen run by that old institution —a wife. It was unnatural, and a committee of women ought to break up the mess before the offenders get too much into the habit of celibacy and make a mess of their lives. The poor fellows are starved at heart, however replete in stomach, and each starts a dog for a companion. Alas! some of them go to the dogs in other ways. A ten-thousand-miles-away-from-home feeling has many temptations connected with it.

A person who is only middle-aged feels quite antique at Hong Kong, not so much by reason of the enervating climate as because there are scarcely any old people in the colony. All leave when they can afford to do so, and when still young. Age and awkwardness at games are considered here un-pardonable sins.

There are beautiful and, I believe, comfortable cemeteries

for Hindoos, Mahommedans, Protestants, and Roman Catholics, overlooking the racecourse in the Happy Valley. In this valley are played golf, cricket, and other games, and when officiating at a military funeral I used frequently to hear an illustration of the truth that "in the midst of life we are in death," for the shouts of football players would rise up and mingle with the recitation of those very words or with the three volleys after the service which proclaimed that a soldier had played out his game of life upon earth.

Polo is played all the year round, but the ponies do not appear to have their hearts in the work. Game can be found in the New Territory, and for those who can content themselves with clay pigeons there is a gun-club in Hong Kong.

The L.R.C.—that is, Ladies' Recreation Club, or, as some read it, Ladies' Recrimination Club, is managed with great care by ladies. Gentlemen are eligible as subscribers.

With the races the Hong Kong season closes, for soon after the weather begins to get warm. Great then is the disappointment of the ladies if the race-days are cold or wet, or otherwise unsuitable to the costumes they have planned and perhaps imported ten thousand miles for this occasion.

On either side of the grand stand temporary mat houses are put up. In these society "tiffins," gambles, flirts, and regales itself with tea and ices. But nothing at the races is so interesting as the two miles of road from the terminus of the Peak tramway to the course. Each day, chairs, rickshaws, tramcars, and pony carriages convey people of every costume and colour in the Far East to the Happy Valley. The crowd is so sober and orderly that it might be going to church.

I never could care which horse came in first, but the human races always amused me. I liked looking at Chinese jugglers pretending to run swords through boys; at dentists making believe that they draw teeth and put them in again; at the curious arts of medicine-sellers ; at the solemn efforts of Indian soldiers to be jolly and funny to a tom-tom accompaniment. I treated myself to an entrance ticket, price one cent, to several shows containing such things as a duck with three legs, an optical illusion which made a human head look as if it were separated from the trunk, and a deformed dwarf that seemed to be only half human. Do the Chinese ignore Western inventions? Certainly not, for I saw them at these races paying cash to get electrical shocks and to hear phonographic wonders.

It would be well if the residents of Hong Kong, instead of indulging in the excitement of *fan-tan* at Macao, which is distant three hours by steamer, were to go through the yellow-scarred heights and investigate the beautiful valleys and quaint villages that are in our New Territory. Even at Macao it is not necessary to gamble, for there are interesting manufactories and beautiful gardens to be seen. There are, too, trips to the Ringing Rocks and elsewhere that can innocently fill up a week-end.

CHAPTER II

TIENTSIN AND PEKING

SOON after arriving at Hong Kong, I was offered an
indulgence, or free passage, in a transport ship which
was going up to Taku to bring back soldiers from Tientsin
and Peking. "You may be in time to see the Forbidden
City," said the officer in charge of transports, "before it
is shut up preparatory to the Emperor's return. It is very
hot up there at this time of the year, and you would have a
good deal of roughing, but you will never have such an opportunity again." There is a charm about forbidden things, and
as I wanted to see this most exclusive city and the other
sights of Peking, and reflected that there were as many
belonging to my military parish to whom I might be of
use in Tientsin and Peking as in Hong Kong, I started on
the 25th of July, 1901.

On the fifth day we arrived at Wei-hai-wei and put in for
orders. There were several large ships of war in the harbour
and bands playing upon two of them, but no one paid any

attention to our arrival for a considerable time. At last
a young officer sauntered on board with a message that
we might go on our way, but too late to admit of our doing
so that night, so we had an opportunity of seeing the then
much-talked-of Wei-hai-wei. A large hotel has been built,
and Wei-hai-wei is becoming a seaside resort as fashionable as
Cheefoo, another port where we remained a day on our return
journey. At a little distance were pointed out to us the
native walled town of Wei-hai-wei and the fine new barracks
in which the Chinese regiment, organised by England, lived.

In a day and a night we came to Taku Bar, and were
transferred into a launch which brought us some miles to
Sinho, passing the historic mud forts at the mouth of the
Peiho river. Each fort had on it the flag of the nation that
gave most assistance in taking it.

At Sinho we got into the military train which was used by
soldiers of all nations, but worked by British Royal Engineers.
Surely a more miscellaneous collection of military officers
never travelled in any train; we were British, German,
Russian, Japanese, Austrian, and so forth; the Chinese were
crowded like cattle in trucks without seats.

From Sinho to Tientsin there was scarcely anything to be
seen in the flat landscape except reeds, Chinese graves, and
salt-heaps; but everywhere were signs of the Boxer trouble
which had only just ended. All the dwellings on either side
of the railway were burned, and this was the case all the way
up to Peking. The burning was done by the foreign armies,
to prevent the houses hiding Boxers, by the Boxers themselves, and by the pillaging mob that followed them. In
fact, every one seemed to have been burning everything. No
attempt was made to distinguish between innocent peasants
and Boxers. The officer commanding a battery of British
artillery told me that with great trouble he had collected
a number of coolies to move his guns. The colonel of a
passing Russian regiment came to him and asked him to give

them up, for he said, "I've got orders to kill every Chinese met between Tientsin and Peking." And yet it was said that there was no war with China!

Of course we were much interested in seeing the marks of the fierce fighting that had recently taken place at the railway station at Tientsin. If the Russians and the British Marines had not made the grand stand they did there, Tientsin would have fallen into the hands of the Boxers and the Imperial troops. We visited the native city and saw a very interesting temple, and the fine new road along the river, which has been made in the place where formerly stood hundreds of native houses. Along this and in other parts were the settlements of British, American, German, French, Italian, Japanese, and other soldiers. I have always liked studying foreign armies and comparing them with each other, and here was a unique opportunity for doing so. Truly it was a kaleidoscopic picture of military movement and varied uniforms. Most critics were of opinion that the discipline and transport arrangements of our Anglo-Indian army were superior to those of the others. Certainly a German officer told me that the Indian soldiers could not have any strength with such thin legs, and that they would be cowardly in battle. He did not know what muscle was in those legs, or that the men he sneered at were born fighters.

These encampments may have helped to cause the plague of flies from which we suffered. James the First said to a fly, "I have three kingdoms, and yet the only place you could go was in my eye!" The Tientsin flies during the hot weather when we were there were so numerous that they had to make places for themselves inside and outside our eyes, on our food, everywhere. The enormous amount of matting-covered baggage, and the number of transport animals to be seen everywhere, enabled us to realise, to some extent, what active service is like.

After six days we left Tientsin and started for Peking. The country on both sides produced fine crops of millet, of hemp, and of other cereals.

When I saw Cairo, I thought that I would never again see such an out-of-the-common city, but, compared with Peking, Cairo is quite commonplace.   If Southey could say of Exeter that " it is ancient and stinks," what would he have thought of the assorted odours of that old curiosity-shop—Peking?

The first thing that astonishes the traveller as his train glides into the station, near the Temple of Heaven, are the walls and gates of the Chinese, Tartar, Imperial, and For-bidden Cities, cities which are situated one within the other. The circuit of these walls is twenty-five miles; they are fifty feet high and forty broad.   At intervals there are enormous castellated keeps or gate-towers.   In the embrasures of these are, or were when I was there, fixed boards upon which were painted the muzzles of imaginary cannon.   This was intended to terrify an advancing enemy, and perhaps to deceive Kuanti, the god of war.

When I got into that vehicle without springs or seats, called a Peking cart, which the Rev. F. Norris, chaplain to the British Legation, the friend at whose house I was to stay, sent for me, I knew for the first time what a really bad road means.   It is not exaggeration to say that sometimes we sank a yard in a mud-hole or between stones.   My friend's house was a large Chinese one, and the first thing he did was to show us over it, and to explain in what respects it differed from an English house.   Like most other Chinese houses, it had only one storey and the three-sided courts into which it was divided were turned to the south.   Before the outermost court was a screen intended to ward off evil spirits.   These beings are supposed always to fly straight, so that anything which turns them aside frightens them away.   For this reason the Chinese have made Prospect or Coal Hill, which one can hardly believe is artificial, outside the Imperial City.   We

SOUTH GATE, PEKING.

To face page 36.

climbed up this screen against evil spirits, and had a fine
view of Peking. It did not look like a town at all, but like a
splendid park, covered with trees; this is because almost every
house has at least one tree in its compound. The yellow
roofs of the Imperial buildings were pointed out to us, and
also the green-tiled ones that distinguish princely and ducal
residences.

Most of the houses in Peking that are not palaces are
hovels. No two houses are on the same line. The object
of this is to deflect evil spirits, who are not able to turn
a corner. To further drive away or catch these gentry,
clay or porcelain dogs or lions or bottles of sorts are put on
the ridges of many houses. We may remark that to serve
the same purpose netting is sometimes placed upon the corner
of the sail of a junk.

The next day was Sunday, so we went to the Legation
Church and were entertained at lunch afterwards by the
Ambassador. Two or three of those present had been in the
siege, and they showed us some of the sandbags used, a
stable into which millions of rifle-bullets seemed to have been
fired, and a place where the last order issued was written up
in chalk. Underneath were the words, "*Nil desperandum,*
two bottles of beer." All this was very vivid, especially as I
was wearing a straw hat lent to me in which were two bullet-
holes.

One day we visited the Lama monastery, but that day is
almost a blank to me. I was bewildered with the summer
heat, with the strangeness of everything, and with the
impatience of my companions, who did not care to see sights
but only to "do" them. I retain, however, a dim recollec-
tion of the main temple of the monastery with its three seated
figures of Buddha in the centre and its eighteen Lohans, or
Genii who await transformation into Buddhas, along the sides;
also of a temple beyond this in which is a gilt wooden statue
of Maitreya, the coming Buddha, not seated but standing and

with his head touching the roof, seventy feet above. In vain repetitions of the name of this divinity fifteen hundred priests spend most of their time. And yet these clerics are sometimes guilty of what is nearly as bad in them as simony in an English clergyman. They sell to tourists the small brass or gilded Buddhas that are everywhere to be seen. Gods were not cheap the day we visited the place, and we could get none, but I have seen several that were bought there.

A great contrast to this repository of idols is the Temple of Confucius. In this are no idols. There is simply the tablet of the sage standing in the centre in a wooden shrine with the tablets of some of his most eminent disciples on either side. Before these are a few gilt bronze censers and some other articles of altar furniture. In an adjoining court we were shown the ten black granite drums on which verses in ancient characters describe a hunting expedition of the Emperor Siuen in the eighth century B.C.

Words cannot describe how Peking looks and smells upon a wet day, but we had during our stay this experience. The only cleaning or repairing that has, as a rule, ever been done to the streets is to throw dirt and refuse into the middle from either side. In process of time two great dykes full of ink-black stagnant water have been in this way formed. In one of these, if a person were jostled off the street, he might be drowned, and probably Peking is unique in this as in other things, that people have been drowned in her neglected streets. My friends would not venture out on this wet day, so I amused myself looking into shops and learning the customs of the people in their homes. When they saw that I was interested in them and was making overtures of friendship, they would invite me to come in, show me their things, and offer tea, cakes, a pipe or a cigarette. Imagine a Chinaman's reception were he to try and get into the houses of London people absolutely unknown to him by simple civility! I was followed by a crowd, but always by a good-natured

LOO-MAN-TZE STREET, PEKING.

To face page 39.

crowd, and on one occasion they became so pleased with my smiling confidence in them that, taking me by the hands, they brought me into a mosque and showed me sacred books and other curious things.

The great breadth of Peking's chief thoroughfare is concealed by two lines of booths that have sprung up in a kind of ditch that extends on either side. Behind these booths fantastic poles, gilded signboards, carved woodwork, waving streamers and lanterns prevent passers-by from ignoring the shops. In this broadway may be seen *literati* nodding behind saucer-like spectacles in screened sedan chairs, boys perched on the tails of diminutive donkeys or bestriding shaggy ponies bitted with a cruel arrangement of wire; ramshackle waggons drawn by mixed teams of mules, asses, and oxen yoked together by entangled rope traces. There are people from Thibet, Manchuria, and Mongolia, those from this last place frequently in charge of strings of camels far finer than I have seen elsewhere. A man sits on every sixth animal and drives them.

What is that enormous red and gilded thing? It is a catafalque or bier, and it is carried in the funeral *cortège* by from sixteen to one hundred and twenty-eight bearers according to the rank of the deceased.

At every street-corner there is something that calls together crowds. They are now gazing at a man who swallows a large ball and a sword, and who puts wooden skewers up his nostrils and into his eyes. A snake-charmer charms street arabs as well as snakes. The story-teller seems to be much appreciated, judging from the number of open-mouthed listeners he has. Acrobats perform feats and musicians tweak a single-stringed guitar. Gambling proclivities are pandered to by a sportsman, who backs a well-nourished fighting cricket against all comers. People who possess only one pair of shoes get them mended while they wait by cobblers sitting at street-corners.

Pedlars call attention with rattles and curious cries to the carved jade snuff-boxes and other curios which they have spread upon the ground. Those who would keep their heads cool amid all this excitement have them shaved by a wandering barber. He uses no soap, and his apparatus is very simple—two sets of boxes, one containing drawers for cash and razors, and a seat for the person to be shaved; the other a stand that encloses a pan of lighted charcoal for heating water.

It seems strange to have an invitation to lunch or attend a polo match in the Temple of Heaven, but that is what we had, as we knew some British artillery officers quartered there.

The Temple of Heaven is in a park, of which the walls are three miles round. Here on the Chinese New Year's Day the Emperor, who, like Melchizedek, is high-priest as well as king, prays for a blessing on his people and offers a bullock whole and without blemish. The altar consists of a triple circular terrace of white marble, each terrace being surrounded by a richly carved balustrade. In this balustrade a curious symbolism of three and its multiples was pointed out to us. Hung-wu, the first Emperor of the Ming Dynasty, A.D. 1368, prohibited all prayers but his own to God. "What a confusion," he said, "there will be above; what intolerable annoyance, if you people call all upon Him." Should a common person presume to worship his Father in heaven he may be punished by Chinese law with eighty blows, and even with strangulation.

At the great festival which celebrates spring the Emperor also officiates as Pontifex Maximus, or high-priest. This time it is at the temple of the god of agriculture, where at the close of a religious service he ploughs, or pretends to plough, a little bit with a plough which is painted yellow. Imperial representatives do the same in the provinces with red ploughs. The same encouragement which the Emperor gives to the

TEMPLE OF HEAVEN, PEKING.

To face page 40.

production of food is given by the Empress to that of clothing. At a ceremony in the ninth moon she publicly gathers mulberry leaves and gives them to silkworms.

The officers' mess at which we lunched was in a building called the "Hall of Fasting" (there was no fasting at our lunch); it is so called because the Emperor spends here fasting the night before New Year's Day, when he goes to the Temple of Heaven to pray for his people. The roof of the Temple of Heaven is made of beautiful blue tiles, to represent the sky.

On our way back to the house where we were staying we visited the Imperial City and thought that we had never seen anything so beautiful as the artificial lake filled with the sacred lotus-plant. The lake almost surrounds the marble bridge, over which we passed into the city. In this city are the houses and offices of Court officials, and within this the *Sanctum sanctorum*, or Forbidden City, where reside, each in their own suite of apartments, the Emperor, the Eastern and Western Empresses, and the Empress-Dowager.

Most of this City of Palaces or Palatial City might be described as a series of reception-halls made in the shape of portals or gates. One is particularly impressed with the beauty of the colouring of the roofs of these one-storey vestibules, and with the carving on the marble steps that lead up to them. The thrones in them, two of which I desecrated by sitting on, seemed rather shabby. The Emperor gives audience to the different people who visit him in different halls according to their rank.

We inspected the private apartments of the Emperor and of his wives. The furniture was of carved blackwood, with a mixture of European chairs and sofas. Jade ornaments abounded. There were many clocks, pianos, and harmoniums, but most things had been removed. What had not been removed was the dust of sleepy centuries. When I sat upon the bed of the "Son of Heaven" and noticed the small, close room in which it was, I said to myself, "Here is a man, owning a house so large that it is called a city, who sleeps in a room no bigger than a garret!"

In the pavilion of the Empress was a piano and a small organ. The much finer pavilion of the Empress-Dowager, which was crowded with musical-boxes, mechanical toys, and foreign rubbish generally, had in it some really fine embroideries. A large bronze lion with one paw resting on a globe and the other on a crushed diminutive lion was pointed out to us near the Emperor's garden. It is emblematic of China ruling the world and trampling her foes. Rather ironical, we thought, at that period.

It is eight miles from Peking to the Summer Palace, but to me, riding over the road on a fine little pony which my host lent, it did not seem nearly so long, so interesting were the novel sights which were to be seen. There was, too, the excitement of feeling that Boxers might fire or jump upon us at any moment, for the country was still in a very troubled state. As, however, the British officers who were my companions had each at least one revolver, I felt quite safe.

It is said that the Russians took five hundred cartloads of loot out of the Summer Palace, but, indeed, all nations seem to have taken a hand at that game. The wonder was that so many beautiful screens and other things were left in the rooms used for a British officers' mess, where we lunched.

I may here say that for the credit of their professed Christianity I hope that the stories not only of looting but of far worse things which European soldiers did were exaggerated. Talking of the foreign troops, an able official who had been in the British Legation when besieged said to me that they "made a hell of Peking. A rage for looting "seized the officers, and they left the men to do what they "liked. I found in one house seven women who had "hanged themselves to prevent being ravished. I saw a

A LESS IMPORTANT STREET, PEKING.

To face page 42.

"Russian soldier bayonet a mother and dash out her baby's
"brains on a big stone. Another Russian deliberately shot
"a man whom I saw walking over a bridge. The soldiers,
"all except the Japanese, seemed to have gone mad. Their
"eyes looked murder."

After we had seen the beautiful grounds of the Summer
Palace, the artificial lake, the marble boat, the bridge of
sixty marble lions, the bronze ox, and other things, we
climbed a hill and got a view of a very wide and well-
cultivated plain below, and of the ruins of the old Summer
Palace which the British and French burned in 1860. There
was at the top of the hill an Imperial domestic chapel, in
which was a statue of Buddha that had been blown down
by Italian soldiers, and another on its last legs.

From Peking I returned by passenger steamer *via* Cheefoo
and Shanghai to Hong Kong, and was by a chapter of
accidents detained four days at that dirty, muddy place
called Tonku, from which the steamers start. The delay,
however, enabled us to see some characteristic life in the
villages around. Oh, the filth and smell of those collections
of mud hovels !

We could hear that the northern people were very different
from those in the south of China, for the coolies who loaded
and unloaded ships spoke to sailors from the south in pidgin
English, as neither party understood the Chinese of the
other. We could see, too, that the northerners were far
more muscular, because, the heat being great, many of
those who worked upon the river wore no clothes at all,
not even a loin-cloth. It was fortunate that the British
matron who demands fig-leaves even for statues in museums
was not there.

We went to have a nearer look at the battered forts
on the much winding Peiho and the camps of the troops
of several European nations. The coming and going too
of ships full of soldiers also interested us.

FIVE HUNDRED GENII.

lychees, loongyens or dragon's eyes, whompees, persimmons, pommeloes, and with other kinds of fruit-trees.

Then appear lofty square structures of granite which are used by the rich as storehouses and by the poor as pawnshops. There are about a hundred first-class ones, and they are in all parts of the city as churches are in a British town; and does not Canton worship Wealth, of which these storehouses are a sign, more than any other god? Every evening incense sticks are burnt in the little niches outside the shops where the images of the god of Wealth are placed.

To prevent being lost in the mazes of Canton I hired a guide, and with him in one chair I started in another for a day's sight-seeing. The first place visited was the hall of five hundred genii which was built in 1847. These gilded figures represent the disciples of Buddha, and one of them, dressed as a Western, probably erroneously, is said to stand for Mr. Marco Polo, as our guide called the traveller. No two figures are alike, though they all have hideous ears. One has more than the usual number of eyes, to show that he is a great observer; another has very long arms, to signify that he can reach everywhere; another has figures of children sprawling over him, and to him mothers pray for male issue.

Near this hall is the "Doctor Temple," dedicated to the god of medicine. In this are sixty inferior idols, and before the one having a number corresponding with the years of his life up to sixty the sick person prays for recovery. If over sixty, he begins to count again.

In the temple of another "Medicine King" a great many fans are presented by worshippers on the god's birthday. As the Æsculapian deity on the morning of this day is supposed to have returned hot and weary from the mountains, where, in search of medicinal plants for the service of men, he had spent several hours, his votaries fan the idol by which he is represented and then leave the fans as offerings.

Our next visit was to the temple of the Five Rams, on

which the five genii who preside over the five elements of
Earth, Fire, Metal, Water, Wood, descended from heaven
bearing blessings. The rams are said to have petrified, and
the interest of the temple centres in five roughly hewn stones
which are supposed to be the genuine animals.

Need it be said that we did not go into each of the one
hundred and twenty-four temples of Canton? We did, however, visit one more. This was the temple of the god of the
city, or, as foreigners call it, "The Temple of Horrors." This
Chinese Madame Tussaud's was not as gruesome as others
of the kind which I have seen elsewhere. On either side
of the entrance court are life-sized wooden figures representing people undergoing the tortures inflicted in the ten
kingdoms of the Buddhistic hell. They are being bored
through the middle, sawn between two boards, precipitated
upon turned-up swords, boiled in oil, extinguished by the
descent of a red-hot bell. People are having their eyes and
tongues pulled out. Others are being transmigrated into
lower animals. One figure is being ground, as if he were
rice, by a hammer worked by the treading of a coolie. This
is the braying a fool in a mortar spoken of in Scripture.
A dog waits to lick up the blood. There is a mirror in
which the man sees the deeds for which he is being punished.

In this temple there is a curious votive offering. One merchant accused another of fraud. The accused hastened to the
shrine and declared his innocence. Shortly afterwards he
died, and to the wrath of the god before whom he made a
false statement his death was attributed. The accuser put
up an offering in the form of an abacus, which is an
instrument for performing arithmetical calculations by balls
sliding on wire. Upon it is inscribed: " Man with man
has many reckonings, with God he has but one. That
great Being seeth in secret."

The Flowery Pagoda has nine stories, but the so-called
five-storied one is not a pagoda but a watch-tower and a

THE TEMPLE OF HORRORS.

To face page 48.

barracks. From it we had a good view of the White Cloud mountains and of the yamens of the Viceroy, Governor, and Tartar General. Asylums for those who have "no oil in their eyes" (the blind) and for old people were pointed out to us, also a village inhabited by lepers.

The mint, which is the largest in the world, is near here. I have visited it more than once, as its English manager is a friend of mine. It can turn out two million coins each day; but the Chinese coins made here and elsewhere are not nearly as highly esteemed by the natives as British coins of the same value. If a coolie be offered a Chinese ten-cent piece and a Hong Kong one, he will say, " Give me the piece with the foreign devil on it." I hope that His Majesty Edward VII. feels complimented.

Our next visit was to the " copper-jar water-dropper " or water clock, which is five hundred years old. It is composed of copper vessels placed one above the other upon step-like platforms. In the bottom receptacle is a float with an indicator passing through it which, as the water flows in, rises and shows the time. When leaving the room in which the clepsydra or water clock is placed we noticed a small bundle of " time sticks " which reminded us of " King Alfred's candles." Each of the sticks, which are about thirty inches long, burns for twelve hours, and in this way measures time.

The potter's field, as the execution ground literally is, for clay pots are dried there, is called the "Horse's Head," from its form. It is small considering the terrible amount of business that is done in it. Many skulls were lying about the day we visited this Golgotha. In one corner was a cross upon which criminals sentenced to be cut into pieces are bound.

The " city of the dead " is the most unique sight in Canton. In each of its one hundred and ninety-four small houses is a corpse lodged at the rate of twenty-five dollars for the first three months, and then at a reduced price until the geomancers decide when and where it should be buried. Silk or paper lanterns and representations of fruit adorn the roof. There are large screens in each apartment between the coffin and the door. Tea, fruit, and any kind of food the dead person particularly liked when on earth are placed for him on the altar before the coffin each morning. Cardboard servants wait upon him with cardboard cups of tea, with pipes, and with other requirements. Two smiling paper females show his spirit the way to heaven. The people who thought of and made this "city" must believe what we profess to believe—the communion of saints.

I was so much interested in the "City of the Dead" that I went again to see it on my second visit to Canton. Failing to get a guide, I hired a chair. The bearers, either not understanding the order they got or thinking that a prison is a city of the dead, carried me to the Nam Hoi magistrate's prison, one of the two filthy establishments in which Cantonese law-breakers "do time," and, if they have no money to bribe, a very indefinite time too. We noticed that the street leading to this prison was full of gambling dens, a fact which is eloquent of much. Canton is probably at present the greatest centre of gambling in the world. On coming to the door of the yard, where the prisoners, with chains round their necks and on their limbs herded together, the gaoler demanded twenty cents. Having paid my money, I tried to go in, but it was only a "look see" through the door that the fee carried. And perhaps this was enough, for, as the gaoler explained, if we did go in the prisoners would probably take everything we had on us or about us. "The place is too full," he groaned, "and half of the prisoners should have their heads off." The poor wretches were indescribably dirty. The eyes of most of them glared with hunger from out of their parchment-looking faces. My companion threw a five-cent piece among them, and there was a scrimmage, as at Rugby football—in grim earnest, however, and not in play.

A fortunate few whose friends had brought them something to supplement the regulation ration, which is the smallest portion of rice that will keep body and soul together, were cooking it in a corner. It was pathetic to hear the prisoners using the polite formula as we went away, "Go slowly," and, looking at their chains, "Excuse our not going with you to the gate." On one occasion we visited the Pwan-U prison. This contains women as well as men, and it is even worse than the one described. We were surprised that in a city so large and with such a bad reputation for crime as Canton there should be only two prisons and so few inmates in them, until we reflected that those who can bribe do not go to prison and that it is cheaper to cut off the head of a criminal than to put food into his mouth. The Chinese see no sense in feeding those who will not earn a living for themselves. Two years ago it was said that about a hundred executions took place in one particular week at Canton. This may have been an exaggeration, and it certainly was considerably over the weekly average. It was after the New Year's holidays, and the work of the headsman had got into arrears.

But in Canton horrors are forced upon those who least desire to see them. Once I had to pass, on going from the steamer, a man who had been strangled with thin ropes in an upright wooden cage for a robbery which he committed, or was said to have committed. On returning to the steamer next day, the corpse, taken out of the cage, was lying on the jetty.

We visited silk-weaving shops, and halted to see ivory carvers and those who wear out their eyes inlaying green and blue kingfisher's feathers upon gold and silver ornaments. We saw jade stones being cut with wire saws, and tobacco shaved from blocks with planes. Even the manufacture of little red candles for domestic shrines, and of big ornamented ones for temples, was interesting. Each trade has a separate location in the city, and nearly the whole of one street is

4

devoted to the sale of beautiful blackwood furniture. Tourists who like that sort of thing buy pictures on rice-paper representing the punishments inflicted in China, or subjects that are even less decent. We go a little further, and there are wholesale tea-stores or shops dealing in dried sea-products or in rice, millet, and other kinds of grain.

Nothing impresses one who visits a Chinese city for the first time so much as the signboards that hang perpendicularly from shops and hongs. A good one is a valuable piece of property. In bright colours and gold are inscribed the sign of the firm and some such words as " Never-ending success"; " By Heaven made prosperous "; " Trade revolves like a wheel "; " Virtuous and Abundant "; "Health and happiness rest on all who enter here "—this last over an opium-smoking den! Hints like the following may be read : " Gossiping and long sitting injure business "; " No credit given: former customers have taught caution." The shape of the signboard and its colour, as also the colour of the letters upon it, indicate different trades. The brightly painted large paper lamps that hang over the shops also add to the cheerful picturesqueness of the streets of Canton and of other Chinese cities. I liked the market gardens at Fati because there I saw growing upon trees cumquats, carambolas (Chinese gooseberries), and other curious fruits which I had never before seen, except plucked, on street stalls.

We also enjoyed a railway trip which we took to Fatshan, a prosperous, and even comparatively clean, town, twelve miles from Canton.

But it was the street life that interested me most. I had been warned that the picturesque charms of Canton had to be paid for by smelling stinks that are said to rank after those of Amoy and Peking. I was agreeably surprised, and think Canton the least unsavoury (which is not saying much) Chinese town I have visited. To be sure I am hardened in this respect, for have I not smelled Naples

and Valetta, and was not my last station dear, dirty
Dublin? In Canton, as in other Chinese cities, it is only
banks and pawnshops that are closed in front. Other shops
are quite open, and you can look at articles being manufactured
on the premises similar to those on sale. In the streets are
peripatetic vendors and tradesmen of all kinds. There is the
cook with his portable kitchen, and the gardener with his
basket of flowers and vegetables slung from his shoulders
by a bamboo pole. One sees in the streets travelling
blacksmiths, itinerant porcelain-menders, ambulatory seal-
cutters, migratory bankers, and peregrinatory makers of
sugar puppets. In the unhalting procession there comes a
coolie with a tub of water at one end of his pole and a
chopping-block at the other. After a long chaffing palaver
about the price, some one orders a pound and a half of carp.
The seller nips a fish four or five pounds in weight out of his
tub, puts it on the chopping-block, slices it up by the back-
bone, and leaves the remainder flapping upon the block. The
author of " Chinamen at Home " tells us that when on one
occasion he remonstrated against such barbarity with a
native Christian, he was thus answered: "I am a very
tender-hearted man, sir; I could not be a butcher and kill
cattle, but a fish utters no cry."

Books, most of them of the "penny dreadful" kind, or
even more voluptuous, are spread out for sale at the street-
side, and so are sheets of pawn-tickets.

The Chinese have no objection to publicity. They take
their meals in the street, they wash their feet, sitting in front
of their houses, in a basin of hot water. They get their
teeth drawn amidst an admiring crowd, by a dentist who has
round his neck a ghastly string of fangs as testimonials of
his skill.

The names of the streets are such as these: The Street
of Benevolence, the Street of Ten Thousandfold Peace, the
Street of a Thousand Beatitudes, the Street of One Thou-

sand Grandsons, and so on.   A particularly unfragrant street
is called the " Street of Refreshing Breezes " !   By a similar
touch of perhaps unconscious satire one of the noisiest streets
in Peking is called the " Street of Perpetual Repose."   At
the entrance to most streets there is in Canton, as in
other Chinese towns, a gateway, which is shut up at night
by means of upright wooden posts.   Over one of these
gateways my attention was called, by a friend who knew
Chinese, to the name of the street which was put up.   It
was the " Street of Increasing Virtue."   I had myself
remarked the increased number of gambling dens, fortune-
telling establishments, and other rascalities which it contained.

Many of the streets are roofed, to keep them cool, with
matting or with plates of thinned oyster-shell fastened together.

About three hundred thousand people live in sampans,
house-boats, and huts raised on piles in the Canton rivers.
They keep very much to themselves, and they are not allowed
to marry with those on shore.   Each sampan, though barely
twenty feet in length, shelters under its movable roof of
bamboo basket-work probably six people on an average.
The women, generally with a child hanging in a red bag
fastened to her back, work the boats.   They and the children
never leave them, but many of the men labour on shore
during the day and return at night to their sampans, which
they can easily find in the different water-streets, for every
boat is bound by law to keep its own appointed place.

In the majority of cases, however, the men go on land as
little as do the women, and then it is difficult to see how they
earn a living.   Certainly they are most thrifty, and very
ingenious in inventing ways and means.   They dredge, for
instance, for coal which has been dropped from steamers, and
also try to pull up, with an instrument covered with hooks,
purses or other lost property.   Many of them are like that
people of whom it was said that they earned a precarious

living by taking in each other's washing. It may be said of the Chinese generally that they rake the sea with the same untiring industry with which they cultivate the land. No phase of life is unrepresented among the water population of Canton. Kitchen boats supply hot food at a very cheap rate. The barber, in a tiny boat, paddles himself in and out among the crowd of sampans, attracting attention by ringing a bell. The river-doctor also gives notice of his whereabouts by a gong or drum. When his medicines prove fatal there are floating biers to convey the dead to graves on land. Sadder than these biers are the boats tenanted by lepers. These afflicted people solicit alms by holding out a long bamboo stick, from the end of which is suspended a small bag.

There are boats that sell oil and boats that sell firewood. That one with a bundle of sugar-cane hanging for a sign from the masthead sells fruit and vegetables. There are boats for the sale of flowering plants, and others that sell perhaps nothing but bean-curd. There are fish-boats and boats for the sale of pork. There are crockery-boats, clothing-boats, and so on.

Flower-boats are fitted up with coloured glass and with wood-carving brightly painted and heavily gilded. They are lighted by a number of lamps and of reflecting mirrors. In them wealthy citizens give dinner-parties, which are enlivened by richly dressed singing women. Whether flower-boats are or are not improper depends upon those who visit them. There are floating hotels, and even floating joss-houses, and from the latter often proceed deafening sounds of drums, gongs, pipes, and cymbals.

Slipper-boats, so called because shaped like a Chinese slipper, i.e., enclosed at the toe and wide open at the heel, are intended for speed. They are propelled by four men, or two men and two women, uniting their strength on two oars only.

No matter how crowded a sampan is, room is always found for a family altar, on which are placed small gods and ancestral tablets.   And the poorest buy flowers for its decoration. Many of the boats that carry passengers quite glitter inside with gilding and red paint, and though so many people live in them, one need not be afraid of vermin, for water is plentiful, and the boats are continually being washed.   Over the sterns of nearly all of them are suspended long baskets, in which are kept hens, ducks, geese, and perhaps a pig or two.   The family cat is nearly always tied by the neck, lest she should stray away and get into a neighbour's pot.   Too often the women who work the boats by day are prostitutes at night.   These are nicknamed "Shuey-Kee," or water-fowl.

I was greatly pleased with a little excursion which I once took to the White Mountains, eight miles from Canton.   The Monkey Temple or the Stork Temple affords a resting-place at night.

CHAPTER IV

ON THE WEST RIVER

A bolt from the blue—Kong-Moon—How cold the tropics can be—Pirates —Dutch Folly—A silk country—Rafts—Lepers—Objects of interest— High-handed ladies—Soup and rats—Ducks—Tigers—Wuchow—A "pencil pagoda"—Cheating boats—A fire.

THE first attempt I made to go from Canton up the celebrated West River was prevented in this way : my companion, the Rev. E. L. Cowan, chaplain of H.M.S. *Glory*, and two other men who, besides myself, were the only first-class passengers on the steamer, had five hours after starting sat down to "tiffin" in the little saloon which was on deck, when the captain, looking out, said, "There are soldiers learning to shoot on the paddy fields." "Oh, I want to see Chinese soldiers," cried I, running out and followed by Mr. Cowan and one of the other passengers. The soldiers had their backs to us, and fired several volleys. Then my friend, who was standing on one side of me, fell, and exclaimed, "I am shot." The other man, who was a little behind me, said, "I am shot too." It seemed a bolt from the blue, and I could not take in the situation. Had the soldiers turned round and fired upon us, or what was it?

Mr. Cowan was so badly wounded that he was brought back to the Naval Hospital at Hong Kong next day by H.M. gunboat *Sandpiper*, which fortunately was not far distant. Of course I accompanied him, and so ended our unfortunate outing. The British senior Admiral, the Consul, and others, held an investigation, and the explanation which the Chinese authorities gave was that our steamer happened to get into a battle between soldiers and pirates, and that the volley which we received was one from the latter intended for the former. "If you do not believe us," they said, "we can show you twenty-seven bodies of men who were killed then and there." Dead bodies, however, can always be shown in China.

On another occasion I went to a busy town on the West River called Kong-Moon, which means water-gate. The number of things that are here made out of bamboo surprised me, as did also the simple and ingenious tools used. It is the centre, too, of the palm-leaf fan manufactory. The journey there was not very comfortable. As there were three opium-smoking Chinese in the one little cabin of the steamer, I preferred to lie out on deck, but even with two pairs of trousers on, three shirts, five coats, and a blanket it was too chilly to sleep. How cold these tropics can be sometimes! The noise, too, was very disturbing, for the Chinese, who lay all round me, never ceased clearing their throats (even high-class Chinese do this, and spit everywhere) and talking in unmusical tones.

I lay awake looking at the cold clouds and at the bars which divided the decks into compartments. These last are necessary on West River boats, because pirates are wont to take passage amongst their inoffensive countrymen and in the quiet of the night make a sudden attempt to seize the ship. They can be shut off by the iron gates and bars.

A year after my friend had been wounded I made another attempt to go up the West River. As I got on board the steamer and saw the guard of Indian watchmen now considered necessary, and heard every one talking of the activity lately displayed by the pirates, I began to doubt the wisdom of my undertaking.

An old missionary is said to have dispersed a band of pirates by taking out his false teeth and shaking them at them. The pirates who now infest the West River are not so easily frightened. Not long ago they shot one Englishman dead and wounded another on a Chinese steamer. They came on board as peaceable passengers, but the accidental dropping of a revolver on the part of one of them and the torture that drew from this one the names of his *confrères* resulted in the capture of five or six, the others being shot or escaping. The captured ones had their nails pulled out, their ankles broken, their eyelids, and afterwards their heads, cut off.

Many interesting places were pointed out to us as we started on our trip. We particularly remember a small island called Dutch Folly. In the early days the Dutch, obtaining permission to erect a hospital here, landed barrels and cases of medical comforts. One of the cases burst open, and arms and ammunition fell out. The Chinese looking on observed, " What fools the Dutch must be to attempt to cure the sick with powder and ball."

During the first two or three hours we passed large rice-fields that looked like British corn-fields because, being watered by the river, they were not divided into little chess-board plots as is usually done to facilitate irrigation. The banks of the river were for many miles planted with bananas for the sake of the fruit and also because the roots keep the earth from falling away.

Beautiful hills after a while came into view, and upon the top of several of them were graceful pagodas. The Gorges, unfortunately, were passed at night, so we saw little of them.

The silk country of the West River was announced by the number of mulberry shrubs that were grown to feed the " precious ones," as silkworms are called, and by the presence of the large junks armed with old cannon, which carry away valuable cargoes of silk.

We stopped at several prosperous-looking towns to let passengers out and in. The massive towers of numerous pawnshops broke the monotony of the low roofs. Here and there, embowered in large venerable-looking trees, were temples or the houses of wealthy families.

We passed several rafts carrying timber. The rafts take months to drift down the river, and accumulate so large a quantity of wood that they look like islands. Huts are built on them, sometimes a little village in which the crew and guard live.

Large flat-bottomed boats were also seen loaded with matting, which is here made in large quantities, or with twigs and coarse grass to be used for fuel in brick-kilns.

On the third day we saw a great many plantations of sugar-cane, and the bamboos which are the glory of the West River bowed their beautiful ostrich-feathered heads in greeting.

Several lepers paddled out to the steamer in small boats furnished with matting coverings, which were made purposely low in order to hide their hideous wounds and the stumps of members that had rotted away. The captain threw to them bits of wood upon which money was fastened. This was to remunerate them for keeping bamboo rods stuck up as a warning against rocks and shallows.

The captain was very kind in pointing out the Mark's Head, a rock which rises 1,410 feet from the river, the Cock's Comb Rock and Weeping Widow Rock, so called from the appearances they present, the celebrated marble caverns which looked purplish black at the distance from them where we were, a large tea plantation, a hill where pirates are buried heads downwards, and other places of interest.

In many parts of China they do not now build temples or even keep existing ones in repair, but at several of the dangerous corners of the West River may be seen temples or shrines which have been lately built, or at least painted and decorated afresh. Money was collected for one temple by

ladies of the congregation in a rather high-handed way.
They asked every man for a certain sum according to the
value of his property. If their demand was not complied
with, they refused to take less, and threatened to post the
names of the niggards on the city walls.

At Pak Tai there is a temple of the god of the North which
is much frequented. People beginning a business ask his
blessing, and if they succeed present a tablet on which their
gratitude is expressed in gilded characters. A settlement or
accounts between merchants, drawn up at the end of the year,
is sometimes brought to the temple and burnt, so that in this
way it may reach the god and be registered. Here too
masters and servants ratify their engagements. If a man is
charged with theft and asserts that he is innocent, he is taken
before the idol and asked if he will declare his innocence in
its presence. If he does so, his accuser is generally satisfied.

When we came to Sam Shui, the steamer was soon surrounded by boats, from which a sale began of cakes, eggs,
fruit, melon-seeds, all kinds of pickles, dried fish, snails, and
soup. A passenger asks for the last : first the salesman dips
a bowl in the river to wash it ; then he takes some chopped
onion, a dried shrimp or two, a few pieces of almond, also a
little finely chopped carrot, turnip, and ginger ; to this he
adds a bit of fresh fish. All these things are raw. The bowl
is then filled up with boiling rice water and a few drops of
soy, with a sprinkle of salt added to bring out the flavour.

Those were looked upon with envy who could afford to pay
ten cents for one of the many spatch-cock rats (split open and
dried) that hung up invitingly. The rats sold for food,
however, in these parts are not always dead. A friend told
me that in the town of Sam Shui he saw a man when walking
past a shop start and jump aside. A living rat, hung up by
the tail to let people know that that sort of delicacy was sold
inside, had bitten his shoulder.

We passed several duck farms. These are large rafts

roofed with rice straw, in each of which thousands of ducks are housed. The rafts are moved every day to a new place, and the ducks land and pick up snails and other luxuries. I was told that certain ducks are taught to look after the flock, as dogs are trained to shepherd sheep. When the owner of the ducks thinks that it is time for them to go to bed he whistles, and the shepherd ducks drive their charges on board. Indeed, the whole flock hurry of their own accord, because the three or four ducks that arrive last are given sharp knocks on the head, and this makes them careful not to come in last again.

To supply these duck farms there are establishments where eggs are artificially hatched with heated chaff and earthenware stoves. The Chinese delight in ducks, especially when the birds are split, salted, and dried in the sun. As there are no sheep, or very few, in the south of China, but ducks innumerable, it has been suggested that the words "All we like sheep have gone astray" would be more intelligible to the Chinese if they were altered into "All we like ducks have gone astray."

We heard nearly as much talk about tigers as about pirates on the West River. One first-class liar claims to have shot seventeen of the former; second-class liars have only seen tigers. A friend of mine really did shoot a man-eater that had killed ninety human beings. In the tiger's lair were found the remains of an old man carried off the night before. The villagers were delighted when the beast was killed, put their fingers in his wounds and sucked the blood to make them strong. My friend waited three nights in a tree, under which a dog had been tied to attract the tiger, for tigers are as fond of dog as are some Chinese. On the third night the great creature walked stealthily to his doom. He sprang upon the dog and flattened him to death, and then received himself the two balls that finished him.

Being of a peaceful turn, I and the two other European

passengers amused ourselves by practising with a rifle on coloured stones and other inanimate objects on the banks.

At last we came to Wuchow, the terminus of the steamer. The city is thirteen centuries old, and has a population of about fifty thousand. It climbs up the hills in the background for some distance, but seen from the river it looks like an agglomeration of tumble-down shanties. There are, however, three rather fine temples, and opposite one of them a gateway having three arches elaborately carved. The Yamen and dyeing works are worth a visit, and one ought, if time permit, to go to the top of the Peak of Wuchow to see the magnificent view.

In the Pagoda a light is kept burning when a Wuchow candidate for a degree is competing, as long as the examination lasts. At another place on the West River a "pencil pagoda" was pointed out to us. It is so called because it was built by a winner of a degree. Students now go and worship there before going up for an examination, in the hope of being equally successful.

At Wuchow boats of a peculiar shape are used. They have deep, bulging sides, with very narrow upper works. They are built in this manner to evade the customs, as when loaded it is difficult for the officers to ascertain how much cargo there is on board. This is, of course, well known, but it is winked at, and allows of a number of squeezes being introduced on both sides.

The large amount of wood in Chinese houses and the carelessness of their inmates cause fires to be very common. Not seldom they are kindled by those who wish to rob during the confusion. Every fire that destroys ten houses must be reported at Peking. If eighty houses are burned, the head official in the city is degraded one step. If they cannot bribe off, the people through whose carelessness the fire originated have to stand for a certain time in the street wearing the wooden collar called the "cangue." This explains

the fuss there was at Wuchow when, during our stay, two
houses burst into flames.   Immediately people began beating
upon cans, drums, trays, cymbals, or blowing upon a bugle or
large shell.   Soldiers belonging to different corps ran to the
scene to prevent every one except themselves from plundering.
Some carried spears, gingalls, and blunderbusses, others
revolvers and rifles, in the use of which they were probably
very inexpert.   A military mandarin followed on a very small
pony at a more dignified pace.   He knew that if the fire
caused a riot and the riot led to a rebellion, which in many
provinces is always on the point of breaking out, that he, like
the Ephesian town clerk, was in danger of being called in
question for the day's uproar (Acts xix. 40).   Then the fire
brigade appeared, and they were a curious sight with their
gaudy banners and their hand pumps.   They had no "water
dragons that save from fire," as the Chinese call the fire-
engines at Hong Kong.   The Wuchow folk who could assist
no other way endeavoured to frighten the fire demon by
discharging volleys of fire-crackers.   Truly a homœopathic
remedy!

On the return journey I stopped at Shiu-hing, and stayed
two days with a missionary friend.   He brought me to see
a large Buddhist monastery which, like all establishments of
the kind, is situated amidst precipitous scenery.   The trees
which the monks planted, some of them centuries ago, are
a beautiful monument to their nameless memory.   The
wood of one tree that grows here, called Hung Shu, when
pounded into an aromatic powder, is used for making joss-
sticks.

CHAPTER V

A general resemblance between Chinese cities—Wall literature—Oysters—
Mice steeped in honey—Pewter ware—People very civil—Country round
Swatow—Thatched men—Amoy celebrated for its pigs, its graves, and
its dirt—The Temple of Ten Thousand Rocks—Pailaus—The Min River
resembles the Rhine—The "Bridge of Ten Thousand Ages"—Soapstone—Foochow a centre of missionary effort—Apology for a good
house—Not luxury—A friend's grave.

THIS chapter consists of notes made during a short leave
spent at the above-named treaty ports and their
neighbourhood, but first I would remark that there is a
general resemblance between Chinese cities. In all that I have
seen, except Peking, the streets are only wide enough to admit
of two sedan chairs passing each other, and any one who
likes makes the way even narrower. There are on both sides
of the street fruit-stalls, temporary restaurants, and tables at
which sit gamblers, fortune-tellers, and medicine-sellers.
Old things that look as if they had never been new are spread
out on matting for sale. You may have to step over people
covered with terrible sores, who have been dumped down in
the street to die or to get cash from those who pass. There
is a great noise of bargaining, for the lower class of Chinamen
haggle for a cash at the top of their voices. Yet with all the
din and hurry there seldom occurs an accident or an interruption of good nature.

From time to time the traffic, which consists only of

human beasts of burden, of coolies carrying chairs and other
loads, is impeded by a wedding or funeral procession, or by
the shabby-grand retinue of a fat Mandarin. After this,
perhaps, come a dozen or more blind people, each resting his
hands upon the shoulders of the one in front of him—literally
the blind leading the blind. You will often see a procession
in honour of an idol. The idol is carried in a gaudy chair,
and is preceded and followed by banner and lantern-bearers.
A horrible sight, or rather smell, in all Chinese towns is that
of buckets of night-soil which are carried away for manure.

The streets are generally paved with granite flags, but the
pavement is irregular and in many places broken, and a
careless step lands you ankle-deep in foul mud. The streets,
too, are slippery with decayed animal and vegetable filth.
Dogs abound, and are nearly as dirty and have nearly as
many sores as the beggars. There are shelters, like dog-
houses, at the upright wooden bars which divide the different
wards, but these are not for dogs but for watchmen. On the
dun-tiled roofs of the one-storied houses in which most
of the inhabitants live, seed, firewood, and other things
are dried. At long intervals, paper or other lamps, provided
by interested shopkeepers, show up the darkness, so to speak,
of Chinese towns at night.

Once at Amoy we walked into so many pools of black
water and tripped over so many paving-stones that we had
to buy a bamboo torch and get a boy to carry it before us.
We learned then why every self-respecting Chinese carries
with him a lantern at night.

A feature of Chinese cities is wall literature. It suggests
the " agony " column of a Western newspaper. Mixed up
with trade advertisements and with notices of lost property,
sometimes consisting of human beings, there are announce-
ments of remedies for every disease, pills for the cure of
opium-smoking, lists of subscribers to a coming festival,
warnings against profaning paper or female infanticide. It

is scarcely necessary to add that wall literature has often been directed against foreigners, and especially against missionaries.

The beggars rouse our indignation, chiefly by the way they ill-treat children.   A sobbing woman bends down dramatically over a little child who is forced (what pain to a child!) to lie as still as death.   The passers-by are meant to think that the child is dead, and give money.

Swatow, though situated upon a small, muddy peninsula, is a very important place because of its fine harbour.   From it large quantities of indigo, sugar, and oranges are exported. Great numbers of oysters are found and artificially cultivated in the flat mud shores.   The Chinese dry their oysters, and seldom eat them fresh.   Oyster-shells are, like most other things, put to good account in China.   They are scraped down until they are nearly as thin as glass, and used for windows, and for many purposes which glass serves with us. I have been told that a favourite dish at Swatow is mice steeped in honey, but it has not been my good fortune to come across it.

Swatow being a treaty port has had a foreign settlement assigned to it on a high rocky island.

Pewter ware is a speciality of Swatow.   I saw in a shop for the sale of tobacco pipes some made of this material having bamboo handles three feet long.   There were also to be seen elaborate water-pipes made of pewter like the more common brass ones.

The Swatow people were very civil, and one man brought me to see several guild-houses or clubs.   By shaking my own hands in Chinese fashion and showing a tooth of mine which is cased with gold I seem to get an *entrée* into any house I want in China.   A beard also procures for me much respect in a beardless nation.

I took several walks in the neighbourhood of Swatow, and admired the fine trees that sheltered the villages.   Not so admirable, beneath the shadow of these trees, were the un-picturesque, malodorous concrete vats where dreadful manure is collected.

The orange groves around Swatow look beautiful, and the fruit, when not picked unripe, which is the Chinese custom in reference to fruit, are sweet and luscious.

When one travels in a cargo steamer, as I did to Swatow, one must do as the cargo does, and as rain prevented the landing for three days of the perishable goods on board, we saw rather more than we wanted of Swatow. However, the rain showed to us a specimen of the people's ingenuity in the coats of cocoanut fibre which they put on to shelter themselves. These coats are made like the palm-leaf rain coats worn by coolies in wet weather in other parts. The wearers look as if they were thatched.

The population of Amoy is estimated at a hundred thousand. There is an outer and an inner city divided by a ridge of rocky hills. On the hillsides are many of the large horse-shoe graves in which rich people are buried, and five millions, so it is said, of a less costly kind. These last consist of round mounds of white concrete, and at a distance the burial-place looks like a washing green or a collection of white beehives. When I expressed surprise at the number of graves a native remarked, "Yes, Amoy is celebrated for its pigs and its graves." It is also celebrated for being the dirtiest town in China, but from a distance it looks picturesque, lying as it does along a boulder-strewn bay. Here, as at Swatow, the foreign residences are all on an island separated from the city by a narrow strait.

Among the many things that are made at Amoy may be mentioned artificial flowers for the adornment of ladies' heads, and for offerings to the Imperial dead. Only the graves of royal people are allowed to be decorated with either natural or artificial flowers in China.

I visited the Temple of Ten Thousand Rocks which is situated

AMOY.

To face page 66.

amongst enormous boulders. It contains three fine gilt representations of Buddha, and images of eighteen of his disciples, also gilded. Below the images were the usual big candelabras and censers. A thin smoke curled up from the slow combustion of blocks of sandalwood, or from sheaves of smouldering joss-sticks standing in a vase. The pony on which I rode was a wonderful little creature. Like a cat it ran up and down the steps of the steep streets and so-called roads.

We were also advised to visit the temple of the white antelope and that of the tiger, but we could not spare time.

We saw in the neighbourhood several handsome pailaus. These are honorary arches erected to commemorate virtuous widows and other deserving people. It is thought that, in addition to being thus commemorated, virtuous widows will enter this world as men in their next term of existence, which would be as great promotion for them as it would be for an American man to become an American woman.

As we steamed up the Min River to Foochow we were continually reminded of the Rhine. The town is nine miles from Pagoda Island, where ships anchor.

Most of the European community live at Nantai, which is connected with Foochow by the "Bridge of Ten Thousand Ages," said to have been built eight hundred years ago. And certainly the bridge was no scamped work, but looks as if it were intended to last ten thousand ages. It is built of slabs of granite resting upon forty-nine ponderous pieces of the same material. Some of the slabs are forty-five feet in length and three in breadth. A number of street stalls are daily established upon one side of this bridge for the sale of sweetmeats, fruit, and the many curious things which Chinese coolies eat. Here too you may buy ornaments made of a soft reddish stone called soapstone which is found in the neighbourhood. Often the head of an executed criminal is here exhibited. The last time I passed over the bridge two thieves were dying, partly of starvation and partly of strangulation, in two upright cages surrounded by a jeering crowd.

The tide of busy life moves as restlessly beneath the bridge as above it, and I saw nearly as many boats of all shapes and sizes here as at Canton.

There are very fine trees in the vicinity of Foochow, and the city itself is called " The Banyan City," on account of the great number of bastard banyan-trees in and near it.   The " whiskers " of these trees that hang down from the main branches are curious.   Another name for Foochow is the "Three Hills," because of the three hills that are enclosed by its six to seven miles of thirty-feet-high walls.   Before the tea trade began to fail Foochow was, after Canton, the busiest city in China.

Like Amoy, Foochow is a centre of missionary enterprise. Ask Europeans in China, who sneer at and pretend to despise missionaries, where some information can be obtained, or where you can stay in places where there is only an unclean native inn, and they will reply, " Go to the missionaries."   I experienced the wisdom of this advice at Foochow.   The hotel was quite full and I did not know what to do.   " Call upon Archdeacon Wolfe " some one suggested; " he will make you all right."   I did so, and that fine young man of over seventy years, said, " Of course you will put up with us, and I will show you what we are doing here."   After he had brought me to the churches and preaching halls which he has built or rented in different quarters of Foochow, it seemed to me that the Archdeacon performed more than archidiaconal functions—that he had a diocese to look after.   And yet as he said, " When I came to Foochow forty years ago there were only two Christians; now there are twenty thousand, and a similar advance is going on all over China."

The Archdeacon pleaded guilty of having an excellent house, and apologised for the crime in this common-sense way: " For a missionary and his family to live in a healthy

FOOCHOW.

To face page 68.

house is cheaper than to live in one that will make him ill, and necessitate his being invalided home at the expense of his Society. Besides," he continued, "when we bought and built our houses things were cheap and the houses cost us very little." So, too, when walking up to a school for Chinese girls at Foochow, I admired the pots of flowers on either side of the path, the lady who manages the school remarked, "Mr. Sutton, the seed merchant, is good enough to send to us a present of seeds every year, but there are many critics, who, if they saw those flowers, would see in them another example of the luxury of missionaries." I may here say that at a Church of England mission, lately established in far-away Kwe-lin, I know a young missionary whose housekeeping expenses are a little under £10 a year. This is not too much luxury for a gently bred University man. I was also much interested by a visit which I paid when at Foochow to Miss Oxley's School for Blind Boys. These unfortunates, who in their homes were being eaten by vermin and utterly neglected, have been so well taught by this self-sacrificing lady, that they greatly astonished me. They read well from books of raised, romanised Chinese characters, sang, played musical instruments, and went through physical drill, in which last they take much pleasure. They are taught to earn their living by basket and other work.

I saw the graves of my college friend, Rev. Robert Stewart and his wife, who were murdered on the 1st of August, 1895, at Hwasang, 120 miles from Foochow. Their two children survived terrible injuries. One of them hid under a bed when the house was entered, and would most likely have been passed over, but, noticing that her little sister was lying helplessly *on* the bed, she threw herself across her body, and received the sword-cuts which were blindly dealt out.

CHAPTER VI

UP THE YANGTZE

Shanghai the Paris of China—Chin Kiang—Nanking—Vain repetitions—
Water-buffaloes—Kiukiang—A wedding celebration—Hankow, Han-
Yang and Wuchang—Between Hankow and Ichang—Cheap labour—
Ichang gorges.

THE Yangtze is the second largest river in the world,
being three thousand miles long, and so broad in
some places that it resembles a lake. Until one has seen
something of the country through which this mighty fertiliser
passes one knows nothing of China. To get rid of this
ignorance I embarked at Shanghai for a holiday, through
a land which may be called the desire of the whole
earth.

First a word about Shanghai. It is on the Whangpoa,
a river which runs into the Yangtze at Wusung. It is the
Paris of China, and many young men are ruined by its
attractions. Not long ago a rich Chinaman asked a friend
of the writer to find an English tutor for his son, as if the
youth were sent to Shanghai to learn English he would be
"ruined by the vices of foreigners."

There are in Foochow Road tea-houses, restaurants, opium-
smoking establishments, and baths of the luxury of which
I had no idea until brought to inspect one of the best of each
by a wealthy Chinese friend. It was fine to see Chinese as
rotund as porpoises apparently enjoying baths.

WHEELBARROW PEOPLE.

[To face page 71]

Even in the foreign settlements there are shops gorgeous with gilding and bright with coloured Chinese characters, in which their owners sit in summer bare to the waist displaying their prosperous fat and in winter their furs and satins.

Every globe-trotter visits the bubbling well and the mandarin's tea-garden, and believes that the latter is the original of the willow-pattern plate. The Bund, with its palatial banks and hongs, is a magnificent thoroughfare. Here in the evening compradores and shroffs, with their womankind painted and powdered, drive about, as do also Americans and Europeans who can afford smart traps. The cotton liveries of the coachmen and grooms are sometimes very fantastic.

A wheelbarrow having its one wheel covered at the top and sides, is the vehicle upon which impecunious Shanghai people drive. You will see one coolie pushing a whole family. I have tried this conveyance, and it made my teeth rattle as it bumped along. Outside the city, if the wind should be aft, a sail is commonly hoisted, and it was to this custom Milton referred when he wrote—

> "Sericana, where Chinese drive
> With sail and wind their canny waggons light."

The Shanghai gardens are a place not easily matched for passing away the after-sunshine hours.

Like another place, the native city of Shanghai is not mentioned to ears polite; but I ventured into it twice. It is like stepping back three hundred years, and a pleasant though unsavoury change from the up-to-dateness of the "Model Settlement." Europeans pride themselves on stupidly ignoring old Shanghai, and think that it is "bad form" to visit it.

Leaving Shanghai at 7 o'clock p.m. in a great white

herded when feeding along the banks. The boy keeps away the flies, and the buffalo so much appreciates this service that he will put his head down and give the boy a leg up with his great horns when the youth wishes to mount. Nearly two years ago some of these herding children reported to their father that there was a buffalo calf in the grass that did not belong to them. The father went and found a tiger lying asleep. He called out all the neighbours that had guns, but none dared fire lest they should fail to kill and be attacked. In the evening the tiger awoke and took his departure in peace. There is always plenty of work for a sportsman along the Yangtze. We saw many deer and pheasants, and every now and then flocks of wild duck and geese almost darkened the sky.

We admired much the silver ornaments that were sold in the shops at Kiukiang. As we were looking into one shop we heard in the back part of the house festive sounds. It was a wedding celebration, and the people made signs to us to go in. We did so, and were most hospitably treated and shown everything. Would an unknown Chinaman receive similar kindness in an English town?

Of the three cities that meet together and almost join— Hankow and Wuchang separated by the three-quarter-mile wide Yangtze, and Hankow and Han-Yang separated by the boat-covered Han—Hankow is the largest. Indeed, the "Million-peopled City" is the commercial centre of China, and the greatest distributing point in the Empire.

I visited the Kiangsi Guild-house at Hankow, and thought that it was finer than even the Swatow Guild-house at Canton. It is less ornate, but more massive. There are connected with it several shrines and two stages for theatrical performances. Outward religion, business, and amusement here combine.

The principal streets of the native town are flagged; the others are cut into deep ruts by wheelbarrows, and always inches deep in mud, because of the spilling of the water that is continually being carried in open buckets on men's shoulders.

The houses of many of the poorer Chinese along the banks of the Han are built on piles, so that the rising of the river may not sweep them away. Those belonging to a lower depth of poverty herd in mud huts, which are removed as the water rises.

Then there is an enormous population afloat. Junks and sampans—two, three, and four deep, "like the teeth of a comb"—reach for miles along the river-banks.

Hankow reeks of tea, for it is the centre from which the Russians import brick tea. I was much interested by a visit to one of the places where tea-dust (only inferior broken tea is used) is compressed in metal boxes into bricks. So many are the Russians in Hankow that there is in it a Russian church. Here I attended a service on Good Friday, which in the Greek Church comes about ten days after our Good Friday.

Opposite Hankow is Wuchang. Here is the large arsenal, where the Viceroy and other officials have their yamens. Having spent most of a day in this town, I crossed over to Han-Yang and visited a large Buddhist monastery. A monk who had died was placed in a sitting position in the square wooden coffin in which priests are cremated. Many joss-sticks were burned at the altar, behind which the box was kept until the cremation ceremony. Not being one of those who like to see China Westernised, I did not visit the iron-works at Han-Yang. Let us hope that more gain even, morally speaking, than loss will come from the disappearance of antique civilisation.

Having spent three days very profitably at the American Episcopal Mission at Hankow, I took passage in one of the smaller steamers that go to Ichang. From this place onwards the river became narrower, so we could study the villagers from a nearer point of view. At some places we were near enough to throw empty bottles to the people.   These they find very useful, and they vied with each other in running and tumbling down the banks to get them.   The girls and women were even more keen for foreign-devil bottles than the other sex, and looked quite gay as they ran after them in the red trousers they wear.

The people seemed contented and even happy.   They were rich in not having wants.   If only poor China could be left alone, and not made to desire things that have not increased our own happiness !

The weather had become warmer, and the pink peach blossoms competing with the plum were beginning to blend with the light green of the willows.   The chief business of the people for miles along the river is cutting and transporting the reeds that grow near the banks.   They are used for many things, but especially for making the walls of houses when they are plastered within and without with mud.   The reeds are carried away on carts having solid or spokeless wheels.   On a lower level sledges are used for the purpose.

We were interested in the bamboo belts that are put round the furnaces in which lime is burned, and wondered if there were anything for which they do not use bamboo in China.

Ten miles below Ichang the dead-level of scenery that we were having altered, and we got to the Tiger Head gorge.   It does not deserve so formidable a name, but there were finely coloured and many shaped mountains at the back.   One peak is crowned by an inaccessible looking Buddhist monastery. Pyramid Hill, opposite Ichang, looks just like the pyramid of Cheops at Cairo.   To counteract the bad influence that might come from it, a monastery has been built on the Ichang side of the river.   This silenced the grumblings and threatenings of the Feng-shui prophets.

Ichang is a walled city of about 85,000 inhabitants.   On the river front are the go-downs and other buildings of the Chinese Imperial Customs.   There are four flourishing missionary establishments, all of which we visited. The long hill behind was covered with graves, which looked like very large mole-hills.

The number of boats and junks that were packed for over a mile along the shore astonished us. The junks are strongly built for the rapids, and some of them are quite handsome with their stained and oiled woodwork looking like varnished pine.

My stay at Ichang, where there is no hotel, was made possible by the thoughtful hospitality of the head of the Customs, Mr. Unwin, and instructive by his well-informed conversation.

Labour is certainly very cheap in these parts. After staying a night at a friend's house, I gave the houseboy a Mexican dollar (not quite 2s.). He turned it over and over, and seemed frightened at the largeness of the amount, and at last handed it back to me. I asked his master what this meant. " Oh, " he said, " they do not understand silver here, only copper cash. Give me the dollar, and I shall give it to number one, and after eulogising your generosity, tell him to change it into cash, and divide it amongst all the servants of the establishment."

At Ichang, to save Europeans the trouble of carrying cash, slips of bamboo having ten or twenty cash written on them in English and Chinese, are supplied for giving to boat and chair coolies. After being carried in a chair by two men for an hour I gave them a slip with twenty cash marked on it, that is the equivalent of one halfpenny in our money. They were overcome with gratitude, for they only expected ten cash, which make a farthing !

Those who track or pull junks with ropes get twenty cents. a day for walking and hauling twenty or more miles, and for taking, like patient mules, the blows of overseers on their bare backs. We talk of the battle of life, but it is for these poor men quite literally a tug of war. The track ropes are made of strips of bamboo, and that so skilfully that they are stronger than hemp ropes.

On account of the great danger of the rapids after passing Ichang, there is a well-supported Chinese Lifeboat Association. The boatmen are rewarded for every life saved.

One of the industries of Ichang and some of the other towns we visited is stamping paper money for offerings to the gods. When the people think of doing this by machinery they will probably think that it need not be done at all.

There remained but little time at our disposal, but the thousand miles which I had come from Shanghai would have been almost wasted if I had not gone further and seen something of the gorges beyond Ichang. Fortunately the current in the river was so weak that the boat we hired got five times higher up than it could have gone in the same length of time six weeks later.

The sides of the first gorge through which we passed were 3,500 feet high, and our motto was "excelsior" until we got to a gorge a thousand feet higher than that. We shall not attempt to describe the fantastic shape of the rocks. Most of them might be designated, what one actually is—pillars of heaven. Wild monkeys are sometimes seen sitting upon them, but they did not think it worth while to come out and see us. One of the arguments of the Chinese for not using steamers after Ichang is that the monkeys would throw down rocks upon them!

We visited at different elevations quaint villages and temples. Some of the cottages were perched on apparently inaccessible little platforms, with the small children belonging to them tied to rocks and trees for fear of their falling over. On lower levels orange-trees flourished.

Between Ichang and Hankow, on our return journey, there was one day quite a sea, or rather a river, on, and it was strange to hear a lady say that she was going to be sea-sick when it was on a river that we pitched and tossed.

When we arrived at a place where we had made the acquaintance of a local mandarin, he came on board and called. He seemed to enjoy the cigar which we gave him, but after a while returned to his own pipe. The stem was about five feet long, but the bowl was very small, and had to be filled and lighted frequently by an attendant, who apparently had no other object in life. Every few minutes this individual walked solemnly forward from behind our visitor's chair, filled the pipe, and blew the fire-stick into a flame. The mandarin opened one corner of his mouth, the boy, who seemed intelligent enough for higher work, inserted the stem, and applied the fire-stick to the bowl.

CHAPTER VII

VILLAGE LIFE

Each village self-sufficing — Drastic measures — Overcrowding — Thrifty husbandry—A Chinese village like matrimony—Lepers—Stay-at-homes —Markets—No roads—Idols punished—Schools—Respect for scholarship—Theatres.

THE rural Chinese live in villages for protection and sociability, and of the men seen in large towns at least half keep their wives and children in villages ten, twenty, or even a hundred miles away. A village is occupied by members of the same clan or family, and all have the same name. Each village, with its special hand and foot industry, is almost self-sufficing, growing much of its own food and clothes stuff. It is also a little principality by itself, for the Government of China, though nominally autocratic, is democratic in its administration and allows a large amount of home rule. Nor are the people heavily taxed so long as they do not indulge in litigation and come within reach of squeezing mandarins.

The fathers and grandfathers of a clan being held responsible by the Imperial Government for the conduct of a village, are entrusted with much power. These greybeards, who are themselves much influenced by elderly ladies with well-hung tongues, will not tolerate scandal in their communities. Indeed, they are only too drastic in their desire that Cæsar's wife should be above suspicion. A friend of mine came across a place outside a Chinese village, not far from the British frontier in Kowloon, where earth had recently been turned up. He asked for an explanation, and was told that two days before a man and woman taken in adultery had been there buried alive by order of the village elders. The culprits were put in two holes facing each other and earth was shovelled in, not all at once, but at intervals of time, so as to prolong their sufferings.

Clan affections and the value attached to posterity prevent, as a rule, the abuse of fatherly correction on the part of Chinese Puritans, but I have heard of a hopeless gambler and opium-smoker being condemned to death by a village council.

What is that noise and crowd in the main street of a village? A man is beating a gong and is followed by another man with his hands pinioned behind him. A lictor close at his heels plies a bamboo on the culprit's fast-reddening back. This "walking punishment" has been ordered for theft by the villagers themselves, and the district magistrate, Gallio-like, cares for none of these things.

It is the business of the headmen in a village to get back stolen property, to prevent the removal of the stones which mark the divisions of land, and to keep the peace generally between neighbours.

In a country with so many poor as China, and where the fields are not enclosed, a "lodge in a garden of cucumbers" or of other kinds of crop, in which some one watches day and night, is a necessity. If a thief is caught he is at the least well bambooed and tied up as a warning for a certain time at the village temple.

In most villages there is a sort of insurance against robbers. Each householder pays so much a year to a constable or watchman, who manages the money. This official recovers anything that is stolen or pays the value of it. If a murder is committed little or no notice is taken unless the family

prosecute, and it requires money to do this.   Frequently the
case is settled without going before the district magistrate
by the village elders.   They put a money valuation on the
murdered one, and give part as compensation to his family.
You can murder for from two to four hundred dollars, but
for a robbery you pay as a rule with your head.

Village houses made of stone, brick, wood, mud, or only of
matting are huddled together, with the result of unhealthy
overcrowding.   Land must be saved for eatables.   There is,
however, a great difference in the villages.   Some are dirty
and tumbledown, others comparatively clean and well built.
Chinese who have returned from Australia and California
have improved many villages in the neighbourhood of Canton
so much that they suggest Devonshire.

A village is generally on ground a little higher than the
rice, rape, millet, peanut, or whatever other crops surround it.
In front there is a pond in which fish are nurtured and slate-
coloured water-buffaloes disport themselves.   For every few
houses there is a concrete threshing-floor and a receptacle for
liquid manure.

In the case of everything except rice the Chinese put a
liquid preparation of manure upon the plant rather than upon
the soil.   This is for economy, as on account of the few
domestic animals that are kept manure is very scarce.   Every
substance convertible to it is diligently husbanded.   For this
reason the cakes that remain after the expression of vegetable
oil are kept.   The plaster of old kitchens, which is blackened
with smoke, because the kitchens have no chimneys, is so
much valued that sometimes new plaster is put on in order to
get the old for manure.

Hair is carefully collected in the barber's shop for the same
purpose, and this must mount up considerably in a country
where some hundred millions of heads are constantly shaved.
The Chinese are market gardeners rather than farmers, and
they keep their plots of vegetables so free from weeds that

one would think weeds would become extinct. Even the tops
of the narrow ditches separating the rice-fields are planted
with single rows of beans.

As a rule the only power used is man power, for that in
China is the cheapest. The simplicity and ingenuity of
agricultural implements call forth our admiration. The
Chinese seem to be able to do almost everything by means
of almost nothing.

When a rice-field has been laid under water and ploughed
by a water-buffalo and his driver wading up to their knees,
rice shoots are transplanted into it by a convenient division
of labour. One person takes the shoots and hands them to
another, who conveys them to their destination. They are
there received by another party of labourers, standing ankle-
deep in mud and water, some of whom dibble holes, into
which they drop the plants by sixes, while others follow to
settle the earth about the roots.

To raise water from a river or canal to irrigate rice, an
endless chain which moves a number of buckets is worked
treadmill style by the feet of coolies, which reminds us of the
Biblical saying, "Thou shalt water thy ground with thy
foot." When possible, bamboo water-wheels, often thirty or
forty feet in diameter, are used.

In the time of harvest the grain is beaten out of the ears
on the edge of a basket.

The inhabitants of many villages can only afford rice as a
luxury. They call themselves "sweet-potato people," for
that is their usual food.

There is much sugar-cane grown in the South, and it is
interesting to see the water-buffaloes working the primitive
pressing mills.

In their care of silkworms the peasants show great powers
of observation. They study the habits, weaknesses, and
idiosyncrasies of the insect to such a nicety that they are
able to regulate its digestion by exact dieting. The mulberry

trees planted for the silkworms are never allowed to grow larger than currant-bushes.

A Chinese village is like matrimony—difficult to get into and difficult to get out of. It is built in this way to puzzle evil spirits or robbers. With the most honest intentions I have wandered about a long time before I could find my way out of one.

I have seen outside a village a number of lepers, living each in a sort of dog-house made of straw or matting. When they saw that I was a stranger they, with other beggars, exhibited their sores, knelt down, knocked their heads on the ground, and moved their clenched hands up and down in an agony of mendicancy.

A leper will sometimes sit on a doorstep and refuse to move until the householder gives him, say, fifty cents. He is offered ten or twenty or thirty, but no! When he sees a good many people approaching he cries out : "You are rich and I am a poor leper ; you must give fifty cents."

Chinese lepers believe that if they can communicate the disease to any one it will be proportionately lessened in themselves. With th's unselfish object in view they will wash in wells and indulge in sexual intercourse. Villagers sometimes become so exasperated with this kind of conduct that they beat lepers to death or bury them alive.

There are many Chinese who never leave their native village and who cannot tell you anything about the next village, not even the distance to it. We may remark that distances between places in China are not fixed quantities, but vary according as the ways to them are rough or smooth, hilly or level. On level ground one mile is called two li, on a hilly road five li ; when the way is very steep it may be as much as fifteen li.

Life in an ordinary Chinese village would be considered by us deadly dull. After work is over there is nothing to do but go to bed. It is not considered respectable to walk about

A Mule Litter.

To face page 85.

aimlessly after the sun has set, and in many places the people greatly fear tigers or evil spirits at night.

> "'Bright shines the moon,' say you? but list, my son,
> Hear my advice and walk not out alone;
> Or if alone, on duty, you must go
> Forget not the red lantern's light to show."

On every tenth day in some villages a market is held and things are sold under large umbrellas made of palm branches stuck into the ground. A great many cats and kittens, tied up by the neck, are on sale. In Great Britain kittens are bestowed to save them from being drowned and girls are given away in marriage, but in China a man buys both pussy and wife.

Leading to market or anywhere else there are no proper roads in the South of China, but only tracks that are sometimes cobbled or paved with slabs of granite. Often there is nothing to walk on except the small banks that enclose the water in the little patches of rice.

In every Chinese village there is an ancestral or other temple, in which gatherings of the clan take place with the usual accompanying feasts. The tablets of successive generations are arranged on shelves behind the altar, and to honour the spirits of the departed incense is burned every morning and evening. The village shop of miscellaneous goods supplies requisites for temple service, such as cardboard and wooden idols, incense-sticks, fire-crackers, and paper money.

Those who desire to see their names posted in conspicuous places sometimes build a second or even a third temple, though it is a common remark amongst the Chinese that the more temples a village has the poorer it is in money and morals.

The idols of one village are occasionally brought to visit those of another, or they may be borrowed if they have the reputation of being able to cause rain. When a god does his duty the villagers are careful of his comfort. If, for instance, a temple at a distance from a village has to be shut up for fear of thieves, a small opening will be left to give the idols air to breathe!

Although instruction is not compulsory in China, nearly all boys are sent to school. Village schools are established by the joint effort of a few families. The teachers are poorly paid (only about fifty dollars a year), as the supply of them is in excess of the demand, but they are much respected. Country families, as we would call them, generally keep a tutor in the house. After staying with a rich family, Mr. Archibald Little wrote: "At table I was surprised to see at the upper seat— that is next to mine—and among my handsomely clad hosts, a poorly dressed, almost ragged, pale young man, who I was told was the 'Lao-sze' (literally, old scholar), or family tutor. It is gratifying to see the extreme respect everywhere paid in China to teachers; their extreme poverty would render them despised in Europe. Villagers are proud of any graduate who may live among them, for in China unbounded respect for learning co-exists with unbounded ignorance, and a literary man can make himself useful in many ways, as, for instance, in writing letters and helping to win a law case." ("Through the Yang-Tse Gorges," page 223.)

The great event of village life is the occasional visit of strolling players. In a very short time a temporary mat-shed theatre is put up on some barren spot on the outskirts of the village; around it cook-shops, tea-shops, gambling booths and the like, all made of bamboo, palm-leaves, and matting, are erected. The place is like a fair. At mat-shed theatres the audience in the pit stand; above there are seats for subscribers and local magnates. Seeing me standing among coolies in a theatre in a Hong Kong village, an Indian policeman came forward and saying, "It will never do for a European to stand here," brought me right on to the stage, which made me feel as if I were part of the show. However, the actors bowed a

welcome, handed me a chair, and did not seem to notice the incongruity of my sitting in the midst of the battle in which they were engaged. When I got up to leave one of the performers insisted on bringing me to see the dresses and other properties behind the stage. Chinese actors wear many-coloured gold-embroidered clothes and hats of a period before the Tartar conquest. Their faces shine with thick paint and threaten with fierce artificial whiskers and beards.

There is no curtain, or wings, or scenery, or stage illusion of any kind, and the play is not divided into scenes and acts. When the actors appear they tell the audience who they are and what they are going to do, and imitate such actions as rowing a boat or riding a horse so cleverly that scenery is unnecessary. Should one of them be killed, he gets up after a decent interval and walks away.

The parts of women are nearly always taken by boys, who imitate well their shrill voices, mincing movements, and even their hoof-like feet. Respectable women do not go to Chinese theatres. The plays themselves may be unobjectionable, but the actors take great license. The motions of the actors are like those of puppets, and if the men fight in a battle they give the impression that they take no interest in self-defence. The only applause that is heard is an occasional prolonged sigh, but the pipes, gongs, and cymbals of the orchestra emphasise important sayings and doings in a way that is very trying to European ears. The play is "long drawn out," or at least seems so; but it is not "lingering sweetness." When the plays are short they follow each other without any interval, and this gives foreigners the erroneous impression that they are all ridiculously long. Fifty-six actors make up a full company, each of whom must know perfectly from one to two hundred plays, there being no prompter. They have also to learn all kinds of acrobatic feats, as these are freely introduced into "military plays." Their diet is carefully regulated, and in order to strengthen the voice they walk about in the open air for an hour or so each day, the head thrown back and the mouth wide open.

A mandarin can command the services of players, as indeed he can of most people. He even gets money from them in this way : he has a warrant made out ordering a theatrical entertainment, in which a space is left blank for the name of the company that is to furnish it and the date when it is to be given. This document he sells to the broker who bids highest for it. The purchaser goes to the managers of the theatrical companies in the neighbourhood, and threatens that if they do not give him a certain amount of blackmail he will put the name of their company into the warrant. It pays to give a good sum to escape this, for the mandarin gives no remuneration to a company, and may keep them incurring great daily expenses for a long time.

After the theatre the next most popular form of village diversion seems to be a faction fight. Two adjoining villages may engage in one, or it may be different parts of a single community. This last was the case when some coolies, returning from Hong Kong, where they had not heard of a war that had begun, landed in the enemy's end of their native village. They were taken prisoners and severely beaten.

The *Hong Kong Daily Press* for November 20, 1903, incidentally mentioned how some villagers disport themselves, when describing a conflagration by which almost the whole of a village near Canton was burnt. Gambling led some companions to form a robber band, of which three members had been executed the week before at Canton. So far was this from dispiriting them that they continued gambling till late at night, and then singed a cat preparatory to cooking it for supper. Some of the sparks from the hair ignited the mat-shed in which they were assembled, and this the houses near it.

The ways in which the population of towns and villages

are calculated are vague and unreliable. You ask an apparently intelligent-looking inhabitant, "How many people are there in this village?" He will tell you the number of big pots there are for boiling rice, or the number of pawnshops there are, leaving it to you to settle how many persons should go to a pot or a pawnshop.

CHAPTER VIII

The unexpected happens—Chinese practices which we think absurd can
be rationally explained.

WHEN we first come to China all things seem to be upside
down, and it is the unexpected only that happens.
Meeting a friend, a Chinese shakes his own hands and not
the hand of his friend, which is more sanitary than is our
custom. If he wants a man to keep away, he makes the
same movement of his hand which we make when we wish
him to come to us. He laughs when he announces the
death of a relative, and a Chinese bride cries at her wedding.
If you go into the office of a European whose hat is on his
head he will take it off; if you go to where a Chinese is
sitting with his cap on the table in front of him, he will put
on the cap. A servant in China should wait at table with
his cap on. At a Chinese entertainment the post of honour
is at the left and not at the right, as with us. If it is a
dinner it will begin, contrary to ours, with dessert, and end
with soup and rice. At home dogs are tied up; in China
cats are, at least those belonging to boat people.

The Chinese are not only at our antipodes with regard to
position on the globe, but they are our opposites in almost
every thought and act. Our shoes are all blackened, the
Chinese whiten the sides of the soles of theirs. To us

observation without sympathy is torture, but the Chinese seem to like to be observed working, eating, or whatever they are doing.

The mourning colour in China is white and not black, and the Chinese must think a white cloth upon a dinner-table as dismal as we would a table covered with black crape. When foreigners come first to China they notice that men wear petticoats and women trousers. As a matter of fact both sexes wear these last, only the peasant women whom foreigners most see do not have either a petticoat or a frock, but only a long jacket; and the literary man, that is to say the gentlemen of China, always wear a long outer robe. A Chinese wears a waistcoat over his coat, and not under as we do. We use our hands to play battledore and shuttle-cock; the Chinese have no battledore and kick the shuttle-cock. If a British boy is puzzled, say, in doing a sum, he scratches his head, but a Chinese boy kicks off a shoe and scratches a foot. Chinese babies are carried not in front in the arms of their mothers, but upon their backs.

The Chinese do not say north-east, north-west, south-east, south-west, but east-north, west-north, east-south, west-south. They say that the magnetic needle points to the south and not to the north. The stern of a Chinese boat or junk is where the bow of a European one is, and at a distance the boat looks as if it were sailing backwards. If a boat is rowed or sculled the men face the direction in which they are going, and do not turn their backs to it as we do. If a boat is hauled up on the shore it is pulled stern foremost. When unloading a ship each burden-bearer in Great Britain hands a tally every trip he makes to the overseer, in China the overseer hands one to the worker.

Fancy the framework of a roof being constructed before the pillars that are to support it! This is done by the Chinese, but like most of their, as we think, contradictory practices, it can be rationally explained. The pillars are not sunk into the ground, but only upon stone foundations, and the weight of the roof is required to keep them in their place.

A Chinaman mounts a horse from the offside instead of the near, putting his right foot first into the stirrup. He holds the reins in his right hand and not in the left. When the horse is in the stable it is placed with its head where we think its tail should be. Many tools, as, for instance, the saw, are used in an almost opposite way from what we use them. Stockings are knitted from the toe upwards. The beginning of a Chinese book is where a Western one ends, and it is read from right to left and from top to bottom. The notes, if any, are placed on the top of the page, and separated from the page by a line. Books are placed on shelves on top of one another, instead of side by side. The Chinese arrange their dates the opposite way to what we do, putting the year first, the month next, and the day last. They turn their fractions upside down, and instead of saying four-sixths, for instance, they say six-fourths. Decimal fractions, however, are their vulgar fractions, or those in common use. Tell a Chinese clerk to fasten together some documents numbered from one to ten, and he will do it in the reverse order. In the perspective of Chinese pictures things get larger instead of smaller.

The Chinese place the family name before that of the individual, saying, as it were, Smith John instead of John Smith. We speak of being killed by lightning, the Chinese of being killed by thunder. In other countries if a man wishes to wreak vengeance on an enemy he kills him, in China he kills himself. To plague the life of an adversary he takes away his own life. He believes that his spirit will haunt and torment the man who has offended, or at least that the mandarins will make it troublesome if a dead body is found on his premises or even at his door. A dead Chinaman is nearly always more considered than a living one, and the most important event in his life is, to speak in an Irish way, his funeral.

In Europe the best places are occupied by the living, in China by the dead. In life a Chinaman pigs it in a hovel little raised above the level of the surrounding swamp; in death he occupies a breezy hill-side spot, commanding often a charming view. In Chinese towns drains are on the surface, which, though less agreeable to the nose, are healthier than our underground drains. Europeans only drink hot water as an emetic, Chinese never drink water cold. A Chinese watchman, policeman, or soldier does not conceal himself in order to arrest thieves, but beats upon bamboo sticks, blows a long bugle, or makes some other noise to frighten them away. We match honest men against thieves, not so the Chinese; they make an arrangement with robber-leaders, and in this way set a thief to catch a thief. If two or more Western people are walking together they will go side by side, but the Chinese invariably walk one after another, having probably acquired the habit by walking on the narrow paths that surround rice-fields.

With us pawnshops are the sign of a poor neighbourhood, in China of a rich one, because they are used as much for warehousing summer or winter articles in the off-season as for " raising the wind." On the roofs of many of them are kept large jars full of vitriol, ready to be thrown down on people attempting to rob them.

Honours in China flow upstream, so that deceased ancestors derive titles of distinction from their worthy offspring. This is a sensible arrangement, because it is by reason of our ancestors and not of our successors that we are what we are. A dutiful son seeks reputation chiefly for the sake of reflecting it back upon his parents, and dreads disgrace lest it should bring reproach on their name. Indeed, it is the duty of a son who has been honoured by the Emperor to ask that a title one degree higher than his own may be conferred upon his father.

In the Western world a lady goes into a room before a man, and in everything else is given the preference. In China she takes a very back seat indeed, and when she speaks to a man she stands up to show respect. Instead of being honoured more than men, she is considered an inferior animal.

At a Chinese wedding the bridegroom is the centre of attraction, and in reference to the bride, there is only the curiosity which is felt to see what sort of a bargain the family made in getting her. We regard a husband and wife as the basis of a new family; in China they are only the latest branch of a family tree. Accordingly the bride goes to live with her husband's family, where she is nothing but an echo and a shadow.

It must seem disagreeably topsy-turvey to ladies, on coming first to China, to find " boys "—that is to say, servant men— doing the work which house- and lady's-maids do at home. The boy brings early morning tea into a room occupied by married people, and enters the apartment of a young lady with little or no warning to arrange her bath. The Chinese think our plan of chambermaids bringing tea and hot water into the rooms of unmarried men no less improper.

To us, uncut nails are disgusting; to the Chinese, nails so long that they have to be protected by cases are very stylish, because they indicate that their owner does no menial work.

When there is a *fête* in a Chinese family, or visitors are expected, the chairs, made usually of marble or bamboo, are covered with embroidered red satin covers, which is the contrary of what is done in Europe, where the furniture is uncovered on important occasions. The Chinaman puts a candlestick into a candle, and not the reverse. The Chinese pluck and eat their fruit unripe, and think that our habit of eating ripe fruit is unwholesome.

To us the idea of a pillow is something soft on which the head rests; to the Chinese it is a rounded piece of wood or lacquer ware, which supports only the neck.

CHAPTER IX

SOME CHINESE CHARACTERISTICS

Fashion and custom differ with locality—What would the Chinese not do if they were unanimous?—Fish-fights and cricket-fights—The braying of a donkey stopped—The Chinaman's expression, his patience, his ability to sleep, his materialism, his integrity, his dirt—Chinese proverbial philosophy—Natural orators—Conjuring—Men of resource—Two impressive things—Early inventions—Why do the Chinese not know more?—Great at organising—Guilds of beggars and thieves—Gambling propensities—Privacy not respected—A debtor and credit account with Heaven—Want of sympathy—Loss of face—Resemblance between the Chinese and the English.

IN order to find out the characteristics of the Chinese people, one ought to see many parts of the country, for fashion and custom differ with locality. "You should be born in Soochow, live at Canton, and die at Ningpo," is a saying that shows how each place is generally a speciality for something. Birth in Soochow is an advantage because the people there are better looking than elsewhere; living at Canton is preferable because especially luxurious; and should luxuries shorten your life, you cannot get anywhere a coffin better than at Ningpo.

Practically the eighteen provinces into which China is divided are as distinct from each other as are the countries of Europe. This is why, in our wars with China, coolies were willing to earn pay and rations by helping to work British guns, and showed the pride of good workmanship when a shot made a lane through their countrymen. I have often heard Chinese belonging to different provinces talking to each other in pidgin English. Curran said of an Irish inn, where he had spent a night, "The fleas were so many and so vicious if they had only been unanimous they would have lifted me out of bed." What could the Chinese not do if they were unanimous?

The Chinese are fond of their children, though they pet them one moment and beat them the next. They seem to prefer birds to animals. Where we would bring a dog for a walk, they carry in a cage a singing bird, generally the yellow-eyebrowed thrush. They do not indulge in cock-fighting, as did our ancestors, but they train quails, thrushes, and even fish to fight. Two bottles, in either of which is a fish, are placed alongside; when the fish grow angry with each other they are put into the same bottle, where they fight it out.

Crickets, too, have an important place in the Chinese sporting world. Two at a time are put on a flat tray with a deep rim, and are tickled on their heads with a hair until they get into a rage and charge each other. When the victor of many fights dies, he is sometimes honoured with a silver coffin. Even those who do not train crickets for the arena keep them in tiny bamboo cages and earthenware jars because they are fond of their chirping.

The Chinese are cruel to animals, but they know how to make them do what they want. If, for instance, they are disturbed by a donkey braying at night, they tie a big stone to his tail, and this humiliates him into silence.

A Chinaman always appears to be looking round the corners of his eyes at you, and to have a meaning that you cannot get at. He gives you the impression that somebody when he was born sat on his nose, and that he has been lamenting the calamity ever since. And yet, though he never lays aside this expression of resigned wretchedness, the average Chinese is not at all more miserable than the average Britisher.

" The highest calling and election," says George Eliot, " is to do without opium and to bear pain with clear-eyed endurance." The Chinese do not do without opium, but they have made their calling and election sure in reference to enduring pain. They can wait without complaint and bear with calm fortitude. They combine the active industry of the most civilised people with the passive patience of the North American Indian.

A Chinese sleeps when he has nothing better to do, like a dog. He can " go to sleep across three wheelbarrows, with his head downward like a spider, his mouth wide open and a fly inside." Indeed, a Chinaman seems to like noise for its own sake.

A Chinese thinks money, and is as uncomfortable as an American until he ascertains the price of everything he sees. Most Chinese are so poor that they can only seek for food; the rest are as hard and materialistic about money. After the day's business the shopkeeper counts his cash with great care, and the click of his little calculating machine brings music to what he is pleased to call his soul. That integrity is a characteristic of the Chinese merchant when he has not been spoiled by foreign examples is shown by the fact that, even in the largest transactions, written contracts are seldom required. His word is his bond. However, I was once a little disappointed in this respect. I asked a seller at a street stall how much a dried fruit was. He answered, " Five cents." My companion, who knew Chinese well, pointed to a label indicating that the price was only one cent. The crowd laughed, and the stall-keeper " lost face." " No two prices " may be put up in the shops, but every Chinese shopman will come down to a persevering bargainer.

Before the Chinese were prohibited from emigrating to the Philippine Islands, the fare from Amoy to Manila was for them 75 dollars first class, 15 dollars second. Those in the latter class had to take a bath before landing, so, in order to escape this terror, many used to travel first-class who would otherwise have gone second. A whole family of Chinese will make their ablutions one after another in about a pint of unchanged water in the same basin. In their heads nearly all Chinese "grow vermin."

Still, the Chinese are not dirty in all respects. Even coolies generally wash their feet when work is over, and swab with a wrung-out cloth as much of their bodies as can be got at without taking off their trousers. They clean their teeth much more regularly than do British peasantry. And whatever their practice is, they have at least a theoretical belief in cleanliness, if we may judge from an inscription which a Chinese placed over pieces of soap in his shop—"Cheaper than dirt." Talking of inscriptions, we may mention that where we put up "Commit no nuisance," the Chinese equivalent is "Respect yourself."

Their proverbial philosophy shows that the Chinese are very thoughtful. Here are a few specimens : "The best and strongest man in the world finds that he cannot escape the two words 'No continuance '"; "Happiness consists in a medium station "; "When you are sitting quietly, and alone, think of your own faults; when conversing with others, do not talk of the faults of others "; "Correct yourself on the same principle that you correct others, and excuse others on the same principle that you excuse yourself"; "He who requires much from himself and little from others will keep himself from being the object of resentment "; "He who pursues a stag regards not hares"; "A gem cannot be polished without friction, or a man perfected without adversity "; "The gods cannot help a man who loses opportunities."

The Chinese call a harmless blusterer "a paper tiger," and compare a man over-estimating himself to a rat falling into a scale and weighing itself. Overdoing a thing is a hunchback making a bow.

BRIDGE AT PEKING.

To face page 90.

You have only to watch their story- and fortune-tellers in the streets to see that the Chinese are natural orators ; you can see that by their gestures, even if you do not understand what they say.   They use very apt illustrations.

I never saw conjuring so clever anywhere as in China. Some of the tricks, however, were not pleasant to look at, as, for instance, when a man put a long, living whip-snake into his mouth and brought it out from his nose, or when he pretended to cut off a boy's head.

A Chinese is nearly always a person of resource.   A young man was accused of knocking out his father's teeth, and was in danger of being put to death.   He was visited by a friend who had taken a high degree.   The friend looked grave, and whispered into the prisoner's ear, "It's a bad case." Suddenly seizing the ear between his teeth, he gave it a severe bite.   "What do you mean?" asked the young man, raising his fist.   "I mean," was the answer, "that you are saved ; you have only to show the marks of my teeth and say that they were made by your father, whose teeth, being shaky, dropped out."

Two small things especially impress foreigners with the skill and ingenuity of the Chinese.   One is the way ivory balls are made and carved, one within the other, to the number of seven or eight ; and the other, the inscription of minute characters inside agate or crystal snuff-bottles.

The compass, printing, gunpowder, water-tight compart-- ments in junks, bills of exchange, and bank-notes were invented by the Chinese.   They had the compass 2634 B.C., and the oldest newspaper in the world—*The Peking Gazette*. They made the longest canal and wall ever made ; they built monumental bridges.   If they see a machine gun or anything else for a few moments, they can turn one out just like it.

The political economy taught by Kouan-tse before the Christian era differs in no way from the teaching of our own Adam Smith and J. S. Mill.   The ancient Chinese economist

draws the same line between productive and unproductive
labour, and shows that in proportion as the rich buy luxuries ;
the poor are deprived of necessaries.

The Chinese studied astronomy twenty-two centuries ago,
and a book of theirs, written B.C. 221, is looked upon as the
first treatise on trigonometry.

Chinese have a strong sense of humour, but the stories
which they most appreciate generally refer to buying and
selling.   Here is one which was told by a friend of mine, who
heard one of them, almost convulsed with laughter, telling it
to another: A clever woman was afflicted with a stupid
husband whom she could not trust to do the family shopping.
Once, however, when ill, she had to send him to buy something that was badly needed.   " They will ask too much for
it," she said, " so be sure and only give half the price mentioned."   A dollar was demanded for the article.   " I will
give you fifty cents," suggested noodle.   " Oh, that is too
little, but we will let you have it for eighty."   Mindful of the
injunction to give only half of what was asked, the obedient
one said, " Very well, I will give you forty cents " !

The Chinese are so clever and sensible that the apparent
irrationality of many of their thoughts and deeds is un-
accountable.   They have discovered and know so much that
we are surprised they do not know more.   Why is it, we
wonder, that people with such an ancient civilisation should
persist in thinking that the earth is square, and that the
cause of eclipses is a huge dog seeking to swallow up the sun
or moon?   The cause of this, no doubt, is their incorrigible
conservatism.   Being shut in by sea, desert, and mountains
led China to think of those without as " barbarians."   Her
exclusiveness kept her ignorant, her ignorance kept her self-
satisfied, her self-satisfaction kept her conservative.

An unfavourable opinion of the intellectual powers of the
race is produced by a habit the Chinese have of keeping their
best arguments last and advancing puerile ones first.   The

following answer of a boatman, when asked why an eye is painted on both sides of junks at Shanghai, is often quoted : "No got eye, how can see? No can see, how can sabee (know). No can sabee, how can makee walkee (travel)?" No doubt the real explanation is the superstition of the good and evil eye which is found amongst all nations.

A man agreed to pay a dollar a day at a Chinese inn, but no money was forthcoming. At length the host reduced the price of his guest's board to half a dollar a day, in order that, as he explained, he should not lose so much by him. A Chinaman is never such a fool as he sometimes looks, and if this reduction was ever made it was because the host thought that he might get half a dollar but could not get a dollar.

The Chinese are great at organising. "Union of hearts," says one of their proverbs, "is the best bulwark." The trade guilds, which are in every town, work together as one man when their interests are assailed. A guild looks after people of its own district, aids them if sick or impoverished, and, when necessary, provides that which a Chinaman values most —a respectable funeral. The social side of the guilds is seen in the frequent feasts and theatrical entertainments which the members provide. The guild club-houses are in many instances very beautiful.

There are life and many other kinds of insurance associations; convivial, chess, literary, and burial clubs. Temperance societies are a very old institution in China, the members of the present ones promising to abstain from rice spirits, or from opium, or from tobacco, or from all three.

Even beggars and thieves have guilds. In Canton and other large towns, the former are ruled by a king, and he is paid so much a year by shopkeepers on condition that he prevent his subjects from tormenting customers. Should blackmail not be given, the guild will send beggars to play hideous music and to clamour loudly at the defaulter's shop. If cash is still withheld, they will drive away customers by

inflicting wounds on themselves or by threatening to expose
their nakedness. Every morning the king of the beggars
sends a certain number of his sackcloth-clad or nearly unclad
subjects to beg a particular district. They also claim a share
of what is left at wedding and funeral feasts. In these ways
poor rates are collected by the beggars themselves.

Owners of property pay so much a year to guilds of thieves
in order not to be robbed. On the gates of farmsteads may
be read, " This household pays yearly tribute to the robbers,
and must not be molested." A common practice is to hire a
member of the guild as a watchman. In a city where there is
a thief's guild, if an outsider attempt amateur larceny or a
professional from a distance fail to report himself they get
into trouble " with the honourable members of the guild of
thieves."

The Chinese never waste anything. A shopman puts up
parcels with half the paper and string used by Europeans.
Servants collect and sell matchboxes and things for which no
one else could find a use. In the country you will notice a
boy up in a tree beating down a single leaf with a stick for
fuel as though it were a valuable fruit. Women, when too
old to work at anything else, collect dry grass for the same
purpose. A very old woman, who was seen hobbling along a
road, was asked why she persisted in walking when so little
capable of doing so. She replied that she was at the point of
death, and that if she managed to get near her home, where
she would be buried, her friends would have to pay coolies less
for carrying her ! A man collects his fowls and then beats
old damp mats or matting. Cockroaches and other vermin
jump out, and the cocks and hens have a meal that costs
nothing.

You give a coolie an old coat that you are ashamed to
give to any one and he will probably get a tailor to transform
it for thirty or fifty cents into two pairs of excellent trousers
for himself.

In one respect, however, the Chinese are not economical, but very much the reverse; we allude to their gambling propensities. To satisfy this taste curious forms of lotteries have been invented, one of the commonest being that of the thirty-six beasts. A group of individuals form themselves into a company and select the names of thirty-six animals which they inscribe on counters. Every morning the bankers hoist up to the top of a high pole a bag, into which one out of the thirty-six counters has been placed, the six last counters being exclusively reserved for the bank. The public stake their money on any one of the thirty-six beasts, and those who have backed the beast whose name is written on the counter in that bag that day win thirty times what they have staked. Butchers often put out a piece of meat as a prize to be given at nightfall to the man who has made the nearest guess at its weight. A few cash are paid to the butcher for the privilege of competing.

The *waising* lottery is in connection with the names of successful candidates at the examinations for degrees.

Every one who has visited Macao or any part of China knows about Fan'tan, or "turn-over." There is no skill in it. The croupier throws down a heap of cash, and each gambler stakes on what the remainder will be when the pile has been counted out in fours.

The gambling excesses which Huc describes seem incredible. He says that people will part with all their clothes and run about at night to keep themselves warm, that last of all they will stake their fingers, chop them off and give them to their victors!

Privacy in China is little respected. A friend of mine had an interview with an official of high rank. He did not wish the business known, so was greatly disgusted when he saw the yamen servants and even people from the street crowding in unchecked by any one to hear the conversation. The liberty that is given to go in and out of yamens is an example of the blending of classes that prevails in China. People will talk loudly about what we would consider private affairs. If a man, and especially a woman, have a grievance, he or she will proclaim it from the housetop. It is thought that one who wishes to be private must be going to say or do something wrong.

The possibility of acquiring merit in another world is the motive, as it often is amongst Westerners, for much of what looks like charity in China. The idea of keeping a debtor-and-credit account with Heaven is one which finds favour with the business Chinese mind. Well for him when he makes up his spiritual accounts at the end of the year if he can carry over a balance of good deeds towards the next year's reckoning! It is not charitable, however, in us to say that the Chinese are charitable only for a spiritual insurance, only to gain merit in another world. They are not less charitable than ourselves. They distribute free rice and tea in time of exceptional distress; they subscribe to hospitals and to asylums for the blind, for the old, for lepers, and for orphans; they support associations for supplying free coffins to the poor. The fine stone or wooden bridges like what we see on willow-pattern plates have in many instances been built by private individuals. So have a large number of rest-houses, pagodas, temples, mosques, and shrines.

The character of the Chinaman, however, is many sided, and he can show a very unsympathetic side. There is to him, as it has been said there is to all of us, something not altogether unpleasing in the misfortunes of friends. From a steam launch I saw a sudden squall sink a junk. There were other junks quite near, but no one would give a helping hand to the men struggling in the water. Our launch had to go a considerable distance to the rescue. The Chinese would say that it was not their business to pull up the drowning men, that perhaps the men wanted to die, that if they rescued them they would have to support them, that it might be a wicked interference with Fate. A Chinese submarine miner in British service was drowned near Hong Kong. Several times after, when passing the spot where the man fell overboard, his mates pointed to it and roared with laughter.

The Chinaman's sense of humour is never so much tickled as when he sees any one in a difficulty. A workman falls from a bamboo scaffold and breaks his leg. All his mates upon the job will stop work to have a good laugh.

The colliding of two rickshas is a standing or rather a running joke; and a man being led to gaol by his queue becomes a target for all the would-be wits along the route. An old lady, known to the writer, slipping in a street of Hong Kong, injured her leg so much that she could not get up. Soon there was a crowd round her, "their hands in their sleeves and idly gazing"—very idly, for no one offered assistance. They seemed to enjoy the accident as much as we would a good number of *Punch*.

Like the Jews who asked, "Did this man sin or his parents, that he was born blind?" the Chinese look upon all grievous affliction as the just punishment for some heinous offence committed in a previous state of existence. Perhaps it is owing to this "serve you right" theory that they have so little sympathy with suffering.

People calmly remark of a man in his presence that he is idiotic. "When the eyes squint the heart is askew" is often said to a cross-eyed person. We read of the mother of the prophet Samuel that when it was thought she would not have a child "her adversary also provoked her sore, for to make her fret." Every Chinese wife who has not borne a son knows what this means.

After cold water there is nothing the Chinese so much fear as ridicule and disgrace or the "loss of face." A district magistrate who was to be beheaded asked that as a special favour he might wear his robes of office in order to save his face!

The Chinese dread any change that may cause trouble or disorder. "Better be a dog in peace," they say, "than a man in anarchy." They are as a people submissive and easily governed. The prospectus of a German lottery was sent to a Chinaman in Hong Kong. Not understanding it, he consulted an Englishman, a friend of the writer. It was explained to him that he need not take a ticket or indeed any notice of it. Meeting my friend a few days afterwards, the Chinaman said, "I thought it best to take one of those lottery tickets; I did not want to have any bobbery with that German Emperor."

Far more than we do, the Chinese believe in the might of right and in the prowess of intellect. They have conquered and will continue to conquer by the arts of peace, rather than by those of war. When vanquished by the Tartars in the middle of the seventeenth century they overcame their conquerors by force of mind and character. They turned them into the black-haired race. The "yellow peril" is, not that China should conquer by weapons of war, but by industry, patience, and numbers.

Englishmen and Chinamen should be good friends, for they have much in common. Both have a great capacity for making, saving, and enjoying money. Both are enterprising in commerce, and both will stick to their bargains. Both build substantial buildings, as, for instance, bridges, and both take a pride in good work.

The Chinese are not less characterised by common sense than are Englishmen, and they have John Bull's solidity, respect for law and conservatism. Neither John Bull nor John Chinaman allow sentiment to interfere with business, and there is nothing they value more than a good dinner.

CHAPTER X

CHINESE FOOD

What a Chinaman does not eat is not worth eating—"That belong cocky-loachee"—"With soy sauce anything will go down"—Flowers eaten as vegetables—Woman's milk sold for aged persons—Eggs one hundred years old—Eating one's walking-stick—Kippered rats—Even house rats are eaten—Cat and snake restaurants—An overrated dish—A coolie can revel on twopence a day—Method of eating—Filial gruel—Invitations—Chinese hospitality—The attack begun again—Two good soups—Curious dishes—Gratitude for repletion.

WHAT a Chinaman does not eat is indeed not worth eating. Everything from root to leaf, from hide to entrails, goes into his unscrupulous stomach. Hawks, owls, and other omniverous creatures find their match in him, and are eaten by him. The attendants of a sportsman gladly eat the badger, civet cat, or fox which he kills. Even game which they catch upon their own bodies coolies crack with their teeth and probably swallow.

The bills, feet, and insides of poultry are sold separately in the market. Who can tell what are in Chinese dumplings, patties, and sausages? The coloured drinks on street stalls look unintelligible even though samples of the fruit from which they purport to be decocted are beside them. A receptacle contains egg soup. We know this because unbroken eggs are placed near it to show that they are in it! A thirst for knowledge made me try everything. "Never venture, never win" was my motto. What looked like "broth of abominable things" was in their vessels, but I was occasionally agreeably surprised when, greatly daring, I tasted it.

A caldron worthy of the witches in "Macbeth" could be filled by a few Chinese hucksters. One could contribute eye of newt, and toe of frog, another several kinds of lizards, a third black-beetles and grasshoppers. In a barrel are what look like dried prunes. "What are those?" you ask a grinning Chinaman. Popping one into his mouth, he answers, "That belong cocky-loachee. Velly good." They are dried cockroaches!

A coolie picks up from a street stall with a wire fork provided for the purpose and eats a piece of candied ginger, of lotus-root, of melon, and of everything in the collection. For each tit-bit he pays a cash or about the fortieth part of a penny. Imagine a British workman doing anything so innocent as eat sweets at a street stall!

There is no drinking for company's sake in China. On occasions when our men treat each other to a so-called friendly glass of spirits or beer the Chinese eat together the sociable seed of a melon. (So fond is every one of dried melon seeds that you may have in some places a melon for nothing if you give back the seeds. Samshu, the alcoholic spirit generally drunk, is distilled from rice, but people only take it in small quantities and then almost invariably with food. Water is always drunk hot, which guards against disease.

A Chinese proverb says that it is well always to have something in the mouth, so when any one has nothing better to eat he chews sugar-cane or munches pea-nuts. Confucius ate little, but was never without ginger when he ate. His disciples are more inclined to follow the second part of this rule than the first. The Chinese are nearly as fond of pickles as are British soldiers—pickled nuts, pickled cabbage, pickled onions, and they like fruits when both salted and sugared. With soy sauce anything will go down. Earthworms when fried crisp are relished, and so are silkworms when they have done their work and nothing more can be got out of them. Locusts are thought to have a better flavour and to be more nutritious if they are thrown into boiling oil when alive.

Foreigners used to classify the beef obtainable in Peking as "horse," "camel," "donkey," or "precipice." The last was that of a beast that had been killed by a fall. In South China the flesh of an ox or of a buffalo is not eaten because these animals are so useful for agriculture, and because, on transmigration principles, ancestors might be inhabiting them. If, however, a thrifty person wishes to use a dead buffalo he calls it "mountain whale," and eats it with a clear conscience. In a book of moral maxims an exhortation against eating beef is enforced by examples of people who have suffered for doing so. Nothing is too bad for butchers. One of these, it is told, bought on a certain day three buffaloes, one of which he killed. At night the two survivors came to him in a dream and one said, "I am your father," and the other, "I am your grandfather." Upon this they were transmigrated into men, and the butcher saw that they really were his father and his grandfather.

To eat venison is to incur the danger of becoming as timid as deer. Pork, which is eaten everywhere in China, is often dishonestly treated. Its weight is added to by being injected with water, the point of the syringe being passed into a large vein. In this way the Chinese water their stock when dead! It is amusing to see a pig lying down trustingly for the mistress of a cabin to pick ticks off him.

The Chinese list of vegetables about quadruples ours. Alas! we Europeans dare not eat their crisp lettuce and rosy radishes, for we know with what they are fertilised. They ruin their fruit, too, for our palates, by pulling it long before it is ripe. The petals of chrysanthemums and of other flowers which we would think a desecration to eat they use as vegetables.

When they do not think that it is made by missionaries from the brains of stolen children, the Chinese are very fond of our condensed milk. They drink cups of it, adding much sugar! Milk from cow or buffalo is seldom used by them as food, but human milk is sold at Amoy for aged persons on account of the great nutritive qualities which are attributed to it. An act applauded in popular story is that of a daughter-in-law who deprived her baby of its rights that she might sustain her husband's toothless old mother.

Rice is the staff of Chinese life, though it is not eaten by itself, but with pork, fish, cabbage, and other relishes. Rice-flour is made into many appetising combinations. Bean meal and bean curds are much used. So are all kinds of macaroni, of shellfish, and of seaweed.

Eggs are preserved for an indefinite time in a solution of salt, lime, and wood-ashes. At the end of forty days they are considered fit for the table, but at the end of forty years still more so. A Chinese host treats his most honoured guest to the oldest eggs in his storeroom as a British host brings from his cellar the oldest wine.

At the table of the Governor of Hong Kong I have tasted eggs which, his Excellency told me, were more than a hundred years old, and which he got as a great favour. They were as black as ink, owing either to time or to the wood-ashes in which they were kept. Eggs preserved in spirits made of rice are very good.

Bamboo sprouts resemble asparagus, but as in common with other vegetables in China they are only half cooked, it is a little like eating one's walking-stick. As malefactors are beaten with bamboo canes, coolies object to be told that they will eat bamboo.

"Hawking duck's blood without licence," was the curious charge that was brought against a woman not long before I left Hong Kong. One is surprised at the number of dried and flattened ducks that hang outside the provision shops at Canton by their half-yard long necks. That the things exposed for sale looking like bits of leather were rats we could not doubt after examining their heads and the tails that curled like the tendrils of a vine. People whose queues are scanty use this food as a hair-restorer. Rat-meat is also thought to cure deafness.

The last time I was at Canton I saw only one bundle of kippered rats hanging outside a shop that used to deal largely in them. I remarked to my companion that the supply of rats fell off apparently at that season. Hearing this, the shopkeeper, who knew some English, in his kind desire that I should not be disappointed, went to the back of the shop, produced two dried cats, and throwing them upon the counter before me, said, " They are eating those now."

The Chinese say that it is only field-rats that are eaten. If this be the rule, it has exceptions, as the two following stories, which I have upon good authority, show. During the plague season in Hong Kong all rats that are killed are dissected by the sanitary authorities, to see if there are plague germs in them. A householder asked his number one boy where a rat that had been caught was, as he wished to send it to be examined. " One of your chair coolies ate it for his breakfast," was the reply.

An English lady who was staying with a Chinese one praised a dish at dinner. " I am glad you like it," replied the Chinese; " I caught that rat in your room this morning." This, however, was in the country where food could not be easily procured.

I have visited the cat and dog market in Canton, and seen hundreds of these animals in cages alive, hung up for sale when dead, and being cooked in different ways. Fortunately I escaped seeing a cat killed, as the man who brought me to the market once did. The front paws of pussy were chopped off, her teeth knocked in, and when thus rendered defenceless she was skinned alive. There are in the same place in Canton shops where boxes and baskets full of snakes are kept.   Some of the reptiles are bought for food, but more of them for medicine.

Outside the racecourse at Hong Kong when there is a race meeting many refreshment-stalls are set up for the thousands of Chinese that assemble.   Last year I counted sixteen upon which dog-meat was sold.   It was fried in oil with water, chestnuts, onions, and chillies.   Dog-meat is supplied chiefly for visitors from Canton, for many Cantonese do not think that they have had an outing if they do not get it.   On two occasions I tried the dish, and thought that it was an overrated one.   It tasted between rabbit and tough mutton.

When dogs are skinned and quartered the yellow variety is distinguished from the black in the market by the bushy tips of their tails that are left.   These guide customers to which they prefer, and opinions differ as to their relative wholesome-ness.   Dogs are fed on rice for some time before they are killed.   I do not wish to convey the impression that cat, dog, and rat are the staple food of the Chinese.   It is chiefly the Cantonese who eat them, and they do so as little, but also as much, as the French eat frogs and snails and the British high game and "walking cheese."   The Chinese think that cheese and butter, which they call "milk cake," or "rotten milk," or "beef-oil cakes," are disgusting.

Written on a wall in a kitchen at Nanking were characters which were translated for me as follows : "One bowl of gruel, one bowl of rice; meditate upon it; it does not come easily." To comparatively few people in China does food come easily ; therefore the Chinese are compelled to learn economical cookery.   In a gang of labourers the smallest boy is told off to cook, and is to the manner born.

A coolie can live on ten cents a day, revel on twenty, and go to the devil on thirty.   He is as well nourished upon twopence or threepence a day as a British workman upon 1s. 4d. or 1s. 6d.   I have often seen one of them take from a street stall and eat a bowl of vermicelli or of flour balls cooked in sugar, or of miscellaneous vegetables covered with different kinds of relishes. For this he would give a few cash coins of which it takes nearly a thousand to make a dollar, and with a couple more cash he would buy a cigarette and then walk away looking more satisfied than those do who lunch at expensive London clubs.

The low price of food in inland China astonishes travellers. The inns are nasty, but they certainly are cheap. Dr. Morrison writes: "For supper, bed, and light, tea during the night and tea before starting in the morning, and various little comforts, such as hot water for washing, the total charge for the six nights of my journey from Chungking to Suifu was 840 cash (1s. 9d.)." This was in 1894, however, and every year the prices are becoming more civilised (?).

Another man, when travelling for the first time in the interior of China, once gave a dollar to his servant to buy a chicken. At dinner-time the servant brought a "huge trencher, resembling a tub, filled with a *fricassée* of little pieces of smoking chicken. 'What? All that?' I cried. 'Yes, sir; with your dollar I got twelve chickens.'" For those who cannot afford to buy a whole chicken or duck or goose, the leg or wing of the bird is sold separately, as with us a leg of mutton is sold.

One would think that eating was the trade of Chinese cities, so many are the restaurants they contain. These restaurants are known by the wood-carving and other kinds of ornamentation outside, and by the plates of brass that cover the stairs in the middle of the shop which lead to the upper dining-rooms.

When a Chinaman does not dine at a restaurant he buys his food at a market, and it is a common sight to see him carry to his house a few ounces of pork and some sprouting beans tied by a straw and attached to his first finger.

As a rule Chinese tradesmen and those whom they employ take their meals together, sitting in a circle in their place of business. Each person fills his basin from a large bowl of steaming rice, and holding it up to his chin with his left hand, shovels its contents into his mouth with chopsticks at an astonishing rate. The operation reminds one of coaling a ship. Then the graceful eater picks up pieces of fish, pork, salt duck, pickled cabbage, cut into mouthfuls to suit the "nimble lads," or chopsticks, out of bowls which are used by all. The meal is washed down with tea or hot water.

On one day of the year the members of a family eat together a festive food called filial gruel or porridge. It is supposed to nourish filial piety, though one would think that a rod would be more effective. A little while before a Chinese dinner-party you are informed that on —— day a trifling entertainment will await the light of your countenance. When the day comes, another invitation stating the approximate hour for the feast is sent, or a servant brings his master's large red visiting-card, which signifies, "Come, for all things are now ready." The hour at which a dinner begins is any time between four o'clock and seven ; its vagueness would upset a British cook.

The guests on arriving are given cups of tea. Each takes his invitation-card from the servant who carries it, and gives it to the host from whom it originally came. This prevents guests coming uninvited.

Just before the guests sit down to dinner the host will probably say, "Gentlemen, will you take off your coats?" Then the servant of each removes the official coat and perhaps the chain of his master.

"When one is eating one's own," says a Chinese proverb, "one does not eat to repletion ; when one is eating another's, one eats till the tears run."

Chinese hospitality is only satisfied so long as the mouth of the guest is filled, and when he gets up to leave an entertainment every effort is made to detain him.

From twenty to fifty or sixty dishes appear at the dinner of a rich man in relays of four or six at a time. Politeness requires that you should at least taste each dish at all hazards. You must do more than this, however, with the last portion of food you are given, which is always a bowl of rice, to fill up any crevice that may remain. To show your appreciation of the feast you must, if you accept this, finish every grain. Occasionally the host will grant a reprieve and say that the rice need not be finished. Even high-class Chinese clear their bowls, which are not changed, by calmly throwing bones and pieces of gristle on the floor, and when eating and drinking they make noises which we would think disgusting. Red paper napkins, five inches by two, are folded beside each guest.

When you think that a dinner is finished it is only for a time, during which cloths wrung out in hot water are handed round for mopping the brow, and the stolidly decorous girls who are hired to play and sing cease performing and come round to fan and talk to you. Then a second edition of edibles is put upon the tables, and the refreshed guests begin the attack once more.

Men always dine by themselves, but sometimes dinner-parties are given by ladies for ladies. An old medical maxim says that the stomach loves surprises. If this be so, my stomach must have been greatly benefited by the two or three Chinese dinners I have attended, for that member was not only surprised but astounded every now and then. It told me afterwards, however, in its own unmistakable way, that the only half-cooked or raw vegetables that were mixed up in nearly all the dishes were anything but an agreeable surprise.

Guests are arranged in parties of eight at tables on which are no cloths. They help themselves with their chopsticks and little porcelain spoons from the dishes placed in the centre of the tables. When the host would compliment a guest he selects a titbit with his own chopsticks and puts it into the guest's bowl, and the guest does the same in return.   Guests also exchange elegant extracts in the same way.

Those to the manner born can do wonders with chopsticks. A certain courtier was so expert that once when a grain of rice fell from the Emperor's lips he caught it between his chopsticks as it fell.   For this feat he was appointed to high office.

The best thing that one gets at a Chinese dinner is bird's-nest soup, but as the excellence of turtle soup depends upon the things other than turtle that are put into it, so is it with bird's-nest soup.   The bird's nest is the least important part of it.   Another soup which tastes better than it sounds is made of sea-slugs.

The following dishes seem curious to the foreign diner-out in China : Frogs, smoked duck, roofs of the mouths of pigs, soles of pigeon's feet, sinews of whale and of deer, sharks' fins, fish brains, fish with pickled fir-tree cones, bellies of fish, roots of the lotus lily.   Sometimes a hundred chickens will be killed to get their brains for one dish, or as many ducks for the sake of their tongues.   Samshu, which is a spirit made of rice, is served hot in beautiful little cups after each course.   It tastes like beer and sherry or beer and whiskey mixed.

After a Chinese dinner it is polite to look towards the host and eructate in his face.   This indicates gratitude for the repletion which his hospitality has caused.   Then there are set phrases that must be used.   The host says that he ought to be killed for the shabby way he has entertained his guest, and the guest declares that he has been treated far better than he deserves, which is probably true.

The Chinese profess only to eat two meals in the day, for they do not count the " piece of heart," consisting of some kind of cake and tea, which they take on rising in the morning or the snacks with which they solace themselves between the morning and evening big meals.

The Chinese catch fish and game in ways that are dark but

ingenious. They train otters and cormorants to fish for them. They use boats on moonlight nights having wooden flaps at their sides descending to the water at a particular inclination, and painted white. The fish being deceived by the light reflected from these boards, leap upon them, and are turned over into the boat with a jerk. Europeans who have seen the public latrines that surround Chinese fish-ponds admire the thrift they reveal, but say, "No fish, thank you," at dinner. In the shops fish are kept alive in tanks.

I have observed with interest an oyster-gatherer at work. To prevent sinking in the mud he kneels with one knee upon a board and propels the vehicle with his other foot. No people eat seaweeds so extensively as the Chinese.

A Chinese shoots snipe from his hip with a gun that has no stock. Artificial decoy birds are often to be seen. Rice steeped in samshu is sometimes left for wild ducks; they eat it, get drunk, and are caught in their cups. The following method is used on teetotal principles. Hollow gourds are thrown into the water and allowed to float about. When the birds have become accustomed to these, men place similar gourds over their heads, with holes to see and breathe through. Then wading quietly along, with their bodies immersed to above the shoulders, they approach the birds, and pull them under water by their legs in succession.

You see a great many people in China so thin that they look as if they had not even a bowing acquaintance with food. In many cases these animated skeletons spend upon opium the little money they have with which to nourish themselves. They literally "eat smoke"—to use their own expression. It may be true that this indulgence in moderation does as little harm as our drinking in moderation; but how difficult is moderation! The Chinese themselves have a saying that "It is not the man who eats the opium, but the opium that eats the man." Even if opium did not directly injure health, it is pernicious, because it wastes so much time and money.

What would China be without its tea-gardens and tea-houses? When a Chinese pays a visit, he is immediately offered a cup of tea.   When he invites a friend to come and see him, he uses the formula, "The tea is ready."   In the hot weather charitable people supply receptacles from which any one who likes can take tea.   Tea is always ready where people are at work.

CHAPTER XI

MEDICINE AND SURGERY

Chinese medicines horrible—They cure, however, the man who is fated not to die—A recipe for ophthalmia—Large doses—A sort of *multum in parvo*—Dosed to death—A Chinaman loves free medicines—" It is his pig "—" A little dragon inside me "—Transforming medicines—To give courage—Blood bread—" Dragon's clothes "—An old remedy—The doctor's shop—A saying of Confucius—Pulses—Due proportions—Three classes of doctors—Payment by results—Simples—Acupuncture—Too patient—Jokes against doctors—Superstitious remedies.

AT Canton there are schools where Chinese men and women are taught Western medicine, and similar ones are being started in other cities. The remedies, too, that are used by native medical men in the treaty ports have been modified by contact with Europeans, but at a little distance from these ports strange and extremely nasty preparations such as physicked our Middle Ages are still prescribed. A missionary doctor told me that when called in to see a man suffering from fits he found him smelling white mice in a cage, with a dead fowl fastened on his chest and a bundle of grass attached to his feet. He had been informed that this would cure him.

What do our readers think of glue made of asses' sinews and of fowls' blood, of bears' gall, of shavings of the horn of a rhinoceros, of fungus grown upon a coffin, of the dung of dogs, pigs, fowls, rabbits, pigeons, and of bats, as medicines? Cockroach tea cheers as little as it inebriates, but is believed to be medicinal. I have been told that a bear's paw when made into soup is a "number one" cure for wind in the stomach.   Other ailments are cured by a decoction of the paws of monkeys.

Toad's eyebrows provoke sneezing, and thus clear the head. For a sick stomach earth-worms are rolled in honey and swallowed alive.

A boy was brought to a hospital of the London Mission with symptoms of fever.   The English doctor not being at home, the boy was taken to a Chinese practitioner, who prescribed a decoction of three scorpions, to be taken internally. The patient was well next day, for as a Chinese proverb says, "Medicine cures the man who is fated not to die."   A recipe for ophthalmia, posted on the walls of Peking, ran as follows: "Take three bright brass coins of the reign of Tao Kwang, boil them in water, and use the lotion."

"Pills made out of a whole stag slaughtered with purity of purpose on a propitious day" are considered valuable remedies.   A preparation from the antlers of deer is given to promote virility.   So are the genital organs of a cat.   For some diseases of children centipedes are prepared.   A Chinese dose of medicine will consist of as many as twenty packages, and a pill will sometimes be as large as the egg of a pigeon.

A friend of the writer asked an Irish countryman what medicine he had taken during a recent illness.   "Troth, your honour," was the reply, "I don't know; it was a sort of *multum in parvo*—the less you take of it the better."   Chinese medicine is seldom *in parvo*, but the less you take of it the better.   Sometimes, however, one sees medicines with a great reputation and hard to get, such as the excrement of mosquitoes, sold in very small bottles.   Ginseng is considered worth eight times its weight in silver because of its "repairing qualities."   A "supernatural fulfilment of all desires" is the result claimed for certain red pills that are very small.

A Viceroy of Canton is said to have been dosed to death by

a native medicine man. He was being treated by a German physician for inflammation of the bowels. Lest Chinese practitioners should spoil the case, the German did not leave the sick man's room for a whole week. Then he ventured to go out, and a Chinese came in and said to the Viceroy, "You are getting on well, but you will be cured much sooner if you will take a little remedy which I have brought for you." The "little remedy" was a kettle full of black stuff. The Viceroy took three doses, and had a viceregal funeral.

A Chinaman is never so pleased as when taking medicine, and the pleasure of getting it, especially if it be quinine for nothing from a medical missionary, overcomes his prejudice against foreign innovations. A man described certain pains and other symptoms, and asked for medicine for the patient. "Is it a man?" asked the doctor. "No." "Is it a woman or a child?" "Neither." Then one in the crowd interposed, and said, "It is his pig."

The head Chinese clerk of a friend of mine said, "I have been vely sick for three days!" "What has been wrong?" inquired my friend. "It was a little dragon inside me, but I took some medicine, and it frightened it away." Chinese medicine would frighten anything.

Nothing is admitted to be beyond its power. An Englishman becoming acquainted with a native practitioner, showed him with paternal pride his three fair-haired little girls. "Their complexions are beautiful," said the Chinese, "but their hair is hardly dark enough. A dose taken three times a day from a bottle which I would send would make a wonderful improvement." He went on with more embarrassment, "There is another thing about them that I hardly like to mention." His friend reassured him. "Well, if you will allow me to say it, they are all of them girls. Now, I have at home some pills which if they take regularly for a couple of months will turn them into three as fine boys as father could wish for."

An infusion from the bones of a tiger is believed to confer courage, strength, and agility.   When the skin of a tiger has been obtained, many bones are sold under its cover that never belonged to that species of animal.   Near Ningpo a large tiger appeared.   The chief magistrate, military mandarin, and a force of soldiers, with two cannons, came to the attack. When the animal was killed, the magistrate claimed it, but the military officer said that it was required for himself and his men.   " It is our duty to be brave, and what better recipe can you suggest for courage than soup made from tiger's bones ? "   Soldiers eat the calves of the legs and the hearts of executed robbers to absorb their strength and courage.

In 1887 it was announced in the *Peking Gazette* that the skin and bones of a palace elephant that had died were to be kept "for His Majesty's use" when unwell.   Flour balls steeped in the blood of executed criminals, and called " blood bread," are occasionally sold to cure consumption.

In the *Shanghai Courier and Gazette* (November, 1875) mention is made of a son cutting a piece of flesh from his left arm and boiling it down as a cure for his mother, who was dangerously ill.   The *Peking Gazette* records an identical act which a daughter performed for a sick father.

A friend of mine who had killed a snake in Hong Kong was asked by a Chinaman for a bit of it.   "What for? " " Me boil him and eat him ; he makee me cunning and wise." " Dragon's clothes," as the skins of snakes are called, are in great request as medicines.   So are the skins of armadilloes.

It is strange that such a clean thing as the peel of an orange should be given as medicine in China, but it is, and that so commonly that you get an orange a few cash lower price if you do not take the peel.

The bite of a cobra or other snake is said to be counteracted by sucking up and swallowing water through an old tobacco pipe.

Here is the old remedy, " a hair of the dog that bit you,"

in a prescription : " For a dog's bite, catch the dog, pull out a few of his hairs and work them into a paste with a little lime and oil ; apply the paste to the wound." The lime and oil may be of some use, but the hair is what is believed in.

Summer brings " dog days " literally in China, for at the commencement of that season people eat dog-meat as a prophylactic against illness.

The consulting-room of the cheaper practitioner is a booth or tent at a street-corner or in a court of a temple. You know it by the long strings of extracted teeth that hang up. On one string I noticed two pieces of jaw-bone, which were not reassuring. There are also dried snakes, many roots, bits of bark, curious herbs, and out-of-the-common dried fruit. Things of no value are made to appear mystically medicinal by being wrapped in silk and stored in small boxes enclosed in larger ones. Those little bottles contain substances that are valued only because they are rare and hard to get. The walls are stuck over with plasters that have done their duty and been returned by grateful patients in testimony of their efficiency.

Outside the doctor's shop there is a crowd hoping to see an operation, and no doubt these idlers help patients to bear without a moan, and often with sweet smiles, the burning, nipping, punching, puncturing, and other tortures which with simple faith they pay to have inflicted upon them. Certainly burning and pinching may draw out inflammation, and are cheaper than the croton oil and other things which we use for that purpose. When a coolie has a cold in his head, he nips with two coins the flesh on the bridge of his nose and gets, or thinks that he gets, relief by so doing.

In China the distinction between a surgeon and a physician is drawn by calling the former an outside doctor and the latter an inside one. An " outer doctor " cut off the two ends of an arrow that had gone through a man's arm and put a plaster on either wound. "But," objected the patient, " the rest of the arrow is still there. "That," answered the medico, "is not my business; you must get an inner doctor if you want it removed."

Queer, too, are the expressions used in describing diseases. A Chinaman will tell you that he has a pain in "the east side of his stomach." Talking of this last organ, we may mention that the Chinese think that the stomach is the seat of intellect. It certainly has a great influence upon our mental efforts.

Confucius said that it is the duty of every man to return his body to the earth as whole as when it came from his mother's womb. In deference to this dictum, Chinese surgeons do not dissect dead subjects, and are in consequence ignorant of the location of even the largest viscera. They only practise external surgery, and will allow an arm or a leg to mortify rather than amputate it. If a Chinese in a European hospital is advised by the surgeon to have a limb cut off, he will sometimes ask the surgeon how many dollars will be given to him for allowing it to be done.

One reason why Chinese soldiers have a tendency to run away in battle is no doubt because any mutilation of the body is considered an act of disrespect to the parents from whom it was received. Our doctors are content with feeling the pulse in one wrist, but Chinese medical men feel both wrists, and recognise 481 distinct pulses. They think that the right wrist reveals the state of the lungs and liver, and the left that of the heart. This last organ, they say, is the husband, and the lungs are the wife, and they ought to act in harmony. Should the patient be a lady, her wrists are allowed to appear beneath the screen behind which she reclines, so that the pulse may be felt. So little do the Chinese guard against infection that a woman will wash the rice for her family in the same stagnant pool at which another woman is washing the bedclothes of a cholera patient. Chinese practitioners say that the tops of plants cure the head and upper parts of a

man and its lower parts his lower parts. They attribute all
diseases to cold and hot influences. If the tongue be white,
the patient is under the cold influence; if yellow, he is under
the hot influence. If the centre of the tongue be white and
the edges yellow, he is under the cold influence inside, and
his skin is under the hot and *vice versa*. A proper
proportion, too, must also be maintained between earth,
metal, fire, wood, and water, the five elements of which man's
body is thought to be composed. There must also be due
proportion between dryness and moisture.

No diploma of any kind is required to practise medicine.
Doctors in China may be divided into three classes—those
who have failed at the literary examinations, those who have
inherited prescriptions, and those who are mere quacks. It
has been said that it is the practice of physicians in Europe
to put that of which they know little into that of which they
know less. How much more terribly true is this of Chinese
medicine-men! In China, even more than in our own
country, the sure doctor is Death, for he only pays one visit.

The Chinese believe in paying physicians by results.
When the last emperor was attacked by small-pox, an
improvement in his symptoms brought a shower of gifts
and honours on the Court physicians. Of these, however,
they were stripped when, the disease taking a fatal turn,
His Majesty "ascended on a dragon to be a guest on
high."

The fee of an ordinary Chinese doctor (known as "horse-
hire") ranges from five cents to half a dollar; but whatever
it is it is wrapped up in red paper bearing the inscription
"golden thanks."

As the medico frequently makes up his own medicine, it is
his interest to put into them many and expensive ingredients.
These are criticised by the friends of the sick person. Could
not this and that item be done without? Sometimes after
consulting aloud, even in the presence of the patient, they

will decide that it is better not to pay so much for physic, but
to let the disease run its course and spend the money on a
good coffin and fine funeral.

Notwithstanding what has been said about Chinese medicines, it is a paradoxical fact that they sometimes cure.
They are largely composed of simples, and in reference to the
physical body as well as to the body politic and to the soul,
simples are often the best remedies.   The Chinese have this
wise maxim, "One sleepless night cannot be compensated
by ten nights of sleep."   They used anæsthetics long before
these were dreamt of in Europe.

Acupuncture is one of the nine branches of medical science
recognised by the Chinese.   There are 367 markings on the
ancient copper figures of the human body that are kept to
guide acupuncturists in their work.   Some of these operators,
however, seem only to follow their own sweet will as regards
the places where they insert their hot and cold needles.   I
have heard of a man being pricked underneath his tongue for
an attack of diarrhœa.   No hesitation is felt in thrusting a
needle into a patient's liver or stomach.

Once, at Shangai, I joined a crowd in a temple court and
saw a man acupunctured for a swollen leg.   About a dozen
needles, like sewing-machine ones, were driven into the limb.
On the top of each needle oiled tow, or something of the kind,
was fastened and lighted.   When the needles became red-hot
the flesh fizzled as though a beef-steak were being cooked.
Superior to pain, the patient chatted and laughed with the
bystanders.

Quacks deal much in acupuncture, as may be seen by the
following case that came before the Hong Kong police court :
On a Saturday afternoon when a tallyman called Li Tong was
returning from work he was accosted by another Chinaman, who
told him he was in consumption, and that the best thing he
could do was to see a physician to whom he would introduce
him.   The tallyman said that he suffered no pain, but

was induced after some persuasion to go to the doctor's house. The physician examined him with bits of scrap iron, told his patient to gaze at the ceiling, pricked his chest with a needle, and dropped the needle on the floor before the tallyman looked down. "Now," he said, "the $13.40 you gave me was for placing the needle in your chest. I want $8 more before I can take the needle out!" The tallyman was wild with terror, and imagined he had razors in his chest, although the needle, said to be in his chest by the doctor, was quickly picked up and hidden away. Li Tong said he would return with the money, ran home, told his people of the needle, and as they already knew what tricks these doctors perform, a gang of them, including the tallyman, returned to interview the doctor. As soon as they entered they demanded the return of the $13.40, and as the doctor refused, a policeman was summoned, and the physician was placed in custody.

It is disheartening the way the Chinese, after experiencing the benefit of Western treatment, will go back to their own remedies the next time they have an attack of the same sickness. An American medical man told me that he found a servant of his whom he had twice treated successfully for fever and ague, having his back scraped with a sharp spoon as a counter-irritant the next time he was attacked by it. It vexed my friend to see skin and flesh scraped off, for he knew that the boy would be prevented from working for days.

Some Chinese are too patient when sick. A man will kill himself by not having his disease attended to in time because he was too busy or because it might have cost something to do so. A patient who was being treated in a mission hospital for an ulcerated neck mentioned, *on the eighteenth day*, that his leg prevented him from sleeping. Upon examination it was found that he had there another terrible ulcer.

Chinese medical men, like their brothers elsewhere, have to put up with a considerable amount of chaffing. Here is a

Joe Miller on the subject taken from a popular book. The King of Purgatory sent lictors to earth to bring to him some skilful physician. "You must look for one," said the King, "at whose door there are no spirits of disembodied patients." The lictors went off, but at the house of every doctor they visited there were crowds of wailing ghosts hanging about. At last they found a doctor at whose door there was only a single shade, and cried out, "This man is evidently the skilful one we are in search of." On inquiry, however, they discovered that he had only started practise the day before.

When a Chinese physician has been long unsuccessful he retires and consoles himself with the adage that "There is medicine for sickness, but none for fate."

Then there are many kinds of faith-healing and super-stitious remedies. Taoist priests are hired to recite formulæ, ring bells, and manipulate bowls of water, candles, joss-sticks, and curious charms. Sometimes the family stipulate that one of these reverend gentlemen shall ascend barefooted a ladder the rounds of which consist of swords or long knives, with the edges upwards, and go through his exorcisms at the top.

At temples of what are called "Doctor Gods" piles of written or printed prescriptions are numbered and kept in stock. A person, after praying and lighting a joss-stick, shakes out from a receptacle one of several bamboo slips with numbers on them. In return for cash the temple-keeper gives a prescription having on it the number that corresponds. If faith is not placed in these cut-and-dried pre-scriptions, the priests are sometimes paid to bring the god out in his chair to look for the kind of herbs that will exactly suit the case.

In the presence of cholera people sometimes practise vege-tarianism as a religious exercise, which cannot be very good for them considering the dirty way Chinese vegetables are cultivated.

Even an educated Confucianist will tell you that he has

cured an ache in his stomach by reading a Chinese translation of a certain Buddhist sacred book.

When a Chinese recovers he often thanks his stars rather than medical treatment, because there is a widespread belief that the five elements of which a man's body is thought to be composed are connected with the five principal planets, the twenty-eight lunar mansions, &c.

A relative or friend of a sick person will visit a temple and beat the drum, which notifies to the god that there is urgent need of his help. To ensure that the god hears, sometimes one or both of his ears are tickled. Then the part of the image is rubbed which corresponds with the part of the body of the sick person affected, and the applicant proceeds to state the circumstances of the case, that the man has several children or aged parents, and so on, depending upon his recovery. On returning to the sick person's house the supplicant brings some ashes taken from the censer standing before the image. These are done up in red paper and placed in the censer belonging to the household, and incense and candles are daily burned before them until the sick person either recovers or dies. I have often seen holy water brought away from a temple to be boiled with tea and drunk as a certain cure. Spells written on paper are burned and the ashes put into water and taken as medicine.

The sight of a mother making a fire of paper in honour of a god and waving over it a small garment of her sick child is very common in China. She thinks that this helps its recovery. There are many curious methods in use for bringing back the spirit of health into the empty garment of a sick person. Curious, too, is the health almanack. This is a small book said to have been made long ago by the head of the Taoist priests. It contains a list of days, with directions what to do on each of them to ward off the evil spirits that inflict diseases upon children.

CHAPTER XII

CHINESE CLOTHES

Many changes of raiment required—Prince Chen—Special clothes for every important occasion—Chinese clothes are in many respects better than ours—Ladies, like insects, should wear bright colours—Colours not thought to kill each other—Official distinctions—A mandarin's answer —Fans—Pockets—Boots and shoes—Hair-dressing—Ornaments and paint—Dress of the poor—A Chinaman's toilet—The queue—Beards.

FASHIONS in Chinese clothes change, but, unlike our fashions, they last much longer than do the garments. There are regulations made by law and custom as to cut and material from which neither man nor woman ventures to depart. Every official must assume his summer or winter costume on a day specified in the *Peking Gazette*. Even if he do not "care a button" himself for these things he has to wear a particular kind of button upon his cap, and no other.

Rich Chinamen have as many clothes as have ladies of fashion in the West, and experience self-respect accordingly. One of them related with pride that when he went on a visit to a foreign country the Custom House officers would not believe that his multitudinous garments were all for his own use, and were not intended for sale.

Owing to the many temperatures of a day in China these changes of raiment are required. On a cold winter's morning a Chinaman puts on jacket after jacket, sometimes thickly wadded ones, too, until he looks like an old-clo' man or a cotton ball. When the day becomes warm he takes the jackets off according to taste, and is found behind the counter of his shop stripped to the waist as in summer. When evening approaches on go the jackets, and he becomes the same dimensions as in the morning. A Chinaman speaks of a day as a "three, four, or six coat cold day." Most coolies keep their legs and feet bare all the winter. One of them when asked by an Englishman if these parts did not feel cold replied, "No more than your face." "My face has been exposed since I was born," said the Britisher. "Me all face," retorted the Chinese.

The story goes that at the coronation of King Edward, Prince Chen, who came from Peking, said to Mr. Chang, the Chinese Minister in London, "Why is it that you do not dress more richly, and why do you not also provide richer dresses for Madame Chang, your wife, and for the members of your suite, for the credit of China, at the Court of St. James's?" "Prince," answered Mr. Chang, "my allowance from Peking is so much. I am a poor man. Why should I, therefore, dress better than my means allow?"

There are special clothes for every important occasion. If a Chinaman meet you on New Year's Day in his ordinary clothes he will not salute, but will apologise and say that he will return to pay his respects when properly attired. "The ancient kings," said the old books, "shook their clothes and ruled the world," and ever since the question of clothes has been an important one in China. After self-adjustment and purification, Confucius puts careful regulation of dress in his enumeration, of the things that enable a sovereign to rule righteously. For ceremonial occasions, well-to-do Chinamen put on garment after garment of rich silk, which prevent anything like rapid movement. Their coats are so long that they look like women's gowns, and the sleeves of these are about a foot longer than the tips of the fingers of those who wear them. In winter they loll about in heavily-wadded, fur-

lined clothes as if they were in bed. And yet in many
respects Chinese clothes are handsomer and more convenient
than are ours. It is generally admitted that women, like
insects, should wear bright colours, but so should men, and
this they do in China, and it adds to the cheerfulness of life.
Nor are colours thought to kill each other. You see men
arrayed as fearlessly as parrots in bright green and blue,
accompanied by deep scarlet, purple, lilac, or orange. The
dress which a Chinese gentleman most commonly wears is a
dark purple silk outer jacket over a bright blue gown. An
"angelic stork" worked on the back and breast of his robe
denotes a mandarin of the first rank; a pheasant, one of the
second rank; and nine other kinds of birds mark nine descending degrees of civil rank. Military grades are indicated by
embroidered animals. The summer hat of officials is made of
finely woven straw; in winter it is trimmed with fur. The
wife of a mandarin has an embroidered robe much resembling
that of her husband. Underneath there is, on grand occasions, a petticoat, also embroidered, which by means of wire
is made to hang square before and behind. This is well seen
when the lady is invited to lay aside her skirt as we ask one to
put off her cloak. Like her husband, a mandarin's wife has
a pearl or bead necklace, the original of which is the eighteen
or one hundred and eight beads of the Buddhist rosary. Some
mandarins are very particular about the way their better
halves or, as they would say in China, their worse halves, are
turned out. A very high one was surprised in the act of
painting his wife's eyebrows. He was sent for by the
Emperor and asked if the report were true. "Yes, your
Majesty," he answered; "but what is there frivolous in that?
Is not everything allowed between man and wife?" The
Son of Heaven was satisfied with the reply.

In summer all Chinese have fans, even a soldier on active
service, and a criminal going to execution. Charitable people
supply them for nothing to the poor. There are masculine

A MANDARIN'S WIFE IN FULL UNIFORM.

To face page 132.

and feminine fans ; the former folds up ; the latter is a fixed
fan of feathers or painted silk, said by a poetess to be
peculiarly appropriate to woman, because, like her, it is much
sought after in spring and summer, but tossed contemptuously
aside in the days of autumn. Many *literati* do not buy
pictured fans, but blank ones, upon which they get distinguished people to paint or write something as we do in
albums. A man of means carries his fan in a worked silk
sheath attached to his girdle, a coolie in the neck of his
jacket. Other appendages to the girdle are a purse, a watch-
case, a snuff-box, and sometimes a knife and a pair of chopsticks. A boy generally follows, carrying a long pipe and a
tobacco-pouch. Old-fashioned Chinese who have no pockets,
except, perhaps, small ones for their watches, use their long,
wide sleeves as a substitute. Instead of saying that So-and-
so "pocketed the book," they would say that he "sleeved
it." The crown of an upturned hat or the space between cap
and head are made to hold unconsidered trifles. Coolies find
that the inside of their ears affords sufficient accommodation
for their cash. Trousers of the same bright colour and rich
material as their jackets come down to the "lily feet" of
ladies. Upon these last hoof-like deformities they wear
beautifully embroidered wrapping cloths, and over these
shoes which are seldom more than two inches long. A
woman nearly always makes her own shoes. If a girl's feet
have not been bound, she will sometimes wear attached to the
middle of the sole of her shoe a clump of wood. This makes
her walk in much the same way as if her feet had gone
through the distorting operation of fashion.

The Chinese man's boot is a kind of golosh of cloth, satin,
or other material (never leather), with a sole an inch thick,
unyielding at the instep. Rags, paper, and almost anything
go to the composition of these thick soles. They have been
made even of Bibles. A man sent to several missionary
societies to say that he could place to advantage any number

of Bibles in Chinese. Bales of them were sent for the good of souls, but it was soles that got them. Missionaries found them in the stuffing of boots and shoes.

You seldom see women in a Chinese crowd. The ladies of the lily feet must remain in the seclusion of their homes, or be carried through the street in closely covered chairs. Those you do see have bare heads, their much greased but seldom washed hair being parted in several places on the crown and ornamented with artificial flowers, with butterflies made of jade, with gold pins, and with pearls. Each district has its own style. At Foochow, for instance, the women are not more noticeable for the silver hoops in their ears than they are for the three silver things like paper-knives that keep their back hair in its place. The hair of Manchu matrons projects on both sides from the head like the long wings of a bat. The tresses of some women resemble teapot handles sticking out from three to six inches behind their heads. A gold ornament representing a phœnix is sometimes worn, the wings hovering and the beak of the bird hanging over the forehead. After a certain time of life a woman wears a silk wrapper or embroidered band which crosses the forehead and fastens behind the ears. In the centre there is often a large pearl. Widows have only white flowers in their hair.

Maidens brush their hair back and wear it in a queue like the men, or fastened in a ball on the side of their heads. When they marry they comb the front hair over the brow in a straight fringe and fasten the back part in a roll. When they are only a month old the heads of babies are shaved and a feast given to celebrate the event. On this occasion master baby receives such presents as head-dresses of different kinds, and a silver label to hang on his breast. When his locks grow they are again shaved, only tufts on either side being left that make him resemble a tadpole.

Jade ornaments are to Chinese women what diamonds are to European. For a pair of vivid green earrings or bracelets

as much as five or six hundred pounds will be paid. Poorer
women have to content themselves with imitations. Many
gentlemen wear rings and bracelets of jade or of some perfumed stone.

Chinese ladies put colour thick upon their cheeks and lips,
and there is no deception about it. The only time rouge
and ghastly white powder are dispensed with is when in
mourning and on the day of marriage. It is thought that
eyebrows should be arched like a rainbow or shaped like a
willow-leaf, so with tweezers ladies remove hairs which
straggle out of the required curve and complete the delusion
with paint and charcoal.

The garments of both sexes of the poor resemble each other,
almost the only difference being that the woman's jacket is
rather longer. They are generally made either of blue cotton
or of a dark brown material which looks like oil silk. The
buttons are made with a needle and thread like those used in
England before the reign of Elizabeth.

House boys, shopmen, and workers who in Britain would
not be so particular, wear spotlessly white stockings, and at
their ankles they fasten very neatly the ends of their double
trousers, or rather of the long leggings which they wear over
trousers. These are attached to the girdle at the waist;
but there is a void space behind that presents an untidy
appearance.

The large shield-like hats of coolies, their rain-coats made
of palm-leaves, and their rope sandals are sensible and
inexpensive. They wear straw gauntlets to protect their
sleeves, though these are scarcely worth protecting.

The Chinese have a saying that "Three-tenths of beauty
is beauty, and seven-tenths is dress," and yet even when they
clothe themselves in their best there is generally something
wanting. A man is walking in a religious or other procession
in gorgeous silks and satins; you look at his lower limbs, and
perhaps you see dirty, shabby pantaloons peeping out from

under the imposed finery. You were not meant to look there!

It is recorded that Confucius used to wear a sleeping dress half as long again as his body. The modern Chinese does not imitate him in this. He either sleeps in his day clothes or, stripping some of these off, wraps himself in a quilt and pillows his head upon a small stool of bamboo or a leather-covered block of wood.

In the morning a Chinaman begins his toilet by taking a large mug, a silver tongue-scraper, a tooth-brush, or a bit of willow twig into the courtyard and cleans his tongue and teeth with much spluttering and clearing of his throat. Then a handmaid pours hot water into a small copper or brass basin resting upon a stand and brings the family or hotel rag. With this her master rubs his face, neck, and hands. Nothing now remains to be done but to tie his drawers at the ankles, put on an outward jacket or long robe, and hitch himself up generally.

In 1644, when the Manchus conquered the Chinese, they imposed the towchang, or pig-tail, as a sign of subjection. Of course it was unpopular at first; but it became a badge of honour and of respectability when a law was enacted that no one in prison or who was guilty of crime should wear it. Now, to call a man "woo peen," or tailless, is to insult him greatly. As a punishment the queue is sometimes cut off a malefactor. When he gets out of prison he generally fastens on a false one. This is convenient, for if wanted again and caught he can leave the loosely fastened appendage in the policeman's hand and escape.

There are many uses to which a queue is put. In a street fight the combatants hang on to each other's queues. A *raconteur* supplements manual gesture with his queue. A queue is sometimes plied as a tawse upon the backs of refractory boys. It serves as a noose in which a suicide can strangle himself and a handle for pulling taut the neck of a man being decapitated. Does a Chinaman wish to explain foreign astronomy? He fastens a weight to the end of his queue and whirls it round his head to illustrate the revolutions of the planets round the sun. A Chinaman desires his queue to be as long as possible, and for this purpose perhaps he uses as much hair, not his own, as the average British woman does in dressing her (?) hair. The queue is also elongated by black braid or, in case of mourning, by white or blue. Young boys wear red, the lucky colour. A well-developed towchang resembles the tail of a cow rather than of a pig, and is not ill-looking. So much time, however, is spent in its grooming that Chinese reformers say that it is a drain on the resources of the nation, and ought to be abolished. Many of them are cutting off their towchangs. Coolies twine their queues round their heads when at work, but it is good manners for them to let them down in the presence of a superior.

The women of China were less obedient to Mauchu mandates than were the men. They were ordered to give up the custom of binding the feet of their daughters, but they paid no attention to the edict. It never has been easy to get women to obey.

Chinamen do not seem to be able to grow hair on the lip or chin as readily as they do on the back of their heads. Then social usage only allows a man to have a beard when he is forty years old, or when he becomes a grandfather. This, together with the Chinese respect for age, causes any one with a long beard to be greatly venerated. A man with a nice beard puts over it a bag every night and keeps it neat with a small comb which he always carries with him. An Emperor noticed that the beard of one of his ministers was finer than his own. He asked him what he did for it. The minister said that he did so-and-so—any amount of operations. Then said the Emperor, "If you spend so much time on your beard you have little time left for your duties. I degrade you."

CHAPTER XIII

HOUSES AND GARDENS

The height of impertinence—A patriarchal encampment—In harmony with surroundings—Inside a house—No concealment—Houses as uncomfortable morally as they are physically—Chang Kung—Chinese inns—House-boats—The Yamen—No repairs—A potter's field—Landscape gardening—The flower hermit—Floral calendars.

IT is thought the height of impertinence for a Chinese to live in a house higher than the wall of the town in which the house is situated. Even official and rich people are content with one-storied dwellings. When for family and other reasons they wish to extend, they add courtyard to courtyard until there is a patriarchal encampment. Pictures of European houses of four and five stories surprise the Celestials. They wonder if it is the smallness of our country that compels us to build so high.

Retired officials and other well-to-do people generally reside in or near towns for protection. And they are careful not to display wealth upon their houses lest it should be taken from them. They know that "the elephant is killed on account of his ivory." A man with a reputation for riches might be asked, for instance, to pay a tax on the land he bought during the year. "I bought no land." "Well, but you might or should have done so; therefore pay up."

But though the houses of the wealthy are not showy, they are always in harmony with their surroundings. A Chinaman understands the fitness of things, and would not build a house that would offend or degrade public taste. It must be good to look at.

A tent type of architecture prevails everywhere in temple, in palace, and in private life. The tiled roofs often assume beautiful curves, and the corners are ornamented with dragons and other grotesque figures. Windows only look into court-yards which are ranged one behind another. Until lately, when glass is beginning to be used, the windows were always filled with paper or ground oyster-shells which overlap each other. A high wall surrounds every mansion, in order to secure it from fire and robbers.

The entrance to this class of house is by a triple gate leading through a garden. Under the projecting eaves hang paper lanterns having on them the name and titles of the householder and perhaps those of some of his ancestors. These names and titles are also inscribed in gilt letters upon red boards. The sides of the colonnades are embellished with quotations on red paper. Door bells are unknown in the interior of China. You shout "Lai" ("Come here"), and the porter opens the large middle door or a side one, according to your social position.

The doors face to the south and south-west, to catch the summer breeze and the winter sun. Passing through an outer portico or hall, which consists of pillars and an ornamental roof, you enter the reception hall. In the centre of this, chairs with straight backs are arranged, with small tables between each pair. Near the chairs are placed deep spittoons, which are rendered necessary by the universal habit of smoking. The reception hall generally looks on to a courtyard filled with orange, camelia, or azalea trees, growing in large pots placed upon stone pedestals.

The front courtyard of a grand house is open to any one who may choose to wander in; a desire to exclude strangers would be held to argue that there was something wrong going on which the owner wished to conceal. The guest-room has only three walls, the whole of the front being open to the court. It was this Eastern arrangement which enabled the "woman who was a sinner" and the others to approach the Lord Jesus Christ as He "sat at meat."

To the right and left of the reception hall there are with-drawing and dining-rooms. Beautiful scrolls having on them felicitous words, rich hangings, and long shaped pictures of historical scenes adorn the walls. The floors are of mud, wood, or tiling, with no rugs or carpets upon them. In the drawing-room may often be seen a gilt and carved box. This contains the patents of nobility or commissions to offices held by the proprietor. The Chinese are fond of collecting old and curious things, and the cabinets of many rich individuals at Peking and Canton are worth seeing. Europeans may fancy that they pick up bargains at these places, but they only get rubbish which Chinese collectors have refused.

Porcelain vases and copper tripods are everywhere. Bouquets of flowers are considered vulgar, but single specimens which are meant to be separately enjoyed adorn parts of rooms.

The doorways that lead from one part of a house to another are often circular or in the shape of a leaf. When doors are not necessary these fancy-shaped openings are covered with silk or cloth hangings or with bamboo blinds.

The bedrooms are more sanitary than ours are because they contain less furniture. More attention, however, is paid to the carving of the beds than to their comfort. But it is not only the furniture that is carved. Wood carving adorns the cornices of the rooms and the pillars of the doorways. There are no ceilings in the rooms, only rafters.

In nearly every house there are three small shrines, above or before which stand candlesticks made of pewter, flower-vases, and incense-burners. At the threshold is one, perhaps, to the Earth Gods, before which at evening time red tapers and incense-sticks are burned. Then within, generally in the reception hall, stand the Ancestral Tablets and the altar of the Kitchen God with an ever-burning light before them. And of course there is an image or picture of the God of Wealth, for that in China, as also perhaps in England, is the best served of all gods.

In the absence of artificial means for heating their rooms, the Chinese frequently carry with them a little stove. In the north of China whole families sleep together during the winter upon a heated platform called a "kang." The warmth of this kang is said to comfort "like a mother," but it must be as irritating as a step-mother also, for it nearly always contains a multitude of tiny monsters to which the Chinese are too much accustomed to complain.

Kerosine has "caught on" in China more, perhaps, than any other foreign novelty, but oil made of beans, cotton-seed, and peanuts is still used. It has little more illuminating power than to make the darkness of the houses at night visible. One advantage is that the good old fashion of going to bed when it is dark continues.

We have never seen a dwelling belonging to the poorer class of people that could be truthfully described as a "neat cottage." There is a place for everything, certainly, for things which with us would be in outhouses are kept in the houses themselves, but as certainly everything is not in its place. Rather, beds, benches, and tables may be seen mixed up with weaving-looms, spinning-wheels, jars of grain, farming implements, and other things that we do not expect to find in a bedroom or sitting-room. Probably people like to personally watch their things, for where walls are made of adobe or mud it is easy for thieves to dig through and steal. Nor can property-owners have much confidence in the locks and primitive method of chaining doors that are in use.

In Chinese poorer dwellings there are no chimneys, or only

very small ones, and the stalks and grass which heat the cooking-boiler (the " grass which to-day is, and to-morrow is cast into the oven ") make much disagreeable smoke. The benches that serve for chairs are uncomfortably narrow. A mat laid on a couple of boards or on a rattan frame, and a mosquito curtain of hempen cloth, constitute a bed.

From an Occidental point of view, Chinese houses are models of discomfort. They are cold in winter, hot in summer, and smoky all the year round. Everywhere there are draughts. The doors with double leaves are a bad protection, even if they were kept shut, but they never are. It would be a falsehood if a man in China put on his office door the words " Everybody closes the door but you." Small houses have no windows, or only paper ones, which will not keep out wind, rain, sun, heat, or dust.

When foreigners experience the discomforts of Chinese abodes, they say that the people who live in them are not civilised. This, however, is, as the author of " Chinese Characteristics " says, to confound comfort with civilisation. The England of Shakespeare and Elizabeth was civilised, but it was not comfortable, judged by a twentieth-century standard.

Many houses, too, are as uncomfortable morally as they are physically.

> " Two cats and one mouse,
> Two women in one house,
> Two dogs to one bone,
> Will not agree long."

This is as true in China as in other countries, and it is the rule in China for two or three generations of women to live in one house. No wonder that the Chinese have deified Chang Kung under the title of Kitchen God. This worthy lived in the eighth century of our era, and had his family in such good order that with eight generations they simultaneously inhabited the same courts in perfect peace. Even his hundred dogs were so polite that they waited, if any one of them was late at a meal. The reigning Emperor sent for Chang Kung, to inquire the secret of such wonderful harmony, and calling for a pen, he wrote the character for "Forbearance" a great number of times.

In a household it is always the oldest father who rules, a custom which alone would account for the great conservatism of China.

Though Chinese inns are called "Heavenly Union," "Unapproachable Purity," "The Nourishment of Life," and other much-promising names, they resound with hellish quarrelling, they are too filthy to approach, and the only life they nourish is that of vermin. In the little sleeping rooms there is probably no window, and certainly no furniture except a rickety table, a narrow bench, and a brick-lined ledge on which to put the bed you are supposed to bring along with any food you may require. In the room below, or alongside, pigs or goats are very likely to be the occupants.

One reason why these places are not more inviting is because well-to-do Chinese do not use them. Mandarins travel in house-boats on the many and extensive waterways of the empire. House-boats are slow coaches, but then the Chinese have not our insane love of speed. There is a movable sitting-room and two or three sleeping cabins in the centre of the boat. Cooking is done upon the high overhanging stern, where the crew is also accommodated. There are gangways on each side on which walk the men who pole the vessel in the shallows, and the servants when they have occasion to pass from one part to another. Parts of the boat are beautifully carved, varnished, and gilded. The windows are made of glass, thin oyster-shells, transparent paper, or gauze. For the mat sails used in junks canvas ones are often substituted.

The fare (called "water-legs") on Chinese passenger boats is only about a penny of our money for thirty or forty miles.

To spend time in them must be cheaper than to pay house-rent.

The yamen (literally "official gate") of a mandarin is his combined private and official residence. It is generally a mixture of grandeur and meanness. The roofs and walls are red, the colour that distinguishes Government buildings. Under the cover of the porch of the entrance gate is kept the official chair, and near it the lanterns, tablets, execution swords, and umbrellas that are carried in procession when the great man goes out. Over the entrance door and over each successive door as you proceed inwards are hung red lanterns. If the mandarin be of high rank there will be three or four great gateways to separate him from the vulgar herd. The gates are generally of thick wood, and upon them are painted grotesque door gods, or celebrated officials of heroic size and intimidating features. Each gate has a central part and two leaves. The former is only used by the mandarin himself, his equals and superiors.

In the centre are the private rooms of the official, of his wife, and of his concubines; then come the offices of his secretaries, the waiting-rooms, and a court or reception-room. Around the yard are the buildings where servants and "runners" live.

The Chinese spend much money in building their houses and temples, but they seem to begrudge what is necessary to keep them in repair. Eaves and corners filled with expensive gods, holy men, emperors, and devils; scenes from the life of Buddha in five-coloured porcelain covering some of the walls; corners in heaven and peeps into hell; heroic sized gods looking like the giant in Jack-and-the-Beanstalk and grinning from either side of the entrance—these carved things are in the rich man's dwelling, the yamen, or the temple, but the place they adorn is a magnificent ruin which is seldom or never repaired. Rock-work and summer-house fall to pieces. That expensively made pond in the garden might be beautiful

RECEPTION ROOM IN A YAMEN.

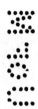

if it did not contain so many dead cats and dogs and were not covered so thickly with oily green slime.

No garden in China looks at first glance better than a potter's field. The plants are put in glazed and ornamented pots, arranged in rows along the walks, but not planted out as in our gardens. Soon, however, you come upon pretty bits of trellis-work and zigzag bridges leading to grottoes with horseshoe doors. Grotesque figures are produced by training certain shrubs over a framework of wire, so as exactly to take its form. Evergreen dragons, dolphins with great eyes of china, and mandarins with china or wooden hands, head, and feet are the forms most generally to be seen. Shrubs are made to take the shape of birds, fans, junks, bridges, houses, and flower-baskets, tall evergreen pagodas are adorned with little china bells hanging round each storey. There are always many distorted and dwarfed trees. These miniatures have every characteristic of the full-grown—indeed, of the aged tree—with gnarled and twisted roots and branches, although they are only a few inches high. Rock-work and summer-houses, the last erected on artificial islands, are features in most gardens. The visitor is impressed with dark caves and rushing cataracts, his gloom being increased by the trunks of trees blasted as if by lightning and the intro-duction of a house thrown down by the fury of a pretended tempest. Then there is a sudden transition, and we see only what is calculated to charm with brilliant colour and beautiful form.

In most gardens there are tanks for goldfish and a pond which is beautiful with the flowers of the famous lotus lily. This plant, rising as it does from mud, is emblematic of Buddha being evolved from lower stages of existence. So sacred is the lotus that the frugal Chinese waste nothing of it. They delight their eyes with its flowers and their stomachs with its seeds and roots. The leaves are dried and sold to tradesmen to wrap purchases in.

10

In 1783, Ch'ên Hao-tsŭ, who called himself the "Flower Hermit," wrote a work on gardening entitled "The Mirror of Flowers." From a translation of the preface we quote the following: "From my youth upwards I have cared for nothing but books and flowers. Twenty-eight thousand days have passed over my head, the greater part of which has been spent in poring over old records and the remainder in enjoying myself in my garden among plants and birds. People laugh at me, and say that I am cracked on flowers and a bibliomaniac; but surely study is the proper occupation of a literary man, and as for gardening, that is a rest for my brain and an antidote against the ills of old age. . . . If a home has not a garden and an old tree, I see not whence the every-day joys of life are to come."

We have quoted this Chinese White of Selborne, because he expresses sentiments about a garden which are shared by nearly every one of his countrymen who have had the advantage of culture.

The flowering of favourite plants and trees is watched for eagerly. Floral calendars are found in every house above the poorest, and excursions are made into the country, not to drink at a public-house or to kill something, but to enjoy roses, peonies, azaleas, camellias, chrysanthemums, and other flowering delights.

The object of the owners of Chinese gardens is to imitate the beauties and to reproduce the inequalities of Nature. By grouping rock-work, by making artificial hills, and by bridging over streams they produce a panorama full of surprises and fresh points of view.

CHAPTER XIV

SERVANTS AND LABOURERS

WHY do we call a male servant in the Far East "boy"
regardless of his age? The reason is said to be that
when Europeans first went to India one caste, called Boyee, or
Bhoi, were found willing to undertake menial duties.

We have all heard of the Chinese cook who used to break
an egg and throw it away each time he made a pudding
because on the first occasion when he was shown how
to make a pudding an egg happened to be bad.

Chinese servants, like the rest of the nation, are very
conservative, and when once you get them to do what you
want they go on in a comfortable groove. Sometimes, however, this stereotyped way of working is not convenient, as I
found when crossing the Pacific. Sea-sickness prevented
my appearance at the *table-d'hôte* dinner on the first day,
and on the second when I did come I partook of scarcely
anything. On recovering my appetite it was difficult to
get from the boy who waited upon me more than I had taken
the first day. And yet one could not be angry with those

picturesque Chinese who served so deftly, and moved about as noiselessly as ghosts in their long, white gowns.

A lady offered her laundry-man a dollar a month extra if he would sprinkle her clothes with his hand instead of with his mouth. He accepted the dollar gladly, but continued his good old way. This is an illustration of the fact that stubbornness often coexists with much faithfulness in Chinese servants. Of one such his master used to say that he was in a condition of chronic indecision whether to kill him or raise his wages.

It is better for the peace of mind, and even of the stomach, of householders not to go much into their kitchens in China. One mistress confided to a friend whom she met in the Peak tramcar at Hong Kong that she had seen her cook, stripped to the waist, rolling with a rolling-pin a cake or pie on his bare chest!

Certainly the way a market coolie carries food for his master at Hong Kong is anything but appetising. In one hand there will be a live fowl, a bit of bacon, and a beef-steak; in the other, dried fish, a pigeon, and mutton cutlets tied up without any covering. It is worse if he puts the dinner in a basket, because then he sticks all kind of heathen messes of his own alongside of it.

A lady who understands Chinese well told me that she once overheard her cook saying to a messenger boy, "Now, remember, you can only have it half an hour, and must then bring it back, because missus says it is to be given to the dogs." Inquiring from the messenger what he was carrying, the lady discovered that it was soup meat, which, after making soup for her own household, was being lent for the same purpose to the cook of a neighbouring house.

Another friend was much pleased with her house-boy until one day she caught him brushing his hair with one of her ivory-backed brushes.

A cook when too much found fault with will take his

revenge by expectorating into the soup. On the other hand, if you treat cook well he will get you out of many a difficulty. Should there be a brace of snipe or of quail too little, he will make two birds of flour for master and mistress.

It is quite wonderful how your number one boy writes out the *menus* considering his small supply of English. Of course he puts "bold beef" instead of "cold beef" and "stewed Irish" instead of "Irish stew," but he will do his best to spare the feelings of your guests. One house-boy was much embarrassed, for the principal dish at breakfast was to be devilled turkey. "Devil very bad word," he said to himself; "how can write?" The dish appeared as "D——d turkey."

Knowledge, however, does not always go with zeal. People are proud of the number of foreign labels on their trunks and valises. A friend of mine had a cabin trunk of which he was especially proud. He invariably showed it to his friends as one of his treasures. It was covered all over with labels. One evening, on going home, his boy met him with smiling face, and, obviously expectant of "cumsha" for his unusual diligence, informed the master that he had "makum clean that ole bag!" The boy had carefully scraped the portmanteau clean of every scrap of paper, and he could not comprehend why the owner swore.

There is almost as much division of labour in a household in China as in India—a servant for each department, and one or two with no work in particular and two or three to help them to do it. Then no Chinaman is so poor but what he can find a poorer to do part of his work. A coolie earning six dollars a month will pay another one dollar a month to help him, and he in turn will give a lad a few cash that he himself may have more leisure for his opium pipe. Fortunately the wages are low as compared with the West, but foreigners in the treaty ports have to give more than double what native employers in the interior give.

A Chinese servant is continually asking to go and bury his father. He has two or three fathers wanting interment every year. Servants will decamp bag and baggage, some of it yours, without any warning. True, the departing one leaves a substitute, but the substitute is nearly always an inferior article, and will soon go, leaving a still worse one. So you may begin housekeeping with a stock of good servants, and find at length that your house has become a den of thieves and idlers. A house-boy in the employment of a family in Hong Kong announced that he wanted two or three weeks' leave to go to Canton to "catchee his wife." He brought another boy to take his place. Interviewed by the lady of the house, the substitute said he had another pidgin, but had two weeks' leave and could take the place of his "fiend" for that time. He did not appear to know much about housework, and the lady asked him if his master was a Chinaman. With all the dignity imaginable he replied, "No! my master belong King of England, and Emperor of Great Britain; me Government servant-boy!"

Servants are supposed to feed themselves and, as they profess to despise our food, they of course do not eat it. And yet it goes, even the cheese which they say is disgusting. It may be that our eggs are not taken, for some Chinese do not care for these unless a hen has sat on them for about twelve days.

One Chinese servant will ask another a question which is, when literally translated, "Do you eat your master or eat yourself?" The meaning is, "Does your master feed you, or do you board yourself?"

I have known honest Chinese servants, one in particular, who returned after several years and gave to his master money he owed. And even those who are no more honest than the rest of us will not allow any one but themselves to steal from their masters. There is honour, too, amongst these thieves, and they limit their peculations by certain clearly defined restraints. A house-boy will say, for instance, "Five per cent. business, ten per cent. thief pidgin." From prince to pauper, however, the squeeze system prevails in China, and in this respect servants only follow their masters. The servants in a large establishment, official or domestic, sometimes form themselves into a company for business purposes. Each in his particular "pidgin" or line of business secures a percentage upon all sales, purchases or other financial transactions. The proceeds are placed in a common fund, and dividends declared at stated times to each according to his rank and work. Nor is such a combination as criminal as it seems, for it is known and understood, and to some extent is regarded as compensation for the low wages that are given.

We used to give the wages of the coolies who carried us in chairs to the house-boy to pay them, until we discovered that he deducted a squeeze out of it. When remonstrated with he said that the chair coolies would have had no respect for him if he had not done it. Number one boy, as a rule, engages, pays, and dismisses the other servants, and it is best for your own peace and for that of the household not to interfere.

"What are servants coming to?" growled a Hong Kong friend to me. "Only this morning my gardener said, 'I no stay with you; you too cheeky a master.'"

Are Chinese servants always ungrateful? Our experience says "No," and also that those who most loudly speak of ingratitude are owed nothing.

So good an authority as Rev. G. H. Smith thus writes in "China in Convulsion" of the faithfulness of some of the servants of murdered missionaries: "In repeated instances, servants who have been sent away for their own safety returned on the eve of a riot, saying simply: 'I heard that you were to be attacked to-night, and I thought that I ought to be here to help you.' Many of them voluntarily served as couriers at the imminent risk of their lives, not once or twice, but constantly, and in this way many were killed."

If I said that I knew one Chinese servant who practised the fine art of telling truth, readers who have lived in China would think that I was a poor artist in this line myself. We are liars ourselves, but we think that the Chinese are greater ones because they lie from different motives. Their mendacity shocks us because it is not the same kind as our own.

It is a common experience in China to have a servant several years and never once to have seen him out of temper. One reason is that the servants despise their employers too much to be provoked by them. They do not show surprise at anything masters and mistresses do.

" Of all people," said Confucius, " girls and servants are the most difficult to behave to. If you are familiar to them, they lose their humility; if you maintain your reserve, they are discontented." So there was a " servant question " in China even in the time of Confucius, and there is one now, but it is much more easily answered in the Celestial Empire than it is in England. What would not the perplexed British matron give for service as clean, clever, and silent as that performed by Chinese boys ? Sometimes they do what we do not want done, and leave undone what we do want, but as a rule their instincts guide them right. Number one boy arranges the meals after a little talk with his mistress. Should unexpected guests come, he is equal to the occasion. There is no danger of his forgetting to send the coolies to market, for he gets his " squeeze " on each article purchased. He will then, turning himself into a parlourmaid, lay the table and arrange the flowers. The house-boy will look after master's clothes so well that master will never know where he has put them, but the boy knows, and can always produce them. The sleek-headed amahs, with big jade earrings and baggy trousers, are fond of and kind to the children committed to their care. So, too, are the coolies who carry the children's milk-bottles or

CHAIR COOLIES AND MARKET COOLIE.

To face page 158.

push their perambulators. It is a mistake, however, to allow children to be much with Chinese servants, for the habitual talk of these people is filthy, and children learn enough Chinese language to understand them.

It is a pity that when British people came first to China they did not teach servants pure English instead of the ridiculous thing called "pidgin English." New-comers think that they can learn this in a few days, and that it consists only in putting double " e " to the end of words, and using mongrel terms such as " chow " for food, "chop-chop" for immediately, and so on. At a boarding-house in Hong Kong I heard a lady who had lately arrived saying to a servant, " Boy, catchee me one piecee saltee chop-chop." So I could not help remarking, " You would be just as intelligible and more respected if you only said, ' Salt, please.' " The chair coolies have now learned this wretched jargon, and so if you want to be carried, for instance, to the house of the Bishop of Hong Kong, you must order them to go to " No. 1 Topside Joss Pidgin." Educated Chinese, however, resent it as an impertinence to be spoken to in an infantine strain. One of these replied to a globe-trotter, " I understand Chinese, French, German, Italian, and English, but I have forgotten the language of childhood, so please do not address me in that."

It is in the north of China, however, that one experiences the comfort of really good service. At Peking and Shanghai the servants seemed to me to be thought-readers, anticipating every want before it was expressed. At the latter place I stayed for some days in a house from which the master and mistress and every European were absent. None of the servants could understand a word of English, and I could not speak their language, yet I had everything I wanted to eat, and everything I wished done as soon as I thought of it.

Every visitor to Japan notices the cheerful industry of the people. The industry of the Chinese may not be so cheerful, but they are "all at it, and always at it," and indeed must be, for, as their proverb says, "to stop the hand is the way to stop the mouth."

In many parts of China an ordinary labourer can be hired for from ten to sixteen cents (2½d. to 4d.) a day. A coolie will carry on his shoulder eighty catties (107 lbs.) forty miles in one day for the equivalent of from seven to nine pence of our money. Much of their payment remains with the middleman who hires out the coolies. Certainly the necessities of life are cheap, but even so the poverty is great.

In China, however, there is less of that contrast between grinding poverty and arrogant wealth which is the rule in Europe. The Chinese are not snobs, and are not ashamed of poor friends and relations. In the north labourers come from their work and sit down in the farmhouse on the same bench with their employers round the fire. When supper is served all eat together.

The cheapness of labour puts men and women to what we would consider unworthy uses. One occupation is this : a man sits or lies in a state of nudity, and eggs are put all around until the heat of his body hatches them. The human hen or cock may occasionally leave the nest for a few moments, but must hasten back before the eggs get cold. After a three weeks' hatch he looks very white and wretched.

I have counted as many as sixteen coolies carrying a great stone. As I saw their ant-like movements I understood how the remains of antiquity that astonish us were built. They took "time for their fulcrum and patience for their lever."

So accustomed does a coolie become to carrying loads attached to a pole resting on his shoulders that if he cannot divide his burden he will fasten a stone of equal weight to the other end of the pole rather than carry the load some other way. The instinctive knowledge that coolies have of the application of force is marvellous. Give one of them a bamboo pole and a piece of rope, and he will shift a log that would seem to require an ox or even an elephant.

Coolies, both men and women, have a great dislike to being photographed. One day we saw a group of the latter, who were picturesque in their ugliness, and tried to get a snapshot at them. The coy ladies, however, strongly objected. They hid their faces behind their umbrella-like hats, and when we tried to get at them by a flank movement they took to flight, and saved their faces by making good use of their feet. One reason why the camera is an object of dread to ignorant Chinese is because they think that it draws the soul away from the person photographed. The coolie women upon whom this photographic attack was made carried the baggage of troops with whom I was on manœuvres in the country. Mr. Thomas Atkins called the ladies " The Amah Brigade."

Speaking of nicknames, we may remark that the one a chair coolie most dislikes is to be called a horse without a tail. " Coffin-chisel," or one that makes coffins, will greatly insult any coolie.

Centuries ago the Chinese made use of the principle of co-operation between capital and labour to which we are now turning as to a sheet-anchor in our twentieth century of Christianity. You are sometimes astonished when a Chinese merchant introduces to you as his partners young men who in England would be junior clerks. Even the coolie packing tea-boxes says, " *We* are doing well this year," and works with a will.

Not long ago I heard in Hong Kong two men discussing the removal of a large quantity of earth in connection with some building. One said to the other, "Would this be done cheaper by rice-power or by steam ? " By rice-power he meant coolies fed on rice, and it seemed a brutal way of speaking of man made in the image of God. One thing, perhaps, which makes us think of men as machines in the Far East is the fact that they draw us about in ginrickshas or pull-man-cars.

Treadmill work is thought too severe for prisoners in England, but coolies do much of it in China. They propel boats by working with their feet a wheel in the stern ; they smooth cotton by peddling on large granite blocks, so that the blocks move backwards and forwards ; they husk rice by stepping upon heavy clappers. In coal-mines worked without foreign machinery men, who are bondsmen, are to be found toiling up to their waists in water. They are nicknamed " frogs," and have, as a rule, sold themselves into slavery because of gambling or family liabilities.

The coolies with dull, downcast eyes who carry enormous loads up the Peak at Hong Kong wear no clothes in summer except small drawers. Some of them look like skeletons covered with parchment and spotted with bruises and sores. The veins and sinews of their legs are all knotted. They never beg. Because of this, and in return for the lesson they taught me in patience, I used sometimes to give a coolie a piece of money. He would look at it with suspicion. "Did I want to make him a rice Christian ? " Finding that I had no design upon his faith and morals, he would take the money with a sickly smile and say, " Cumsha (a present), all right." Most of the materials with which the houses on the Peak have been built were carried up by coolie women. They may be said to have borne the houses on their shoulders. They go at a jog-trot pace, which experience has taught them is easiest. One sees coolie women coaling steamers, breaking stones, pulling big stone rollers, and doing generally the hardest work.

A pathetic sight in the streets of Hong Kong are the "16th Lancers," as our soldiers call the sixteen coolies who draw about the cart of manufactured ice. They haul for all they are worth, and surely each of these sixteen lancers are worth more in God's sight than they look to be to those who notice them only with derision in the streets.

CHAPTER XV

The most important of life's duties—Wives married, concubines loved—
The go-between—Presents interchanged—Betrothed from birth—Married
to a tablet—The wedding ceremony—Teasing the bride—Parents-in-law
must be remembered—"Sifting four eyes"—Pretended reluctance—
Mother-in-lawed—The seven reasons for divorce—A paradox—Thought
disgraceful for widows to marry.

WHEN parents get their children married they are
thought to have performed the most important of
life's duties, though they, no doubt, sometimes make as
great blunders as the young people would make if left to
choose for themselves. Certainly there is human nature in
Chinese young men, and they do fall in love and flirt, but not
with girls whom they marry. To these they are engaged by
their parents, and often they never see them until the wedding.
Then it is said they sometimes start back in pain and dismay.
It is considered improper for men to be seen speaking to their
fiancées, or even to their brides. One young man did venture
to talk in public to the girl he married, and the proceeding
was so unusual that the members of his family made an entry
in writing every time they saw him doing so, and chaffed him
unmercifully. "We marry our wives," said a Korean gentleman, "but we love our concubines," and this is the case very
often in China, though, of course, when a man gets a good
wife, love for her will be likely to come to him after marriage.

157

The family to which the boy or young man belongs generally begin negotiations. They do so by means of a go-between, who may be described as a professional liar. "To lie like a match-maker" is a common expression. This woman—the go-between is frequently a woman—is furnished with a card stating the ancestral name and the eight characters which denote the hour, day, month, and year of birth of the candidate for matrimony. The go-between takes this card to the family indicated, and tenders a proposal of marriage for a daughter. Should the girl's parents entertain the proposal they show to a fortune-teller the eight characters which tell the exact time of birth of the young people, and he, after examining them, says whether the betrothal would be auspicious. If, for instance, the girl was born on the day dedicated to the goose, and the boy on that of the fox, negotiations would terminate, because from time immemorial foxes have eaten geese. Should, however, the respective days be favourable, the families interchange cards upon which a formal agreement has been written. The parents of the young man send with the card gold or silver bangles for the girl, and for her family pig's feet, a pair of fowls, two fish, eight cocoanuts, &c. The girl's family send with the card five kinds of dried fruit, artificial flowers, vermicelli and cakes of ceremony for distribution amongst friends. On the top stack of these cakes small dolls made of flour are stuck. A pair of geese are sent, not to cast a reflection upon the intellectual condition of the youth and maiden to be married, but as an emblem of domestic bliss, these birds being reputed to be good family birds.

Some children are betrothed from their birth, so the time between betrothal and marriage varies from a month or two to eighteen or twenty years. Two persons having the same surname are not allowed to marry. As there are only about a hundred recognised family names in the Chinese Empire, this is a serious limitation.

When a girl "spills the tea," that is, loses her betrothed by

A WEDDING CHAIR.

To face page 189.

death, she is sometimes married to the tablet which represents his spirit, and goes to live with, that is to say, to be a drudge to, his parents. If a girl dies before betrothal, her parents betroth her to the spirit of some man. This is done by writing their names on tablets in a temple. This prevents her spirit returning to torment the family.

The first moon of the Chinese year (February) is considered the most felicitous time for marriage. It is in this month that the peach-tree blossoms, and hence there are constant allusions to it in connection with marriage.

The first part of a wedding procession consists of lantern-bearers, banner-bearers, and those who carry the tablets upon which are inscribed the names of the man and woman who are being married. Some of these bearers wear extraordinary-looking head-dresses. Two or three large red official umbrellas are then borne past. In the middle comes the glass chair of the bride, which is highly adorned with doll-like symbolical figures.

On the arrival of the bride at the bridegroom's house a woman who has borne male children and who lives in "harmonious subjection" to her husband, approaches the door of the sedan chair and utters felicitous sentences. In some parts of the country the bridegroom unlocks the chair, in others it is one of the women. A boy six or eight years old, holding in his hands a brass mirror with the reflecting surface turned from him and towards the chair, invites the bride to alight. This she does, and is then lifted over the threshold, on which charcoal burns in a pan, to prevent her bringing evil influence with her. She is now conducted over a floor covered with red carpet to her room, and is there met by the bridegroom. Both simultaneously seat themselves, side by side, on the edge of the bedstead, each trying to get a portion of the other's dress under him or her. Whoever can do this will, it is thought, have to submit to the other.

After sitting thus in silence for a few moments the bride-

groom takes his departure and waits in the reception-room
for the reappearance of his bride.   When she comes they
worship together heaven and earth and the ancestral tablets,
and this worship is the essence of the wedding ceremony.
A table is placed "before heaven" in the front part of the
reception-room.   Two lighted candles and a censer containing lighted incense are put upon it.   There are also placed
upon it, as omens of prosperity and harmony, two miniature
white cocks made of sugar, five kinds of dried fruit, money-
scales, a bundle of chopsticks, a foot measure, a mirror, and
a pair of shears.

The bride takes her place by the table on the right side of
the groom, and both of them kneel down four times, each time
bowing their heads towards the earth in silence.   They then
rise up, change places, and again kneel down four times,
bowing their heads as before.   The ancestral tablets are now
placed upon the table, and the bride and bridegroom kneel
down and worship these eight times, as they did "heaven
and earth."   On rising, two curiously shaped goblets connected together by a red silk or red cotton cord, and containing wine and honey are held to the mouths of bridegroom and
bride, and then changed so that the bride sips out of the one
just used by the bridegroom.   A bit of the sugar cocks and
some of the dried fruits are also given from off the table to
each of the pair.   Eating from the same sugar cock and
drinking wine from the same goblets are symbolical of union
in sharing their lot in life.

After this the bride and bridegroom dine together, and it is
now for the first time in his life, frequently and always for
the first time on his marriage-day, that the latter sees the
features of his wife.   She wears no rouge on this day, so he
knows what share of unadorned beauty he has got.   The
bridegroom eats as much as he likes, but the bride must not
take any food except what is sent to her by her own family
for seven or fourteen days.   She sits dignified and composed

beside her feasting husband, and does not open her mouth either to eat or to speak. It may be observed here that it is only on his wedding-day that a man in high-class life deigns to dine with his wife.

Some time during the afternoon the male guests sit down to dinner, but they are paying guests, for each sends before the entertainment a present in money. I saw one of these feasts, and was astonished at the large amount of pork, and of cakes with pork in them, that were served. Even uninvited neighbours are allowed to come in during the evening to see the bride, and they frequently indulge in jests and indecent liberty of remark about her which she must hear with not only composure but indifference. The girl is pulled about, and her feet, her dress, and her appearance generally closely scrutinised. She is told to stand with her bound "lily" feet upon a small inverted wine-cup. If she fail to do this, the friends say, "How awkward!" "Give tea to your husband" may be the next order. If she obey, they remark, "What an obedient wife!" Should she sulk and pay no attention, they will condole with her husband on having got a vixen for a wife. This is called "lao-shing-fang"—teasing the bride.

Chinese wedding festivities generally last at least two days. The first day the male friends of the bridegroom are invited to shed their light on the occasion. The second is the woman's day, when female friends are bidden to the marriage.

On the morning of the second day the newly married couple, amid the noise of fire-crackers and other demonstrations of interest, come out of their room together and proceed to the kitchen for the purpose of worshipping the god and goddess of the kitchen. It is expected that the bride, in attempting culinary operations, will succeed better in consequence of paying early and respectful attention to these divinities. The bride will also have to proceed to the ancestral temple to worship there her husband's forefathers.

On the third day after marriage the parents of the bride generally send an invitation to their son-in-law and his wife to visit them, and this visit is paid with much ceremony. Indeed, a man is not allowed to forget his father- and mother-in-law. Every year, upon their birthdays, he is expected to make them presents of pig's feet, vermicelli, wine, and large red candles, with, perhaps, some money.

Two or three days before the wedding the dowry of the bride-to-be, which consists of many pieces of furniture, is carried in a procession through the streets to the house of the man's parents. The Chinese are said to buy their wives, but they themselves deny that this is the case, because the money given to the bride's parents by the husband-to-be is intended to be used for her outfit. At a grand wedding near Canton which a friend of mine lately attended it took seven hundred coolies to carry the bride's clothes and furniture. The entertainments in connection with the event cost something like ninety thousand dollars.

It may be remarked here that at a marriage in South China the bride presents her husband with a pair of shoes, thus signifying that she places herself under his control. In the story of Ruth her kinsman plucked off his shoe, as a sign of his renunciation of his claim to marry her. In Psalm lx. 8, "Over Edom will I cast out my shoe" means, I have renounced Edom.

A custom called "sifting four eyes" is observed as an omen of prosperity. One by one the wedding garments for the bride are placed in a sieve and moved backwards and forwards over a brass vessel having in it burning coals. Those who hold the sieve repeat some such words as these: "A thousand eyes, ten thousand eyes, we sift out; gold and silver, wealth and precious things we sift in." A similar ceremony, called "expelling the filth," is performed in reference to the bridegroom's wedding suit in order to ward off pernicious influences.

CHINESE BRIDE'S VEIL

To face page 163.

Girls must cry for three days before their wedding, and pretend not to care to eat or to drink or to do anything. This is to prevent people saying that they want to be married. For the same reason, when the time comes, on her wedding-day, for a girl to leave her home, she hides herself. Her mother calls her, and searches all over the house, crying that she has lost her daughter. Then she comes upon a room fastened inside; surely it contains the fugitive. She knocks frequently, but there is no answer; and the coolies who are to carry the wedding-chair, and the musicians who are to accompany it, are clamouring that they cannot wait longer. Under these circumstances I knew of one mother who threw a bucket of water in at the window to drive out her daughter. When there has been enough makebelieve of reluctance, the girl opens the door and is dragged, struggling and tearful, by her mother, not exactly to a stool of repentance, but to the bridal chair. Sometimes the girl does not hide from her mother, but pretends that she is hindered from taking a seat in the fatal chair by the girls of her own age, who cling to her, weeping.

Great interest is shown by a girl's female friends when, the day before her marriage, her hair is done up in the style of married women of her class, and she tries on the clothes she is to wear. On the eventful day, just before she takes her seat in the wedding-chair, her toilet is completed by one of her parents putting on her head a sort of tiara and a veil of pearls or flowers so thick that her features are completely concealed.

Before starting, however, for her future home, one more ceremony—for luck—is observed. Members of her family, taking a bed-quilt by its four corners, hold it in this way before the bride as she sits in her chair. Then one of her assistants throw into the air, one by one, four cakes, in such a manner that they will fall into the bed-quilt.

When the quilt containing these cakes is gathered up and

brought into the house, the procession starts amid the sound of fire-crackers and of music, which sounds to Europeans like the noise of cats trying to sing bass with sore throats. A Chinese marriage makes plain our Lord's parable of the man who had not on a wedding garment. All the people in the wedding procession wear red or red and green coats or cloaks—red being the colour for marriage, as the colour for funerals is white. These red garments are lent for the occasion, and the boys, many of them street arabs, have nothing to do but put them on. The man in the parable was so insolent that he would not even do this, so he deserved to be cast into outer darkness—that is, far away from the lights and festivity of the wedding feast.

Perhaps the ordinary Chinese married woman does not in practice obey her husband much more than does the British; but she must obey her husband's father and mother. The latter she calls "mother," or "mother-in-law-mother." If she receive a present she must hand it over to her mother-in-law. This mistress not seldom beats her, and may call upon her son to do so too. Should she strike back she may be brought before a magistrate and receive a hundred strokes of the bamboo. And yet there have been mothers-in-law who were conquered by the tact and forbearance of their daughters-in-law. Dr. Williams quotes the following, translated from the moralist Luhchau: "Loh Yang travelled seven years to improve himself, during which time his wife served her mother-in-law and supported her son. The poultry from a neighbour's house once wandered into her garden, and her mother-in-law stole and killed some of them for eating. When the wife sat down to table and saw the fowls she burst into tears. Asked the cause of her distress, she said 'I weep because I cannot supply you with all I wish, and because I have caused you to eat what belongs to another.' The mother-in-law was so affected by this that she threw away the dish."

A Chinese gentleman does not eat with or talk to his wife, or make her a companion in any way. Nor can the poor thing indulge in talking to him, for loquacity is one of the seven reasons for the divorce of a wife recognised by law in China. The other six reasons are childlessness, wanton conduct, neglect of husband's parents, thievishness, jealousy, malignant disease.

There are, however, three conditions under which the above seven reasons fail to justify divorce; viz., if the wife has no home to go to, if she has twice shared the period of three years' mourning for a parent-in-law, and if she has risen with her husband from poverty to affluence.

The position of a married woman is shown by the proverb, " You must listen to your wife, but not believe her."

It is certainly not true that a Chinaman always limits himself to one unceasing wife, but polygamy is the exception and not the rule. Number one wife is the legal official one, though " little wives," or concubines, are permitted. Probably Chinese husbands do not treat their wives worse than do British, but they have greater power to do so. If a husband kills his wife he is strangled, unless he can prove her guilty of infidelity or want of respect for his parents, in which case his action would be considered praiseworthy rather than culpable. If a wife kills her husband she is tied to a cross and put to death by the " Lingchi," a degrading and slow process. A Chinaman addresses his wife as " Er—rr," indefinitely prolonged, and she speaks to and of him as " Great mandarin."

Still woman, however she may be regarded in theory, possesses a knack of asserting herself in her own home, with a recuperative power which will even bear up against the costermonger's fist, and the paradox is sometimes seen that in China, where woman counts for so little, she reigns supreme in households, and if she be an Empress-Dowager, in the empire.

Widows are obliged by custom to wear a white, black, or blue skirt, when they wear any skirt at all. Hence the expression, "Marrying the wearer of a white skirt," applied to a man who marries a widow. It is considered rather disgraceful for a widow to marry. If she do so she must go in a common black chair carried by two men only, from her residence to that of her intended husband, and not in a red bridal chair. When Chu Hsi was asked if a poor lone widow without means of subsistence might marry again, he replied, "What you are afraid of for her is cold and starvation; but starvation is a comparatively small matter, and loss of reputation is a great one."

So highly esteemed is the widow who does not marry again, or the maiden who, on the death of her affianced spouse, vows to remain single, that frequently triple arches of fine carved stone-work, called pailaus, are erected in their honour.

CHAPTER XVI

DEATH AND BURIAL

Death and social position—No help given to the dying—More light—"The devil who follows"—Like an Irish wake—Sacerdotal ventriloquism—The first lifting of the coffin—A "white affair"—When at the point of death Chinese put on their best clothes—One reason why Chinese coffins are so large—A "charming retreat"—A favourite present—Uncomfortable graves—A Mandarin makes sure of a lucky tomb—"Blood burial"—"Won't even leave his carcase"—"Buying the water"—A hint—Flat beer.

FOR everything connected with death in China rigid rules are laid down, either by law or by custom. Even the name of what is elsewhere the great leveller is not common to all. Emperors are said to "crash"; princes to "demise"; ministers of state to "stop"; officials to "resign their dignities"; and it is only the common people who "die." According to rank, too, is the height of the mounds on people's graves, and the number of yards they enclose. A sliding scale is also provided as regards the avenues of stone figures, which lead up to the sepulchres of the great, or rather of the wealthy.

In China even more care and money are expended upon funerals than upon weddings. If they can get money in no other way to bury a parent in good style, sons will sell all their land, and even pull down their house and dispose of the timbers. People like to have a description of a grand funeral placed upon record in their family history.

It is hard to get one's dying done in China. Nobody
will help you with it. The Chinese do not care what noise
they make in a room where a person is *in extremis*. Those
who have never noticed the individual when in health will
crowd in for a look when they hear that he or she is passing
away. "Oh yes; she'll die. My sister had this disease
and died, so of course this one will die," says one with
a sepulchral tone of voice, and the others comment on the
phases that strike them as most hopeless. It is no wonder
if the patient do die. As the dead cannot see in the land
of shades, their relatives light candles immediately after they
die to enable them to find the right path. In some localities
one of the family will go upon the roof of the house and
call the deceased by name. This is done to bring his spirit
back. In parts of China a lantern is often carried, even in
the daytime, with the coffin when going to be buried, to light
the spirit. I have seen a paper lantern, with a looking-glass
attached to it, carried by the chief mourner. Those who can
afford it buy a pearl and put it upon the forehead of the dead
to give more light. A pair of small mirrors are placed in the
coffin for the same reason.

Another help to find the way is believed to be furnished by
the King of Hades himself, in the shape of a " little devil "
which he sends to be servant and guide to the dead man.
For this "devil who follows," as he is called, the family
place a pair of chopsticks, a small bowl of rice, and a
little paper-money, when they make provision for the supposed gastronomic and financial wants of their deceased
relative. If he were not supplied with rations and pocket-
money the " little devil " might become offended and led
astray.

There is also sometimes made in the same room, or in a
room adjoining the one in which the corpse lies, a bamboo
contrivance resembling partly a bridge and partly a ladder.
The bridge aids the dead to pass rivers, and the ladder

enables him to climb steep places, should he meet such impediments in his journey.

There were obsequies at a house opposite where I stayed at Peking, so I saw something of what was done. One was occasionally reminded of an Irish wake. First a soul of the deceased (each man is believed to have three) was called upon to occupy the tablet prepared for it, with much wailing and chanting on the part of relatives and priests. Sacerdotal ventriloquism is appreciated on these occasions, for by means of it a pretended conversation can be carried on with the dead person. A second soul would go to the grave with the body, but the third had to be attended to, and this was done by the priests burning a life-sized Peking cart, pony, and driver, made of paper and bamboo. Burning sends things into the spirit-world, so the soul would find the equipage waiting to convey it to the city temple, where one soul of every person is supposed to go to learn the decision as to its future fate.

The first lifting of the coffin by its bearers is the signal for the relatives to hasten out of the room. They do this fearing lest, if any mishap should occur, the spirit of the deceased would take vengeance on those who were present when the removal took place.

In Chinese funeral processions there is much dramatic ceremony, with not a little that is shabby and ludicrous. Banners, lanterns, official umbrellas, screens and tablets shining with lacquer and glittering with gilt are carried before and behind the coffin of a notable, but the bearers are dirty street loafers, who have had red and green cloaks thrown over their rags for the occasion. Sometimes the hired cloaks and banners are made of very costly embroidered silk. The eldest son of the deceased is clad in bamboo sackcloth, having characters which mean "Alas, alas, my father!" on his back. In his hand there is a white wand with streamers of white linen or paper fastened to it. Other near relatives are covered with white cloth, and their limbs, which were supposed to have been enfeebled with grief, are supported by the arms of friends. A funeral is called a "white affair," because of the colour of the mourning. The chief mourners have little balls of wool suspended from their heads over the eyes to represent tears.

No Chinese widow looks well in her sackcloth weeds. The mourners throw their heads from side to side and wail loudly. I have seen them just before the funeral started kneel down and knock their heads upon the ground. One girl did not do this last sufficiently on the occasion referred to, so a woman came behind her and banged her head on the street.

When they think that they are on the point of death, some Chinese put on or have put on their best clothes, so as to be presentable in the other world. Clean attire is given to criminals about to be carried off to execution. As the Chinese have a dread of the dead, they perform as many as possible of the last respects before life has quite left the body. It is said, though I cannot vouch for it, that men's paper shoes are put on the feet of a female corpse, so that in the next world she may be on the same footing with men.

In the middle class, as many as twelve garments, including a fan, will be used in dressing a corpse. This is one reason why Chinese coffins are so large. They are made of four half logs, and resemble the trunk of a tree. The joinings of the logs are closed, and made air-tight with cement and varnish. Coffins are covered with red lacquer, or with black, or with no lacquer at all, according to the rank of the deceased. I saw a lacquered coffin which cost three thousand dollars.

When a great Chinese travels he brings with him "timber of age," or "longevity boards," as a coffin is euphemistically called. Insurance in China, instead of having reference to the comfort of survivors, entitles the man who insures to grave-clothes and a "charming retreat," or coffin.

A favourite present for a son to give to a parent is a coffin. It is presented with laudatory speech, and the hope that there may be no immediate use for it. The gift is stored in the hall and shown to visitors with pride. Some people keep in temples the coffins they intend one day to occupy.

A corpse in a massive, sealed-down coffin is often kept in the house where he or she died until a lucky place and time for burial have been discovered by Taoist priests, who are not in a hurry while money is forthcoming.

A missionary thus writes : "A next-door neighbour of ours died, and his wife kept him so long that it was getting to be unbearable, and the hot weather would make it worse. We tried to persuade her to bury him, but she said, 'No! I cannot possibly do it, for the ground we have found contains only the dragon's head and two claws, no body. It must have a whole dragon.' After three months no place had been found!"

Woe to those who put their ancestors in uncomfortable graves. A family are unfortunate in business and consult a priest. He says that he has been credibly informed from the other world that a parent or grandparent is causing the trouble, because he has been buried in an uncongenial spot. The unresting one must have a change of quarters. The family agree to this, and the priest, after testing many sites with an instrument like a compass, fixes on a new one. For this an enormous price is often asked by the owner, who has to share with his Reverence. The coffin is taken up and buried in the new grave.

The ideal spot in which to be buried is on the side of a hill, facing running water. The hill being unavailable for cultivation no loss is suffered by the living. This no doubt is why the hills near cities are all dotted with graves. A military mandarin, to make sure of getting a lucky tomb, had some of his hair and finger-nails interred in different places.

Another occasional cause of delay in burial, is the rule that there must be no funeral while any lady of the household is *enceinte*. It is consoling for those who have not the rent of their house ready that they cannot be turned out so long as an unburied body is under the roof, and naturally they are in no hurry to bury the body. The term "blood burial" is applied contemptuously to a funeral which is thought to have taken place too soon and without all the customary preliminaries. The corpse is believed to have blood in it, not having had time to dry up. It should remain aboveground for at least seven times seven days.

You may come across coffins awaiting burial where you least expect to do so. Sitting on a stone near Foochow talking to a man, he said, "We had better move." Looking behind me I saw in a corner three coffins.

In the country round Shanghai coffins containing bodies may be seen everywhere. Some are covered with straw and other coverings.

The Chinese say, "If he who attains honour or wealth never returns to his native place, he is like a finely dressed person walking in the dark"—it is all thrown away. Most Chinese do manage to return, if not before they die, certainly when that event takes place. Indeed it is one of the counts in the Australian indictment of the Chinaman, that he not only sends his savings to China, but "won't even leave his old carcase behind to manure our lands." If the captain of a steamer brings back the body of a Chinese passenger dying on board, he will probably receive an embroidered banner, emblazoning his "benevolence."

"Buying the water" is an important part of Chinese obsequies. The eldest son who is chief mourner, accompanied by friends and the inevitable gong and pipes, goes to the nearest river, throws cash into it and fills a bowl with water to be used in washing the dead. This washing and the other offices preparatory to interment are done by persons so despised that they are not allowed to enter a temple.

After the grave-clothes have been put on, the corpse is tightly bound around with several pieces of cloth, two of which are white and one red. They are tied in knots of a kind which are considered auspicious or of good omen. A piece of gold or silver, a pearl, a jewel, three cash or three sorts of grain, are put into the mouth of the dead person, according to the rank he had in life.

In order to ascertain the wishes of a deceased person, two coins are put into his sleeve and the arm is shaken. An affirmative or negative answer is supposed to be given by the relative position in which the cash fall.

For some time after a person dies his family offer to him at their meals a small portion of food and drink. When they decide to discontinue doing so, they indicate this decision by presenting a few pieces of firewood, a little uncooked rice, a small measure of oil, some salt, and a quantity of paper-money for marketing. This is a hint that the dead must procure and cook his own food for the future.

An Englishman asked a Chinaman how his deceased relative could eat the food offered to him. He replied, "He can eat it as easily as a kinsman of yours can smell the flowers you put on his grave."

The order of a funeral procession is something like this: A man precedes the whole, strewing paper which represents money, in order to bribe into good-humour any malignant spirits that may be loafing around. This is called "buying the road." Then come two men carrying white lanterns, and musicians making a noise, which to Europeans seems much the same as that which the Chinese make at weddings. After the band are carried red boards or squares of purple cloth, having on them letters of gold, detailing the honours and offices of the deceased. The huge coffin, borne by eight, sixteen, or thirty-two bearers, has at its head a crate containing sometimes a living cock. More frequently the bird is made of cardboard and is a stork rather than a cock, but whether dead or alive, cock or stork, its business is to guide the soul of the dead man.

In the north the bier is a great catafalque adorned with satin curtains on which golden dragons are embroidered, Next pass canopies adorned with blue cloth. Under these are pigs roasted whole, dried ducks, trays of cakes, candles, paper-money and other things to be offered at the grave. Living goats or cardboard effigies of different animals and of servants may also be seen. The longevity picture and the tablet of the deceased are conveyed in a sedan chair or in a rickshaw. The procession may be lengthened to taste by repeating its different parts. Of course, many yellow-robed priests tramp along, and they soothe themselves from time to time with pipes and cigars.

When the procession reaches the lucky place selected for the grave, and the coffin is placed on the ground, the mourners beat their heads and wail bitterly while priests burn incense and fire off crackers to frighten away demons. After the grave is filled up the eatables which have been carried in the funeral procession are spread out, and left for a while in order that the dead man may feast on their essence. The spirits of the dead are so considerate that they only partake of the immaterial part of the roast pig, fowls, cakes, and other luxuries that are presented to them, the gross material part of them is therefore brought back from the obsequies and served as funeral baked meats to the living.

At Amoy I saw a priest arrayed in scarlet robes dedicating in a shrine amidst the tombs as much food of all kinds as would have stocked a restaurant, though it seemed to have all been given by a single mourner. In Hong Kong you will see bottles of beer amongst the offerings. If the dead take the spirit from these, surely what is left for the living must be flat !

Married daughters, having passed out of the family, are not always invited to the family obsequies; when they are, they only wear mourning for seven days. At the end of that time they return to their homes in coloured clothes, and adorned with jewellery, so that their husbands may not be saddened by " trappings and suits of woe."

Infants, unmarried people, concubines, and slaves have no ceremonial funerals, and sometimes none of any sort. In the north of China their corpses are not seldom left on the hills to be devoured by beasts of prey.

CHAPTER XVII

MOURNING

AS soon as a death takes place it is officially announced with much wailing at the temple of the local god. The visit is returned promptly by Buddhist and Taoist priests, who scent fees from afar. These clerics blow horns, moan formulæ, ring bells, and beat upon skull-shaped drums. This, however, is not considered noise enough in a house of mourning, so bombs and crackers are let off at frequent intervals, and people are hired to add to the din with shrill pipes and clanging cymbals.

After the coffin of a dead person is closed down a "longevity picture" is put in a bamboo frame and placed in the reception-room, where it can easily be seen. It is intended to be a likeness of the deceased, and is about as large as a child six or eight years old. As a substitute for this a rag doll is sometimes used. On a table set in front of this representative of the person whose death is mourned, are placed every morning for some time water for the deceased to wash with, food, and paper-money; when the day closes all the members of the family bid "good-night."

A rich man announces the death of his father by sending

to each of his friends a sheet of paper about a yard and a half long and broad in proportion, whereon he states that he and his relatives are on their knees, beating their heads upon the ground and weeping tears of blood. When these friends come to pay a visit of condolence they are received by the chief mourner on his knees. The friends also kneel down and worship before the "longevity picture." They are given strips of white cloth called "cloths to cry with." During this ceremony some female member of the family, hid from view behind a white screen, wails aloud and relates the good deeds of the deceased.

For forty-nine days the chief mourners do not shave their heads or change their dress, and on every seventh day they wear sackcloth over their ordinary clothing. For seven days no cooking is done in a mourning family. Food is sent by their neighbours and must be eaten with the fingers as though the intensity of their grief prevented them from using chopsticks.

In the first agonies of grief visiting cards of plain white paper are used instead of the ordinary red ones. After a while salmon-coloured cards are substituted, on which the mourner is described as being in "dutiful grief."

Over the door of a house of mourning are hung white lanterns with blue characters on them, instead of the usual red ones with black characters. On either side of the door white labels are pasted and linen plentifully festooned.

Sons mourn parents three years, because for the first three years of their existence they were nursed by their parents. By a merciful fiction this period is reduced to twenty-seven months. They cannot, when in mourning, present themselves at examinations for degrees, and it is unlawful for them to beget a child. If they are officials they must remove the buttons from their caps and leave their posts.

Sons are supposed to take it in turn to sleep on straw by the coffin of a parent for a hundred nights. A certain Ho Sun, when mourning for his father, was robbed. Seeing the thief about to take a copper pan, he said, "Do me the favour to leave this utensil to get my dear mother's breakfast in." The thief not only left the pan but gave back what he had taken, saying, "I should certainly bring a curse upon my head if I robbed so good a son."

The mother of a man called Li was always very nervous in a thunderstorm, so when she died Li used to go to her grave whenever it thundered, and bending down say, "Mother, don't be afraid, your son is near you."

A widow known to us slept every night beside her husband's coffin, until he was buried after nine months.

A house-boy of ours was "suffered" to go and bury his father. On returning he said that the operation had cost him over three hundred dollars. He paid a good deal for the grave because he wished his parent, who was more than eighty years of age, not to be crowded with others, but to have one by himself, and he had so many friends to entertain that the adage was illustrated—

> "When old folk die
> The rest feed high."

The friends made the usual contribution towards the expenses, but they had too large appetites to be "paying guests." However, it is not so much what mourners eat as what they take away that costs. Each brings home as a memento the chopsticks, bowls, and other things used at table. To furnish these utensils during the long period when open house is kept, often runs survivors into debt and other difficulties.

On the death of the Emperor all Chinamen must leave the front of their heads unshorn for a hundred days, which produces a very untidy appearance. During this time no theatrical performance may be given throughout the Empire.

A newly crowned Emperor has in the Temple of the Imperial Ancestors at Peking to reverence these worthies by kneeling sixteen times, and by knocking his forehead on the ground no less than thirty-six times. All his nobles, too, are required to do the same in order to teach the people the importance of filial piety. Ancestral worship is filial piety gone mad.

When questioned about the obligations of mourners Confucius answered, "Whilst we are unable to fulfil all our duties to our fellows, how can we serve the far-off spirits?" And again : "If we assumed the dead were living and could partake of the offerings presented to them, that would not be altogether true. And yet the heart, with its strong, deeply infixed affections, could not be satisfied without this ministry of sacrifice at the graves." Ancestor-worship may be said to be the Chinaman's religion ; it influences nearly every thought and act of his life.

The eldest son is responsible for the care of the dead in a family. He keeps their graves in repair, and if the bones have been taken out of the graves because the family have changed their abode or for any other reason, he guards the "yellow gold," as the Chinese call what foreigners irreverently designate "potted ancestors." When he has nothing better to do he cleans up the bones of his fathers, and without any training in anatomy he knows how many there should be and even puts labels upon them.

In early spring takes place Tsing Ming, a kind of "All Souls" festival when graves are visited. A table is set before a tomb and on it is placed a paper or tablet with the name of the deceased inscribed upon it. Candles are lighted, incense burnt, and dishes laid on the table containing fish, flesh (of pork), fowl, fruit, and sweetmeats. The eldest son, prostrating himself many times, makes vows and offers up prayers. Paper clothes and trunks to put them in, pipes, servants, horses, sedan chairs, houses, and indeed paper semblances of all kinds of luxuries and requisites are burned, and by this sort of parcel post sent into the spirit-world. Letters to the dead are also transmitted by fiery post.

Sometimes, three days before the actual Feast of Tombs begins, as well as three days after it, a mourner, always a woman, generally a relative, will be paid to sit swaying herself backwards and forwards as she utters a pitiful cry.

Many of the mourners, however, are not professional, but very genuine. "In the dark place where you are, protect me!" will be the cry of one. Another will moan out reproaches to the dead for having died, such as, "My son, you owed it to me, your mother, who reared you, to have lived that you might have been the support of my old age."

The "saluting of the hill," as the Tsing or Ching Ming celebrations are called in South China, because graves are nearly always on the side of a hill, ends, as do most Chinese functions, with a fusillade of crackers.

Streamers of gold-spotted paper are left by those who have swept and repaired tombs. These serve as visiting cards, and insure that credit will be given for the call.

A Chinese does not put mourning on for those younger than himself or for his wife. He may not even attend that lady's funeral.

CHAPTER XVIII

BOYS IN CHINA

A proverb—Nothing so unfilial as to have no children—A boy is petted and indulged for not being a girl—He gets a "milk name" and several other kinds of names—Boys sometimes dressed as girls or as Buddhist priests—Games—Bird's nests not robbed—Betting on flies and oranges —Boys work too much and too young—First day at school—"Backing a lesson"—Mere memory - boxes—Writing—Long hours—Severity— Answer of Mencius—Anecdote of—The trimetrical classic—Another school book—Filial service—The cap of manhood—Parental power— What will the boy be?

"IF one has plenty of money," says a Chinese proverb, "but no children, he cannot be reckoned rich; if one has "children, but no money, he cannot be considered poor." Mencius taught that nothing is so unfilial as to have no posterity. The man who allows his family to die out for want of offspring wrongs all former members of it. Every Chinese wants to have a son, because it is only a son who can perform the funeral and other rites which the worship of ancestors enjoins. "If you have no children to foul the bed, you will have no one to burn paper at the grave." The hungry spirit of him who leaves no son behind him has only a share of the offerings which, three times a year, are made by the charitable public for the benefit of the destitute dead. The cry is not "Give me children or else I die," but "Give me a son or I cannot die in peace." Boys who can make offerings to dead parents are petted and indulged as a reward for not being unworshipping girls. A boy soon learns his importance, and sometimes rules his family absolutely. A Chinese mother never thinks of teaching her male children self-control, but gives them whatever they cry and scream for.

A boy gets a "milk name" twenty-eight days after his birth. Such names are sometimes given as "Little Stupid," "Vagabond," "Flea," "Dirt." This is in order that evil spirits, thinking that the parents do not care for the boys, may not molest them. For the same reason boys are occasionally dressed as girls or in the despised garb of a Buddhist priest.

A boy receives a "book name," such as "Ink-grinder," "Promising-study," "Entering Virtue," when he goes to school, and a third when he grows up and marries.

The few toys which a Chinese lad has are made of clay, cloth, cardboard, reeds, or sticks of bamboo. I have in my possession an ingenious one composed of two nuts, a small stick, and a piece of bamboo. His games are such as throwing bits of clay at a mark, pushing with his right foot a small ball of lead so that it will hit the similar ball of an opponent, striking a short stick sharpened at the ends to make it jump into a "city." A sort of trial of strength may be seen practised in by-streets. Two boys grasp the ends of a bamboo pole, and standing erect and using one leg as stay each tries to dislodge the other from his standing-place by pushing the pole straight from the shoulder. There seems to be a knack in it, for sometimes a little fellow will force back an opponent considerably heavier than himself.

Hop-scotch finds favour in China. So do peg-tops and marbles. The latter are propelled with the second finger of the left hand pulled back and then let go by the right hand. "Blowing the fist" is a noisy game which is played by two or more boys. One throws out the extended fingers of his fists, and while in the act of doing so another shouts

STREET BOYS.

out his guess of the number of fingers struck out from both fists.

A rude species of draughts is played sometimes with little stones. In the schools which have lately been established to teach Western knowledge, American and British games are beginning to be played. There is a Chinese version of Punch and Judy that never fails to attract. Celestial boys do not whistle. In their lighter moments they hum a monotonous chant in a falsetto voice, making a noise like a cat.

Buddhist teaching regarding the sacredness of animal life very properly checks the robbing of bird's nests. "How," it is asked, "would you like to have *your* house pulled down?" A large proportion of Chinese boys live at a distance from the sea, from lakes, and from rivers, and have no better "watering-place" than the mud hole from which the materials for their village houses were excavated.

The Chinese are a nation of gamblers, and they begin the bad habit when very young. You see boys at fruit and cake street stalls throwing little numbered sticks out of a tube of bamboo to ascertain whether they will pay double or be quits for what they have taken. Your boy or servant bets as to whether you will order ham and eggs or fish for breakfast. A rickshaw coolie lays a wager on which shaft of his vehicle a fly will light on first, which is not more foolish than for British boys to bet on horses which they have never seen. The fly at least cannot be jockied. Money is also put on the number of pips that will be found in an orange when it is opened.

But if boys in China have not as much play as British youths, they are supplied with as much or even more work. With literally a premature air of gravity about them they totter along with burdens too heavy for them, the very youngest gathering fuel and collecting manure.

· When a boy is to go to school an almanack is consulted

and a lucky day chosen for the important event. The boy is clad in festal robe, and looks a miniature mandarin in his tasselled cap. He is accompanied by his father, who brings a present for the master. All three worship before a tablet of the god of literature or of Confucius, and then the boy prostrates himself before his master, and knocks his little shaven head on the schoolroom floor in token of his reverence and promised obedience.

In a Chinese school the boys sit on bamboo stools at tiny tables. On each table there is a stone slab, a stick of Chinese ink, and writing brushes. We are astonished at the noise. This is made by all the scholars shouting out at the same moment their lessons. Were they to cease shouting the master would think that they had given up studying. The teacher reads a line and the pupil repeats it. If the boy does not catch what has been said he repeats the last word until he gets something more.

When a pupil has learned his lesson he turns his back upon the schoolmaster, lest he should get a glimpse of the book, and recites it. This is called "backing a lesson." Boys sway from side to side when saying their lessons.

As the vernacular speech and the language of the classics are quite different, the Chinese boy has to commit to memory words the meaning of which he does not understand. It is something like what we should have in our Western schools if our youths were restricted to the study of Latin, and required to stow away in their memory the contents of the principal classics before learning a word of their meaning.

A boy's entrance upon study is called lifting the darkness, and to teach the beginner is "to instruct darkness," but it is not easy to see how the darkness is lifted when the beginner has to learn by rote characters that convey no meaning to him. The little heads of Celestial boys become mere memory-boxes for certain signs and sounds, but no ideas at all are connected with them.

Writing, which is called "treading in the footsteps of holy men," is learned by tracing page after page of copybook characters on transparent paper in a listless round, that knows no Sunday, and no Wednesday and Saturday half-holidays. School hours are from sunrise to 10 o'clock a.m., when the boys go to breakfast, and from 11 o'clock to sundown. Play is considered a waste of time and is discouraged as much as possible. Even when the school hours are over the scholars cannot have a romp, but are required to return to their homes "in an orderly and becoming manner."

"To teach without severity, shows a teacher's indolence." Judging from this Chinese saying the pupil must often think that his teacher is very energetic. There is no sparing of the rod in a Chinese school, and the head of the boy is the place at which blows are generally aimed, as if that would knock brains into him! There are, however, teachers who resort to corporal punishment only as a last resort. These will use such a punishment as making a boy kneel at his seat for a while before the school.

The Chinese show the common sense for which they are conspicuous by never attempting to teach their own sons. Upon one occasion Mencius was asked why the superior man does not teach his own son. He replied that the circumstances of the case forbid it. The teacher should inculcate what is correct; when he does so and his lessons are not followed he becomes angry. In this way he is alienated from his son, who complains that his father teaches one thing and practises another. The ancients exchanged sons, and one taught the son of another.

Mencius himself, it may be said, was carefully brought up by his widowed mother. As a child he lived with her at first near a cemetery, the result being that he began to reproduce in play the solemn scenes which were constantly enacted before his eyes. His mother accordingly removed to another

house near the market-place, and before long the little boy
forgot all about funerals and played at buying and selling.
Once more his mother disapproved, and once more changed
her dwelling; this time to a house near a college, where he
soon began to imitate the ceremonial observances in which
the students were instructed, to the great joy of his mother.

The first book from which a Chinese boy learns is the
Trimetrical, or three-character classic, so called because it is
written in doggerel lines of three characters each. It begins
by warning the youth that "gems unwrought can never be
useful, and that untaught persons will never know the
proprieties."   It informs him that Confucius once learned
something from a mere child ; that the ancient students had
no books, but copied their lessons on reeds and slips of bamboo;
that one learned to read characters which were traced upon
the sand of the sea by his mother, who could not afford
writing materials; that another read by the light of glow-
worms put into a gauze-bag; and that a third, too poor to
buy a candle, studied through a chink in his neighbour's
wall.

Among the prodigies of diligence cited for emulation are
two, who, "though girls, were intelligent and well informed."
Insects, however, like the silkworm and the bee, can teach
diligence as well as girls, and "if men neglect to learn, they
are inferior to insects."   They should be as diligent as the
student who fastened his queue to a beam above him in order
that when he nodded over his task he might be roused to
fresh diligence, or the youth who so greatly preferred books to
bed that he used a round stick of wood as a pillow to prevent
deep sleep.   That boy, we think, little honoured his parents
who, when away from home, would not read letters from them
lest they should take his attention away from study.

Veneration for parents, however, is inculcated by another
school-book called, "The Twenty-four Examples of Filial
Piety."   One example is of a certain Laitze.   This worthy,

when seventy years of age, fearing that his years might
distress his parents by reminding them of their greater age,
used to dress as an infant and play about the room.

A lad is related to have waited on his sick mother three
years without changing his clothes.   Another boy would go
to bed and allow the mosquitoes to satisfy themselves upon
him, then would get up and induce his parents to retire into
the bed and have an undisturbed sleep.   A boy six years old
thrust two oranges up his sleeve at an entertainment.   After
a while they rolled out, and the boy was not only excused but
gained lasting credit by saying they were for his mother.

The mother of a youth was very fond of fish, so in winter
when the water was frozen, in order to catch fish for her, he
would take off his clothes and lie on the ice to melt it.
Another story relates with approbation how a son killed his
child in order to prolong the life of a grandparent.

The service which a filial son does to his parents is, according to Confucius, as follows : " In his general conduct to them
he manifests the utmost reverence ; in his nourishing of them
he gives the highest pleasure ; when they are ill he feels the
deepest anxiety ; in mourning for them when dead he exhibits
every demonstration of grief ; in sacrificing to them he dis-
plays the utmost solemnity."   In the ancient books from
which Confucius himself learned it is taught that filial piety
is the fulfilment of the law.   A pious son will also be an
obedient younger brother ; and he who is both will, while at
home, be an honest, orderly subject, and in active service
from home a courageous and faithful soldier.

In China filial piety holds the place of religion, so that "he
who serves his parents at home has no need to go far away to
burn incense to the gods."   Indeed the length to which this
virtue is brought is sometimes shocking and disgusting.
Think of a grandson going down on his knees and licking
up liquid that had exuded from his grandfather's coffin, or of
the son of a Viceroy killing himself in order to be buried

with his mother—two acts which have been praised beyond measure.

Still, we could do in England with a little more filial piety, with a little more of that which Confucius meant when he said that filial piety consisted in giving your parents no cause for anxiety, save from your natural ailments.

When a youth of sixteen dons the cap of manhood he is taken to the ancestral temple, where his father invokes for him the care of his forefathers "that he may be a complete man, and not fall below their standard of excellence." He is now considered so far a man that he is protected henceforth from the indignities with which he who is "only a child" has sometimes to put up. Soon after this he is married, but continues to live in the paternal home, his bride being neither more nor less than a servant to his mother. But neither at sixteen nor at any age does a man come out from the legal control of his parents. While his parents are alive a son in private life must engage in the pursuit chosen for him, give them his earnings, and obey them in all things. Filial piety requires that a son should follow in the steps of his father. China does not tolerate self-willed hooligans. If a parent require a son to be publicly whipped or exposed in a wooden cangue, with the crime of "Not filial" written upon it by a magistrate, the latter is obliged to comply. A father will even hand over a rebellious son to be put to death by a mandarin.

Physical care is bestowed upon dogs and horses, so that is not enough to give to parents. They must be treated with reverence. This may be learned from a lamb, for it has the grace to kneel when sucking its mother. The Book of Rites enjoins that when parents are in error, a son with humble spirit, pleasing countenance, and gentle tones, must point it out to them. If the parents will not receive the reproof he must again show them their fault. If now, becoming irritated, they chastise the fault-finder until the blood flows from him, he must not harbour the least resentment but must treat them with increased respect. To use in reference to a father a term equivalent to the "Governor" of British slang would be thought shocking. A Chinese father is called "Venerable Father," "Prince of the Family," or "The Family's Majesty"; and children bow low or kneel down when addressing him. Confucius says that if a father is killed a son should not live under the same heaven as his slayer.

A boy in China has not to determine for himself what he shall be, as have British boys. That is done for him by his parents in this way. On the anniversary of his birthday he is placed upon a large sieve, such as farmers use in winnowing grain. On the sieve have been previously laid a set of money scales, a gold or silver ornament, a pair of shears, a foot-measure, one or two books, &c. The object is to see what the child will first take hold of and play with. If the child be a boy, and he take up a book or a pen, he is likely ʊ become a distinguished scholar; if he touch the money scales or the gold ornament it is thought that he will have a talent for making money, and so on.

CHAPTER XIX

GIRLS AND WOMEN

Girls do not count—Why boys are more valued—"Girls may not be drowned
here"—Presents at the birth of children—A "rearing marriage"—"She
is his wife"—Cruelty to child brides—Girls sold cheaply—Sometimes a
girl is only pawned—Hoped to be born a dog—A scandal from which
China is free—Easily pleased—Small feet—"What medicine am I
to give them?"—The *Ying* and the *Yang* principles—Only a "side
issue"—A "Never-to-be-married" sisterhood—A terrible Sin—Concubines, or "little wives"—The volubility of tongues—He had never
chastised his wife—Advice to girls—"That tallest devil!"

A FRIEND of the writer in China asked her amah, or
nurse, how many children Mrs. So-and-so had. "Two,"
was the reply. "Two?" queried my friend, "I thought that
she had five—two boys and three girls." "Yes," answered
the amah, "that is what I said, two children, for girls are not
children, and do not count." A son is required for the performance of ancestral rites, and therefore one proverb declares
that a perfect daughter is not equal to a splay-footed son,
and another, that one deformed son is better than eighteen
daughters as wise as the apostles of Buddha. "Commodity
on which money is lost," is a common periphrasis for a girl.
One unhappy maiden of whom I have heard was named,
"Ought-to-Have-Been-a-Boy," and another, "Not Wanted."

Nothing in our Bible is so hard for the Chinese to believe
as the assertion that Pharaoh commanded the Israelitish boys
to be killed and the girls to be saved. In some parts of China

the charge for vaccinating a girl is only half that which is paid for a boy, as it is found that the people would rather run the risk of their daughter's beauty being destroyed than pay for her at the same rate as a son.

Women are sometimes beaten by their husbands or mothers-in-law for the crime of giving birth to daughters instead of sons. When only a girl is born the midwife finds it difficult to get her fee. Occasionally she is bribed to substitute the bought boy of poor parents for the girl just born. This is called stealing a dragon in exchange for a phœnix.

I have often observed a gourd or log tied round the waist of a boy infant belonging to the people who live in boats. This is to facilitate his being pulled out of the sea should he fall overboard. There is no such handle ever to a female infant, because she is considered of no importance.

It may be doubted whether the crime of infanticide even of female children, except in seasons of famine, is, in proportion to the population, more common in China than it is in Europe. Certainly fœticide is not. It seems to be true, however, that a large number of female children are put to death, or at least allowed to die. A terrible witness to this is a stone standing near a pool outside the city of Foochow. On it is the inscription, "Girls may not be drowned here." Indeed, warnings and threatenings against killing girl children are put up in many places.

In a proclamation against the crime, which was in 1873 issued by the Treasurer of the province of Hupeh, the following reasons which are generally given for it are refuted: Because the parents have too many children, or none but females; because if the mother suckled the child she would not conceive again while doing so; because she wishes to hire herself as a wet nurse.

Parents announce the birth of a child by sending to their friends eggs dyed red, and by inviting them to a feast given in honour of baby's first and sometimes last bath. Presents of different kinds of eatables are sent to the parents. According to the old Chinese ballads a valuable ornament, like a marshal's *bâton*, was usually given to a male infant to play with, whilst a female only received a potsherd, supposed to represent a weaving shuttle : hence to this day one says to an acquaintance, " I hear you have had joy to-day ! " He laconically replies, if it is only a girl, " Plays with potsherd."

Poor parents often sell or give away a daughter when but a few weeks or months old to be the future wife of a boy about her own age. The child who becomes a bride by a " rearing-marriage" is taken home and brought up by the family of her future husband. An English lady when visiting a school observed a bright boy about eight years of age carrying a baby girl. She asked if she were his sister, whereupon the boy looked shy, and did not answer. His brother volunteered the information, " She is his wife ! "

These child-brides are worked hard and sometimes treated as though they were in an English baby farm. The *Peking Gazette* reported the case of a woman who burned the girl who was being reared to become her son's wife with incense-sticks and poured scalding water on her until she died.

Ten years ago when there was a famine at Chaotong three thousand female children were sold to dealers and carried about like poultry in baskets. As I write I hear of wives (in England we can obtain a wife for nothing, but in China a man can always get a price for his wife) and children (chiefly female) being sold in the neighbourhood of Wuchow on the West River, where there is a famine. A lady who has just returned from there said that the steamer was half full of women who had gone to deal in children and bring them to Canton. Some of their girl wares they had bought for as little as 30 cents (7½d.) each. At ordinary times a slave girl will fetch from £1 up to £10 or £20, according to age, beauty, health, and strength. So much is female slavery a recognised Chinese institution that even in the English colony of Hong Kong most of the female servants and prostitutes of the Chinese are slaves. Of course they can get freedom if they have enough sense and knowledge to apply to the authorities, but they seldom have.

It is thought right that a slave girl should be sold to a husband, or in some other way provided with one, when she becomes marriageable. Sometimes a girl is only pawned for a time, and not sold right out. In some localities when a man leaves home he lets his wife out for hire until his return.

It sometimes happens in the case of better-class families that daughters of the house are taught by resident teachers. Except, however, by Chinese who have travelled or in some way imbibed Western ideas, it is not as a rule considered necessary to fit a girl for marriage by any kind of education. The ordinary father thinks that it would be a waste of money to educate one who will be the daughter-in-law of some one else. A common saying is, "If a girl does no harm it is enough; you cannot expect her to be either good or useful."

Being considered "as dangerous as smuggled salt," girls are kept at home for safety. One remarked that in her next existence she hoped to be born a dog, that she might go where she chose! This rebellious young lady was not influenced by the example of an eminent lady of olden times, who for twelve years did not look out of the door of her house. A common synonym for a wife is the "House-back," that is, the person who stops in the women's quarters at the back of the house. She is also called the "Broom-and-dust-pan."

The waste of power and faculty that is caused by the large number of unmarried women in Europe is a scandal from which China is free. Chinese parents take care to prevent this. The great question concerning a girl as soon as she grows up at all is "Is she said?" that is, betrothed. Fortunately the men are not as particular as with us. A

13

man being questioned as to what sort of a wife he wanted replied, "It is enough if she be neither bald nor idiotic."

Small feet, however, are essential. "It is very important," say the Chinese, "that women's feet should be bound short, so that they can walk with mincing steps and sway like willow-trees. They thus show to all that they are persons of respectability." In some localities natural feet are a mark of an immoral life. In the interior of China a girl with unbound feet would often hear such remarks in reference to them as "Just look at those two boats going by!"

This bondage to custom is said to have started from emulation of Yao Niang, the concubine of a prince who lived nine centuries ago. So light was her step that she "skimmed over the tops of golden lilies." But *il faut souffrir pour etre belle*—"Each pair of bound feet costs a Kang, or bath of tears." The bandages are tightened every week until the distortion is complete.

Happily this custom is beginning to loosen its hold upon the Chinese. Anti-foot-binding societies are being established, and I lately heard of one school for girls under the patronage of a reforming Viceroy, the pupils of which were all required to unbind their feet.

Mrs. Archibald Little, who tries to make the lame "leap as an hart," told me that not long ago she gave a party for Chinese girls. The joy of some whose feet had been unloosened was great when they found themselves able to use the skipping-ropes provided for their entertainment. Very envious were others with feet still bound when they could not jump upon their poor stumps. One mother brought to Mrs. Little five daughters, and said that as she heard small feet were going out of fashion she would like the girl's feet to be unbound. "What medicine am I to give them?" "None at all," replied Mrs. Little. "Only take off the bandages and wash them." Then there was the difficulty how to get stockings instead of bandages.

SMALL FOOTED MAIDENS.

To face page 104.

According to Chinese philosophy death and evil originate in the *Yin*, or female principle, while life and prosperity come from the subjection of it to the *Yang*, or male principle. Woman is regarded as "moulded out of faults," and allowed to have no will of her own. In the land of China, as in the Book of Genesis, man is considered the first object in creation and woman only a side issue. Indeed, she is looked upon as lower than this, as an unclean being whose clothes, for instance, would pollute those of a man if put on the same clothes-horse.

Except for coolie women, who do very hard work indeed, there is no employment outside matrimony for Chinese females. And certainly matrimony for them is anything but an easy profession. Some girls near Canton showed what they thought of it by forming themselves into a "Never-to-be-married" Sisterhood. They swore never to marry because they considered marriage unholy and miserable. So much in earnest were the maidens in their strike against wedlock that a band of them ended their earthly existence in the Pearl River because a member of the Sisterhood had been forced by her parents to marry.

The suicide of young wives who cannot bear mothers-in-law and other evils of Celestial marriages not made in heaven is not at all uncommon. "Why didn't you die when you had a chance?" asked a mother of a married daughter who had attempted suicide and been rescued.

A terrible sin which is not unknown in Europe is sometimes committed by Chinese parents. For the sake of gain they will marry a daughter to a man who is a hopeless cripple or lunatic, or otherwise unsuited to a real marriage.

In China a woman cannot return to her father's house after an unhappy marriage. Her sisters-in-law would take good care of that. A father divides his property amongst his boys, and gives nothing to girls. They are expected to marry, join another family, and stay in it.

If a wife fails to have a male child her husband can take a concubine, or "little wife"; but this is only done by men who can afford it, and the arrangement seldom conduces to domestic happiness. The Chinese themselves call it "sipping vinegar," and they have an adage which says, "If your wife is against it do not take a concubine."

But if Chinese girls and women are in other respects defenceless, they can generally get some degree of justice for themselves by the nimble, fiery tongues for which they are famous. Even a mother-in-law hesitates to raise a domestic typhoon by provoking a daughter-in-law who has a gift of abusive language. It is said that what Chinese women have lost in the compression of their feet is made up in the expansion of their tongues. And when their tongues tire they can lift up and shake the corners of their jackets at their opponents in contempt. Who shall say how many villages in China are ruled by the wives or concubines of village headmen so called? When they have a grievance these head-*women* will "revile the street" in a way that intimidates men whose feet are longer than their tongues. A man will often consult his wife before taking an important step or making a bargain. Then age is respected in women as well as in men, and "Give heed to the voice of an old woman; sorrow has given her wisdom," is a popular saying. The greatest mandarin every three months puts on his robes of ceremony and performs in the presence of his mother a series of prostrations. It might even be said that China is a "hen-pecked" country.

Habit is second nature, and it may be that well-to-do (?) Chinese women, being used to a life in which they do little more than smoke, gossip, and visit temples, may think it as well worth living as the hurry and scurry which Western women call life.

Abbé Huc tells of a Chinese husband who beat his wife when he took it into his head that people were laughing at him, because though two years married he had never chastised

the lady.   Certainly the question, "Does your husband
beat you?" is often put to English married ladies by Chinese
women, and a negative answer invariably excites astonishment
and incredulity.   Who knows?   Chinese ladies may consider
castigation a sign of friendly interest on the part of their
husbands, and may in their own way be happy though
married.   In a modern Pekingese play, one of the characters,
a widower, describes the even current of his late married
life by saying that he and his wife lived together as host and
guest.   In China, as in other countries, the host-and-guest
kind of married life is probably more common than the cat-
and-dog variety.

If a Chinese when visiting England, instead of taking a wide
survey, formed his judgment of its domestic life from police
news and divorce-court reports, he would not be more
unreasonable than are Europeans, who say that all Chinese
women are miserable because they have known a few who
were.   Eastern women do not desire the liberty that is
attaining alarming proportions in the West.   They like to
have a part of the house reserved to themselves, where they can
receive female friends and gossip without restraint.   Shock-
ingly cruel they would think a husband who would intrude
upon their privacy and spy out their actions.

Chinese girls have not always been neglected, at least in
the matter of advice.   Indeed, several volumes have been
compiled for their use.   In one of these they are told that
while powdering the face they should remember that the
heart must be kept white and clean.   "In arranging the
head-dress, consider that the heart needs to be carefully
regulated; in oiling the hair, resolve to make the heart
pliable and docile."   The girls are enjoined to learn the art
of cookery, and commanded to imitate a certain Empress who
always superintended the preparation of the dishes which
appeared on the Emperor's table.   Another lady of rank, says
the same authority, used to go into her kitchen at dawn of

day and prepare gruel for her servants, ordering them to eat it before they began their work.

There have been Chinese women scholars, and even authors. A woman called Pan Chao wrote the first work in any language on female education. In this she says that girls and women should be decorous and unassuming, modestly grave, and inviolably chaste.

Others advise women to be not only humble and respectful but, "as though always in fear and trembling," to bear contumely, and to swallow insult. "If their mouths are like closed doors, their words will become proverbial; but if like running taps, no heed will be paid to what they say."

If a lady sit in a carriage beside the man who drives, it must be next to the hand which is occupied by the reins, lest the driver should put his arm around her waist!

As an instance of how earnestly some girls desire instruction, Miss Gordon Cumming mentions that the first pupil of the London Mission School at Peking was a girl who had disguised herself as a boy.

Though respectable Chinese girls have no experience of the joys of being made love to, and would consider kissing (it is an institution unknown, except when learned from foreigners) a disgusting way of showing affection, they have a power which is theirs by natural right. A Chinese who had suffered much in marriage retired with his infant son to a mountain inaccessible to lily-footed women. He never spoke even of the existence of woman to the boy. He always went down to the market alone, until, becoming old and feeble, he was compelled to take the young man with him to carry the bag of rice. He argued "My son has never heard of women and does not know what they are. If he does see one of them by chance I shall take care that he does not speak to her." As they were on the first occasion leaving the market town together, the son suddenly stopped, and, pointing to three approaching objects, inquired, "Father, what are those things ? " The father cried out, " Turn away your head ; they are devils." The son turned away his head and walked home in silence. From that day when he had seen the things and they had looked at him from under their fans he lost his appetite and was afflicted with melancholy. For some time the puzzled parent could get no satisfactory answer to his inquiries ; but at length the young man burst out, almost crying, " Oh, father, that tallest devil ! that tallest devil ! "

Beautiful women are called in China not only flowers and jewels, but the destroyers of cities and of empires. Of some of these beauties it was said that when they washed their hands (with perfumed soap ?) they scented the water, that they shamed the flowers themselves, and that one of them compelled the moon to hide her face. Another, if she did not shame the flowers, made them dance when she sang, so sweet was her breath.

A beauty called Si-Si had the habit of laying her hand upon her heart. Another woman, thinking that it was this gesture which charmed, imitated it and got laughed at for her trouble. She overlooked the fact that it is what is natural, and not what is forced which is beautiful.

For another celebrated beauty the Emperor Han-Wou-Ti built a crystal palace. Other beauties had every step they took sheltered with gauze umbrellas and screens of pearls.

CHAPTER XX

EDUCATION IN CHINA

Germ of competitive examinations in China—The exceptions to those who can compete—Respect for learning—An examination enclosure—Severity of competition—Honours for those who succeed—The examiners "wash their hearts "—*Pons asinorum*—The last made first—Cheating—Tracts distributed by the charitable rich—A noble maxim—Parables and novels with a purpose—Chess—An elegant present—Reverence the characters—Lettered-paper societies—Large books—Penny dreadfuls—Ignorance in *excelsis*—Western knowledge—Christianity wanted.

THE Chinese had competitive examinations as a means by which each capable member of "the learned proletariat" might climb the political and social ladder twelve centuries before appointments in Great Britain were given in this way. The germ of the system was such maxims of the ancients as "Bend the mulberry-tree when it is young," "Without education in the families how are governors for the people to be obtained?" "The General and the Prime Minister are not born in office." Offices are now sold to the highest bidder, but in theory the possession of a degree qualifies any man to be employed by the State. The only people who are precluded from competing for degrees are actors, barbers, boatmen, executioners, descendants of prostitutes, and those who prepare corpses for burial.

Three degrees are given. The first and lowest is called by two words which may be translated "Budding Talent." The second is "Promoted Man," and the third and highest

"Advanced Scholar." The first and second degree is competed for in the provinces, the third only in Peking. To be selected by the Emperor as the best of the successful competitors in Peking is thought more of in China than it would be with us if a man became all at once Senior Wrangler, First Classic, Poet Laureate, and possible Prime Minister of England.

Respect for learning is diffused by this examination system, for the *literati*, or those who have taken degrees, are the highest of the four classes into which the people of China are divided. They have the right of *entrée* into the presence of officials, and they affect a peculiar swing of body, not to say swagger, with the object, no doubt, of showing that they can go anywhere. It is beneath the dignity of these aristocrats to engage in trade, but they are not above picking up dishonest gains at yamens in which they get if not an official at least a tolerated footing. Not one in a score obtains an office, but they all belong to the literary class and share in its dignity and privileges.

An examination for degrees takes place every third year at Peking and at the provincial capitals. The examination enclosure at Canton contains eleven thousand six hundred and seventy-three things like bathing-boxes or cattle-pens arranged in streets, each street being named, and each cell numbered. The examination lasts nine days, but the time is divided into three parts, and a day intervenes between each part. In each cell a student works for three days at a time. The cell or box, which is only six feet long by three broad, is provided with two boards, one of which acts as a seat, the other a table upon which to write. At night the man being examined makes a bed by placing the table on a level with the seat. Rations are provided by Government, and they are thinking of lighting by electricity these old college cabins.

During the time when an examination is held in it a

Chinese city has a far more animated appearance than has a British one when visited by a Church Congress or by a great scientific association.   From twenty to thirty thousand strangers from all parts of the province seek for temporary quarters.   There will be from ten to twelve thousand or even more competitors, and the rich ones will have each his pipe-bearer and three or more other servants.   Infectious disease is not seldom spread by the crowds that assemble on these occasions.   At a recent examination at Canton a candidate died of cholera in his cell.

To honour those who soonest answer the questions and finish the two essays and one poem that are given to all the candidates, the large middle door of the examination estab-lishment is opened for their exit, and they are saluted by three cannon.   So great is the competition at these exami-nations that at a recent one there were fourteen hundred candidates and only ninety-six "leaped the Dragon Gate," or qualified for a degree.   There are Chinese who spend almost all their lives in a vain attempt to win a degree.   They wear larger and larger spectacles so as to appear more and more wise, but they fail to graduate.   To reward those who think that it is never too late to learn, the Emperor confers the highest degree upon candidates of good character who have won the two former degrees, and who have tried unsuccess-fully for the highest until they have reached the age of ninety !

When a man obtains the degree of Saù Tsoi (B.A.), large placards are sent to his friends announcing his success. These placards are frequently posted outside the house of the recipient to show his pride at being able to claim friendship with so distinguished a person.

Great is the ovation that is awarded to a successful candidate on returning home.   Feasts are given, bands of music and pro-cessions parade the streets.   The hero of the hour, wearing square-toed boots, a gilt flower-like ornament in his cap, and across his chest and back the bands of light-red silk that indicate his new dignity, is told by every one that he is an honour to his parents, to the school in which he learned, and to the city or village of his birth. His parents are publicly thanked by the civic authorities for having given birth to so talented a son.

Conspicuous in a Chinese landscape are tall things like masts, each having near the top a triangular boarding that at a distance resembles the nest of a large bird. These are graduate poles, and they are put up in pairs opposite the ancestral hall of a family when one of its members takes a degree. They are never renewed but are allowed to decay and fall down. A graduate may also place a tablet over his ,door to inform people that he has attained to this literary success.

The main gate of the Confucian temple at Nanking is opened only for the Senior Wrangler of the year and for the Emperor.

To insure impartiality the essays and poems of candidates are transcribed in red ink by copyists, and the examiners never see the originals. Before business begins the examiners " wash their hearts " by vowing solemnly in a building called " The Temple of Perfect Justice " that they will examine honestly. And yet the justice of some of them is, to say the least, imperfect. Even the Government allows persons who have more money than brains to purchase the privilege of wearing, like the *literati*, a certain button on their caps, and of being exempt from arrest and corporal punishment.

The eighteen sub-examiners have their rooms behind the cells of the students, and across a small canal is the office of the Lord Examiner. A " Red Flying Bridge " makes communication. Only those essays and answers to questions which are deemed worthy by the assistant examiners are sent across this bridge, truly a *pons asinorum*. Dollars and taels, however, can " buy a recommendation," and get a comparatively worthless essay or poem across

In 1894 the Emperor astonished and frightened the examining board who had looked over the essays and poems, by examining them again himself. There were two hundred and eight competitors, and it took him three whole days to accomplish the task. At the end of that time the list was turned nearly upside down, for three men placed amongst the last by the examining board, were now marked out by the Emperor as among the six entitled to the highest places.

On going into the examination candidates are searched, but only in a perfunctory way, and there are the "padding" and other methods by which things are made easy. "Sleeve editions" of the classics concealed in the sleeves are used as "cribs." Poor scholars for a certain price personate their employers at the examinations. A good trade is done in forged diplomas.

The two chief examiners sent to a provincial city are escorted to the examination hall by the local magnates, by bands, and by soldiers. Each is borne by eight men in an open sedan chair, the seat of which is covered by a tiger's skin. Before each chair are carried, under a richly carved pavilion of wood, the learned man's commission and seal of office.

On the day appointed for paying respect to the literary chancellor and his subordinates the newly-made graduate sacrifices very early in the morning, gets into his official clothes, and starts for the yamen. Graduates of the first degree enter the presence of the literary chancellor together and arrange themselves in order before him. Then at the word of command of the master of ceremonies they kneel simultaneously and bow their heads to the ground three times. This ceremony ended, the graduates take wine with the high officials assembled to do them honour.

Abbé Huc relates the following : During his residence in South China, having occasion to dispatch a messenger to Peking, he asked a schoolmaster, whose home was in the capital, if he would like to send a letter to his mother. The schoolmaster called to a boy who was singing his lesson in the next room, "Here, take this paper, and write a letter to my mother. Lose no time, for the courier is going at once." This struck the Abbé as peculiar, and he inquired if the lad were acquainted with the teacher's mother. Being informed that the boy did not even know before that such a person existed, Huc asked, "How, then, does he know what to say?" To this the schoolmaster made the conclusive reply, "For more than a year he has been studying literary composition, and he is acquainted with a number of elegant formulæ, how then could he not know how a son should write to a mother?" The pupil soon returned with the letter, not only all written, but sealed up, the teacher having merely signed his name. The letter would have done for any other mother in the Empire, and any other mother would have been equally pleased to receive it.

In recent years essays composed by putting together scraps remembered from the classics, in much the same way as we used to make Latin verses, are no longer required. Competitors are now allowed to write their themes in a natural and not in an artificial, stilted style.

It must be admitted that the Chinese system of education, though more absurd than ours, develops greatly the memory. Mr. E. H. Parker, who was Consul in many parts of China, tells us that the commonest Chinaman can trace his descent back by memory for from two to five hundred years, or even more by referring to his "genealogy" book at home.

Until recently, in order to become a master or doctor of war, a Chinese military man had at full gallop to hit a target with an arrow six times in succession, wield an iron-handled battle-axe, and lift stone-loaded beams. Military education has now been brought more up to date, though it never was as absurd as the British system of examining embryo officers in Greek and Roman classics.

But it is not only human beings who are supposed by the Chinese to pass literary examinations. Snakes, turtles, tortoises, crabs, lobsters, and all kinds of water reptiles are regarded as dragons in lower degrees of existence. By success at a great triennial examination held by the king of the dragons, they attain the form, size, and position of perfect dragons.

There is in China what may be called a University Extension movement. Some of those who have themselves passed competitive examinations in the classics admire the teaching so much that they pay men to expound it in open-air lectures in the streets. These men and the public readers, who work on their own account, select a street corner or some other public place, read aloud passages from the classics, and comment upon them. At intervals a pause is made to take up a collection.

Literati also write tracts urging people to reform their lives, and these are bought and distributed by the charitable rich. In a collection of these tracts called "Sayings of the Wise," may be found the noble maxim, "Only practise good works, and ask no questions about your future destiny," and the encouraging assurance, "Human desires *can* be broken off; Heaven's laws *can* be observed."

Fables and novels with a purpose are much used for instruction in China. The following fable, which is directed against avarice, is well known. A priest had a collection of jewels to which he was constantly adding, and of which he was very proud. A friend to whom he one day showed them, after feasting his eyes for some time, thanked the priest for the jewels. "But I have not given them to you," was the hasty explanation. "Well," replied the friend, "I have at least had as much pleasure from seeing them as you can have, and the only difference between us is that you have the trouble of guarding them."

It may be doubted whether any nation pays as much

respect to the things of the mind as the Chinese. Instead of playing golf or cricket or football, Chinese literary folk recreate themselves with poetical tournaments. Sometimes they will condescend to chess as it is played in China, that is with three hundred and sixty-one pawns, divided into two camps, one white and the other black. Once a Chinese Emperor asked a statesman why he wasted at chess time which might be more profitably employed. The statesman answered that the moments during which a man forgets his worries are the most precious of all.

Young men preparing for degree examinations form themselves into reading parties, and literary clubs are got up for mutual help and criticism in the composition of essays and poems. On the occasion of a birthday or marriage no present is considered so elegant as a pair of scrolls inscribed with a complimentary distich. No wonder that in China pens (small brushes), ink, paper, and ink-slabs are called the "four precious things."

A Chinaman is fond of money, but he respects learning and literature far more. A merchant called Liu Hsin offered Yang Hsiung 100,000 cash merely to mention his name in a philosophical treatise of his. The author replied with scorn that a stag in a pen or an ox in a cage would not be more out of place than a man with nothing but money to recommend him in the sacred pages of a book. The most notable men in a neighbourhood are not the wealthy, but the learned.

The Chinese pay much attention to what we would call penmanship, and use the beautiful characters of their language for ornamental purposes. They do not dash off notes as we do, but write them with the greatest care on fine paper of various colours, called "flowered leaves."

When letters were invented, the Chinese say, "Heaven rejoiced and hell trembled." Confucius told them to "Reverence the characters." On account of the power which they exercise upon life and conduct, great respect is shown to Chinese letters or characters, and to every bit of paper upon which they have been written, printed, or stamped. It is said, " If one protects the eyes of the sages (*i.e.*, Chinese characters), it is just the same as protecting his own eyes from becoming blind." Those who do not reverence lettered paper are no better than a "blind buffalo." They will receive the heaviest punishment of hell, and will be born blind when they come into the world the next time. On the other hand, he who collects and burns lettered paper, or forbids another to wipe anything with it, or to throw it into dirty water or on the ground, or distributes tracts on reverencing lettered paper — such a one will add years to his life, will become honoured and wealthy, and will have filial children and grandchildren. One tract says that characters must not be stamped upon the soles of shoes, as they would be trampled upon.

In 1875 a denunciation by the literary chancellor was posted on the walls of Foochow of the "disrespect exhibited towards the written character by shopkeepers, who, in shameless disregard of propriety and ancient custom, have the audacity to print words upon the papers and wrappers used in the ordinary course of business, the character being thus often torn and soiled in a way that excites one's strongest indignation."

The worst thing in the conduct of Westerners, as seen by the Chinese, is their want of reverence for lettered paper.

There are lettered-paper societies in China, that employ men to go about and gather lettered paper from the ground or from any place where it may be desecrated. The societies also build furnaces in shape like a small house or a pagoda, generally outside temples, for burning the lettered paper which their agents collect. The ashes are carefully kept until a large quantity have accumulated. They are then put into baskets, and carried by members of the society, having on their best clothes and lighted incense-sticks in their right hands and accompanied by a band, to the nearest large river, and into this they are poured. Until this was explained to me, I was surprised on coming to China to see paper stuck into crevices in trees, and at street corners small boxes fastened up containing scraps of paper. Were the Chinese such a tidy nation? The boxes have over them four characters which mean "Reverence Lettered Paper," and are intended to hold scraps of paper which people pick up in the street.

Every Chinese volume is composed of smooth drab papers, and is stitched with silk. Volumes to the number of ten or so are kept in a case covered with flowered satin. One history of China consists of three hundred brochures or thin volumes. There are probably more books stored and sold in Peking than in any other city in the world. An encyclopædia of three thousand volumes was burned by the Boxers. On the other hand, there are thousands of villages and many good-sized towns in China where a book could not be bought.

Many of the cheap books now printed contain the filthiest jests. You see the punkah-puller outside an office in Hong Kong, holding one of these "penny dreadfuls" in his hands and pulling the rope of the punkah with his toes.

Even now there is in the interior of China as much ignorance about Western habits and sciences as there is with us in reference to things Chinese. One high official, when sent to Europe, brought a large quantity of salt with him, because he thought there was none there. Another being asked what he thought of Dr. Martin's "Evidences of Christianity," replied that the scientific part of the work he accepted, but *the religious sections*, in which it is said that the earth revolves around the sun, was more than he could believe! In an argument about a coal-mine, a high official at Peking spoke of growing coal, and said that its rate of growth was not known. A man who had purchased to himself a good degree, asked a missionary, "Can your ships sail to the moon?" If the average Chinese graduate be asked whether he knows where England, France, Russia, and America are, he replies, "What advantage would it be? I am not intending to travel."

Still, China is waking up, too soon perhaps for the commercial interests of Westerners, who, if they were wise, would let sleeping dogs lie. In 1898 the Celestial Empire learned with amazement of an Imperial decision that henceforth the leading features of Western science were to be included with the Chinese classics in the examination for degrees programme. The decree was rescinded by the Empress-Dowager, but even she cannot prevent the tide of knowledge from flowing into China. At the examination for degrees lately held in the city of Chao-Chow, in the province of Kwanton, the two candidates who headed the list had been teachers of missionaries—an illustration, by the way, of the indirect influence of missionaries. From the missionaries the candidates had picked up information which enabled them to answer the questions set about things Western. At this examination the following were asked : "What are the five continents of the world?" "Name the highest mountain and the longest river." "Discuss the difference between the Roman Catholic and Protestant religions." "Explain Free Trade and Protection." "How do foreigners regulate the press, post-office, commerce, railways, banks, banknotes, taxation ; and how do they get faithful men?" "Wherein lies the naval supremacy of Great Britain?"

At another examination these questions were asked : "Which Western nations have paid most attention to education?" "State the leading features of the military systems of Great Britain, Germany, Russia, and France." "Which nation is the best coloniser?"

Three out of the nine days of the last examination for degrees at Canton were devoted to European history during the seventeenth and eighteenth centuries. Two of the subject for essays were, "How can Russia best invade India?" "Compare the philosophy of Bacon and of Descartes, and say which, in your opinion, would more improve China." One candidate is said to have made good marks by writing out and commenting upon the Ten Commandments as a basis for law.

A considerable number of well-educated young men belonging to influential Chinese families are being sent from time to time to Japan, the United States, and Europe, to study these countries and gain knowledge that may benefit their countrymen. Large numbers of foreign teachers are employed in China, and the "language without a teacher," or Western books ably translated, sell in large quantities. Even for girls, schools are being provided, and in one of them, got up by an enlightened mandarin, the scholars have to unbind their feet.

Thoughtful Chinese are now afraid that the present zeal for acquiring Western science may prevent Chinese classics, particularly the works of Confucius, from being studied. And without the proprieties enjoined by that sage, the rising generation will be, they think, no better than hooligans. If the classics are neglected they say there will be no reverence for age, or for parents, and mandarins will rage like tigers. Let us hope that the sweet reasonableness of Christianity may prevent consequences like these.

CHAPTER XXI

CHINESE MANNERS

Polished and punctilious—Would the Sermon on the Mount have had a
similar effect?—"Let your movements be graceful and deliberate "—
"Short measure "—" Politeness before force "—Easy to be rude—
"Little bit lie pidgin "—Salutations—A formal call—" Neither boast
nor grumble "—Tea-drinking—" Go slowly "—Foot-binding—" She
more quiet "—Uncut nails—Polite attention—Friendly interest—Pose
and attitude—" In honour preferring one another "—A missionary's
mistake.

WHEN I used to hear people who had just come to
China saying to a servant, " Boy, boy," in contemptuous tones, and never thanking the boy for service rendered,
I was tempted to ask, " Do you know to whom you are
speaking ? Are you aware that that boy belongs to a nation
that was highly civilised when the British were savages ; to a
nation that has probably forgotten as much as we ever
knew ? "

Nor can any one detect the want of self-restraint that
constitutes bad manners quicker than can a Chinaman. He
may say nothing, but he makes a mental note of it. When
the Chinese have not been spoiled by intercourse with
foreigners they are polished and punctilious. Not in Hong
Kong, of course, where so many of us lose manners, but in
the interior of China, if one chair-coolie knock up against
another, he will ask his pardon. Respect is always paid to
a burden. Should even a mandarin when walking meet a

porter carrying one, he will step aside and make his retinue do the same. An English engineer told me that the civility of junk-men in moving their junks when he wanted an unimpeded sight for surveying astonished him.

If you are mobbed in a Chinese town, you should look straight at one or two of the people and say, "Your parents did not pay much attention to your manners; they did not teach you the rules of propriety." A remark like this will make the crowd slink away one by one, quite ashamed of themselves.

A missionary who asked his way, was answered only by the jeers and hooting of a crowd that had collected round him. Turning to them he asked, in excellent Chinese, "Do you thus observe the injunction of your ancient writers, to treat kindly the stranger from afar? Are you ignorant that Confucius said that what we would not have done to ourselves we should not do to others?" In an instant the mood of the crowd changed, the old men bowed approvingly, and a number of young ones jumped forward to show the way. Would the Sermon on the Mount, if quoted in English by a Chinese in a London or New York street, have the same effect upon an excited mob?

A book containing three thousand rules of behaviour is studied in Chinese schools, so that a well-taught lad knows what to do and how to do it on each occasion, and he goes through the prescribed forms as a soldier does his drill.

The second of these rules is, "Let your movements be graceful and deliberate." People who could frame a rule like this cannot see the poetry of motion that we see in our athletic games and dances.

A Chinaman was in doubt as to whether another were a gentleman or not. His dress and general appearance made him think that he was. One wet day, however, he saw the man gather up his fine clothes and leap over a puddle. Here was proof positive, for no gentleman would do such an undignified thing.

Seeing an English lady jumping about at tennis, a Chinaman asked how much she was paid for doing so. Being told that she was a lady of independent means, his next question was, " Why does she not hire a coolie to jump for her? "

Chinese etiquette will not allow people to hasten even to get away from rain. A mandarin who had jumped a ditch in his efforts to escape a heavy shower, was greatly annoyed when he found that a boy had witnessed the performance, and paid him largely to keep secret the deed of shame.

Bulkiness of figure in a man, but not in a woman, is admired, perhaps because it suggests gravity of demeanour. Any undersized individual who does not fill his chair well, they jocularly style " Short Measure."

The ideal of Confucius was moderation or the " Just Medium." The superior man, in manner and in everything else, " turns to scorn the madness of extremes." Though not wanting in energy, he considers hurry and impatience vulgar. His favourite maxim is, " Politeness before force," for he trusts much to concession and conciliation.

Owing to their complex ceremonial code the Chinese can show disrespect to, say, a foreign diplomatist, by methods such as the manner of writing, folding, or addressing a letter, or the omission of any one of a multitude of simple acts which we would consider of little importance.

Talking of the difference between Britishers and Chinese, one of the latter remarked, " Chinese gentleman every time very polite. For example, where English doctor man say, ' You puttee this poultice on small of your back,' Chinese doctor say, ' This concoction of simples will have the felicity of reposing upon the distinguished small of your honourable back.' "

A Chinese will never mind " little bit lie pidgin " in order to be polite. A direct refusal he thinks rude, so he promises readily and trusts to his ingenuity to escape having to perform. This gives the impression that he has an abstract love of falsehood.

When one gentleman meets another he asks, "Have you eaten your rice?" which is equivalent to our "How do you do?" If the acquaintance has breakfasted or dined he answers, "Beg pardon, I have." That is, he begs his friend to forgive his rudeness in anticipating him in eating. Should one of the friends be on horseback he will say, "I will get off and you will mount," meaning nothing by the proposal, for he knows that the friend encountered is going in the opposite direction. If, however, those who ride are in a hurry they do not recognise each other on the road, even though they are friends. If they did, etiquette would require very lengthy salutations. Hence the injunction, "Salute no man by the way."

Should a man see an acquaintance at a restaurant it is good manners to send a boy or waiter to tell him that he will pay the bill—another of these unmeant proposals.

The ceremonial to be observed in making a formal call is laid down in the "Book of Rites," one of the classical works most reverenced in China. The slightest departure from the rules of this book subjects the culprit to the greatly dreaded rebuke, "He does not know the Proprieties," or "He is a not-know-the-Rites-man."

When going to pay a visit, which is done in the morning, a Chinese wears his best clothes, is carried in a chair by four coolies, and is preceded by a servant. A person of little importance must get out of his chair and walk from the outer courtyard, his immediate superior from the next court, and so on, in accordance with prescribed etiquette. The servant who goes before carries above his head the visiting-card of his master, which is a piece of red paper about eight inches long and three inches wide. On it is written the visitor's name and sometimes such an addition as this: "Your humble

Servant" (literally, "Stupid younger brother") "bows his head in salutation." If the master of the house is engaged he does not lie about not being at home, but simply sends his card and a message that he is engaged. If he can see the visitor he comes out, bows many times, asks how he can presume to receive his honourable footsteps, and edges him to a seat of honour in the reception-room. On this the visitor sits, but not until he has coquetted about the room in an ecstasy of humility for the length of time prescribed.

It is proper to inquire about the father of the man you visit in terms such as these: "Does the honourable great man enjoy happiness?" Should you ask, "How many worthy young gentlemen" (sons) "have you?" the friend visited may reply, "My fate is niggardly; I have only one little pup or bug"—son. If the inquiry is, "How many tens of thousands of pieces of silver have you?" (meaning, "How many daughters have you?"). "My Yatows" (forked heads, or slave children), you answer, with a deprecatory shrug, "number so many."

Chinese politeness requires that conversation should be carried on in a low, soft voice, and that there should be no boisterous laughter. Unpropitious words must be avoided. Another prohibition that Americans and Britons might attend to with advantage is, "Neither boast nor grumble." Lady visitors are enjoined not to discuss mother-in-law or household affairs and not to show their teeth when they smile. "Like sheep that be leaderless are many women come together for much talk." On the other hand, all judges of politeness and the gods themselves honour the lady visitor who "thinketh long before opening her lips." Soon after the visitor arrives tea is served, but he must not drink it until pressed to do so many times and until the host has done so first. If cake or fruit be offered it should only be nibbled at during a first visit. A busy clergyman hung up in a conspicuous place in his study the Scriptural motto, "The Lord bless thy goings out." A Chinese host has this advantage over European ones—that he can give a hint to go, to a visitor who is becoming a bore. When he drinks tea or fingers his cup it means that he thinks the interview had better come to an end.

When the visitor rises to leave he remarks, "Another day I will come to receive your instructions"; to which his friend replies, "You do me too much honour; I rather ought to wait upon you to-morrow." Then he urges his guest to stay, or, at least, to "go slowly." If the guest must leave or wishes to leave he clenches his own hands and bows till his hands almost touch the ground. The host does the same, and warmly thanks him for the instruction he has derived from his conversation. The guest says that he has wearied his friend, and apologises. This last remark often is more truthful than the other polite phrases.

Women's compressed feet are, as every one knows, thought "genteel" in China. The fashion, which seems to us as disgusting as does tight-lacing to the Chinese, may have been established for a practical reason. A friend of mine whose servant had asked leave to "go catchee a wife" said to the boy that he hoped the young lady had natural feet. "No," replied the boy; "she has small feet; that much better. She no walkee, talkee; she more quiet."

To us, uncut nails are disgusting; to the Chinese, nails so long that they have to be protected by cases are very stylish, because they indicate that their owner does no menial work.

A Chinese visitor to England noticed as peculiar that in good society people avoid nasty subjects of conversation. In China all classes, and women as well as men, speak freely about the filthiest things.

What we would consider impertinent curiosity is in China polite attention. It is there thought, for instance, to show a friendly interest to ask the age of a person to whom you are

introduced or whom you visit for the first time. Suppose he,
or even she, reply "forty," you must then say, "From your
venerable appearance I would have taken you to be much
older." When Li-Hung-Chang visited Europe, he, meaning
to be very polite, asked ladies their age, why they had not
more children, why they were not married, and other embar-
rassing questions.

The importance which the Chinese attach to pose and
attitude may be illustrated by a dispute between a barber
and a chiropodist. "You should treat me with more respect,"
said the former, "because my business has to do with the
head and yours with the feet." "On the contrary, you
ought to rise up before me," said the latter, "as you have to
stand before or behind your humblest customer, while I am
allowed to sit, even in the presence of royalty." "Well, if
it comes to that," rejoined the barber, "I have, when I shave
the Emperor, the privilege of pulling his Majesty by the
nose ! "

"In honour preferring one another" is a rule which is
more observed in China than where the bumptiousness of
underbred Britons prevails. Chinese politeness requires a
person to overestimate another's things and to speak dis-
paragingly of himself and his belongings. In a Chinese tale
a visitor is represented as having his fine clothes soiled by a
rat throwing down upon them a jar of oil that rested upon a
beam above. Immediately after the catastrophe the host
comes in, and the visitor, smothering his rage, explains the
situation : "As I entered your honourable apartment I
terrified your honourable rat, which fled and upset your
honourable oil-jar upon my mean and insignificant clothing,
which is the reason of my contemptible appearance in your
honourable presence." "What is your honourable name ?"
one Chinese will ask another. "The trifling name of your
little brother is Wang." "What is your exalted longevity ?"
"Very small ; only a miserable seventy years." "What is

your noble mansion?" "The mud hovel in which I hide is in such-and-such a place."

A missionary who had been only a short time at a station in the country and had not learned Chinese ways was asked by a rich man to visit him. "My house is a very mean one and everything dirty in it," he said, "but I shall be proud if you will condescend to enter it." Taking him literally, the missionary replied, "Oh, I should not mind in the least, for I used to go into very dirty houses when I was a clergyman in Liverpool."

If a gentleman ask you to take a cup of tea he will do it in some such terms as these: "Would you condescend to partake of the miserable trash which I call my tea? It is, of course, unworthy to pass through the honourable lips of you or of your friends, but if you would deign to accept it I would feel honoured indeed." And then you should bow low and answer, "Sir, any tea given by one so honourable as you is too good for your humble servant, and I know, as a matter of fact, that no tea on earth excels that which you are wasting upon me." When the cup of tea is handed you must be careful to take it with both hands. By doing this you show that you think the gift too weighty and important to be held by one hand only.

It would be considered a great liberty for any one, except a very intimate friend, to mention a Chinaman's wife to him. He would probably ask, "What the mischief have you to do with my wife?" If, however, the relative or dear friend were to inquire for Madame, he would call her "your most beautiful, virtuous, and accomplished wife," and the other would depreciate his possession by replying, "The dull thorn or stinking woman at home, who is quite unworthy of being mentioned by you, is well."

CHAPTER XXII

THE GOVERNMENT OF CHINA

The "Son of Heaven"—His allowances—Yang Kuo-Chung's flesh-screen—
A College of Censors. A sensible arrangement—Boards—Circumlocution
—The theory of responsibility—The squeeze system—Public appreciation—Peacock's feathers—Mandarins, how distinguished—Bled by
vultures—On the opium-couch—Pay, pay, pay !—"Bring me an honest
man"—A large and dilapidated house—"He is neglecting his duty"
—"The vermilion pencil"—How rank is shown.

THE Government of China is paternal in theory, but in
practice despotic and democratic. The Emperor is
head of the people as a father is of his family. He is the
representative of the Deity to them, and receives as only
gods of the first rank do the highest of the eight forms of
worship. He even takes it upon himself to promote or
degrade gods. An imperial dispatch is received in the
provinces with prostrations and offerings of incense.

One of the appellations of the "Son of Heaven" is "Sire
of ten thousand years," which recalls the "O king, live for
ever!" of ancient Persia. To see the Emperor is to see the
dragon's face, and his throne is called the dragon's throne.
Thus the Old Dragon has coiled himself around the ruler
of China and got himself worshipped through him by one-
third of mankind.

Great retrenchment is taking place in the palace, but the
regulation scale of things before this change began was as

PART OF IMPERIAL PALACK, PEKING.

follows: The Emperor and Empress had three thousand eunuchs to wait upon them, and in order to enable them to bear the weight of their dignity thirty pounds of meat were daily placed before the Emperor, and twenty-one before his number one wife. Every third year the Emperor is supposed to keep his harem up to date by choosing from the daughters of Manchu officers those he wishes for concubines. During the winter months Yang Kuo-Chung (an Imperial ruffian who was massacred A.D. 756) would often cause a selection of the fattest ladies from his seraglio to stand about him, in order to keep off the draught. This was called his "flesh-screen."

When the Emperor is carried out in his chair every one must hide in a house, or if he cannot get a hiding-place fall down as though dead.

And yet the Chinese are no believers in the flunky theory that a king can do no wrong. They think that the Emperor can and does do so if he violate the law. He has divine right only as long as he governs in conformity with the decrees of Heaven. Mencius said, "The people are of the highest importance; the gods come second; the sovereign is of lesser weight." That "the people's hearts and Heaven's decree are the same," is a Chinese maxim which is nothing else, in fact, than *vox populi, vox Dei*.

The first Emperor of the Ming dynasty observed, "The bow drawn violently will break; the people pressed hard will rebel." Another sovereign remarked to his son, "You see that the boat in which we sit is supported by water, which at the same time is able, if roused, to overwhelm it; remember that the water represents the people, and the Emperor only the boat."

A very old Chinese institution is a College of Censors. The business of its members is to report any breach of propriety in courts of justice or on the part of Government officials generally. Even with the Emperor they are bound to remonstrate when necessary. There have been censors who brought their coffins and left them at the door of the palace when they gave the Emperor advice, in order to intimate that they were ready to abide by whatever might be the issue of the advice.

There are in China twenty-six degrees of hereditary nobility, and by a very sensible arrangement a title loses one degree of nobility with each step of descent. In this way wise fathers are prevented from ennobling fools for ever. Titles are often awarded to those who subscribe largely in the case of national disasters. The nobles have nothing necessarily to do with the administration of the Empire, and must themselves conform to sumptuary regulations in reference to their establishments and retinue.

There is no Parliament in China, but there are two councils, which are the organs of communication between the head and the body politic. For the management or mismanagement of departmental matters there are the Civil Office, the Foreign Office, and the Boards of Punishments, of Revenues, of Rites, of War, and of Works. The Civil Office attends to such matters as the granting of precedence and titles; the Board of Punishments is as amiably busy as was the Inquisition of old. The Board of Rites regulates Court ceremonies and the rites suitable to an eclipse, or to any other national "calamity." The Board of War directs an army which, as a national one, practically does not exist; and the Board of Works, seeking to be justified by faith, neglects its constructive duties. The only part of the revenue that is honestly managed are the Imperial Maritime Customs, which are collected and transmitted by European officers under the supervision of Sir Robert Hart. The Wai-wa-pu, which is the equivalent more or less of our Foreign Office, seems to have been created for the purpose of doing nothing at all and preventing any one else from doing anything. It serves merely as the cold water which extinguishes the hot irons thrust into it by the ardour of the foreign agents.

We complain of the red-tape and circumlocution of British Government offices, but they are original and business-like compared to the Chinese. In the latter at least 90 per cent. of the copying and correspondence that takes place is useless. I quote here, from E. H. Parker's "China," part of a proclamation to show the relative rank of officials and the form of their correspondence: "The Magistrate has had the honour to receive instructions from the Prefect, who cites the directions of the Taotai, moved by the Treasurer and the Judge, recipients of the commands of their Excellencies the Viceroy and Governor, acting at the instance of the Foreign Board, who have been honoured with His Majesty's Commands. . . . We therefore enjoin and command all and several, &c."

The Government of China is greatly helped by the theory that every one is responsible for some one: a father for his children, an elder brother for a younger, the headman in a village for all who live in it. So great a protection is this against fraud and injury that police like ours can be done without in a Chinese village. Every one is labelled through the clan system, and when wanted by the authorities can always be found. In China the family is the unit and not the individual. A missionary of my acquaintance told a magistrate that two men who received five hundred blows were not guilty. "I know that," replied the magistrate, "but they belong to the family of those who were, and I could not get the actual culprits."

The following is the punishment for parricide, which is seldom or now, perhaps, never inflicted in the letter. The criminal is cut to pieces ; his younger brothers are beheaded ; his house razed to the ground, his principal teacher is strangled ; the district magistrate and the other high officials of the province are reduced in rank ; the neighbours living on the right and left have their ears cut off because they should have heard and reported what was going on, and those living

in front lose their eyes because they should have seen and
prevented the crime. So engrained into the Chinese is this
theory of responsibility that it regulates their business and
private life; a bank manager holding his number one clerk
responsible for a mosquito getting into the net on his bed!

A magistrate generally does what he likes. In the city of
Kwang-yuan, for instance, the gate which leads to the
largest portion of the city has been closed for a hundred
years. The reason of this very inconvenient arrangement
is that the mandarin's wife was unfaithful to her husband,
and ran away through that gate.

The edicts of Governors of Provinces often terminate with
such admonitions as these: " Hasten! hasten! a special
edict." " Tremble hereat intensely!" " Lay not up for
yourself future repentance by disobedience." " I will by
no means eat my words." " Earnestly observe these things."

But if the mandarin will not eat his words, he may by
covetousness eat the people committed to his care. As a
warning to him not to do this there is painted opposite
the entrance of every Yamen on a detached wall a monster
trying to swallow the sun. It is not their fault so much
as the fault of the system that many Government officials
deserve to be called " bottomless purses." In theory they
have not to buy their appointments but only to pass a good
degree examination; in practice, however, they have. The
number of successful candidates always far exceeds the
number of vacancies, so *literati* who have neither family
influence nor money are left out in the cold. Certainly they
may sometimes borrow money to buy a post, for it is a
recognised form of business, or rather of speculation, to
finance promising youths so that they may gain degrees,
and afterwards appointments which furnish good "squeezing"
opportunities.

The first duty of the newly appointed mandarin is to pay
the bankers or syndicate who have run him; his second to

put aside the amount necessary to purchase a renewal of his appointment, which is generally held on a three years' tenure, or repurchase in case of dismissal; and his third to save something for the time when he will cease to be employed. After this he may begin to consider the public interest. China can never have just administration of laws, a strong army and navy, or anything that a Government should have until she pays her officials properly. The theory is that the superior man will always act as such, and that all he needs is a living wage. So ridiculously little are officials paid that they have to pay themselves by " squeezing " those whose father and mother they profess to be. " The greater fish eat the smaller, the smaller eat the shrimps, and the shrimps have to eat mud." However, some mandarins " squeeze " much less than do others, and it is possible even in a mandarin's Yamen for life to be well led. When this is the case the Chinese Zacchæus is much appreciated and is presented with " a coat of many colours " by a general contribution, or with an umbrella from " ten thousand of the people." This last is made of red silk or satin, has three folds or flounces, and is inscribed with the names of the principal donors in gold letters. Another compliment is for the inhabitants of a town to ask a good mandarin for a pair of his boots and hang them up over a city gateway, or in a temple.

High officials in China receive rewards from Government, but they are as little substantial as are many of the titles and decorations in which our prominent politicians, or at least their wives, rejoice. The Chinese would seem to think that fine feathers *do* make fine birds, for civil and military officers get as a mark of imperial approbation peacocks' feathers, which are of the one-eyed, two-eyed, or three-eyed kind, according to the amount of honour it is intended to confer. The civil mandarins are divided into nine grades, each of which are distinguished by the colour of the stone or metal button worn on the top of the official cap, by the pattern embroidered on the breast and back of official robes, and by the clasp on the girdle.

Every magistrate must keep from thirty to three hundred, according to the size of his district, lictors, runners, collectors and "watchers," or police. These hereditary rogues, as they generally are, pay and feed themselves on their warrants for the most part. Every one, whether a criminal or a witness who is "wanted on a warrant," is bled by the vultures. With arduous and undefined duties, with executive judicial, and at times even military functions strangely intermingled, a Chinese mandarin is dependent on his subordinates at the best of times, but when he succumbs to the "Yin" or the craving for opium, as many do, and spends half his time on the opium-couch, rapacity and misgovernment go on unchecked.

Before beginning a law-suit one must pay to have a petition written and presented to the mandarin. When the case comes into court money must be given to the judge. Your opponents find out how much was given, and add a little more. You then go one better until "justice" is knocked down to the highest bidder. True, in Europe also the longest purse generally wins a law-suit, but justice is not ignored as it is in China. The favourite eunuch of the Empress-Dowager used to be given about £1,000 for obtaining an interview with that tigress.

Each of the eighteen provinces into which China is divided is to all intents and purposes a distinct country. The viceroy or governor is not interfered with so long as he maintains a show of peace within his borders, and sends to Peking not less revenue than his predecessors. He may rob, torture, and kill as much as he pleases. The first means collecting his salary; the second is supposed to extract truth; the third—well, Chinamen are so many that the death of a few hundred or thousand never seems to be of any importance.

Still, there is a limit even to Chinese endurance. The people, particularly the country people, will at times rise and mob or even beat a mandarin whose oppression is more than conventional. Should he complain to his superiors of this treatment, they resent the trouble, and tell him that if he cannot get on with the people he had better retire.

Several years ago some one denounced an under official to Baron Liu, Viceroy of Nanking, who had made away with seventy-five thousand taels. "I know it," said the Viceroy. "Why do you not dismiss him?" was inquired. "Bring me an honest man and I will," was the pathetic answer.

In the XXXIXth Section of the Book of Rites, it is written, "The men of old, in their desire to manifest great virtue throughout the Empire, began with good government in the various States. To achieve this it was necessary first to order aright their own families, which in turn was preceded by cultivation of their own selves, and that again by rectification of the heart, following upon sincerity of purpose which comes from extension of knowledge." The only thing wrong in the present-day government of China is that the officials, their families, and their dependents have little or no knowledge, sincerity of purpose, or rectification of heart. If left to themselves they will never make reforms. The masses of the people are beginning to see this, and they will see it more and more. China is a large, leaky, and dilapidated house, and as the landlord will not repair it the tenants must.

If early rising had the virtue which some attribute to it China ought to be the best-governed country in the world. The official day of the Emperor begins at half-past four o'clock in the morning, and if he is not out of his bed at that hour there are eunuchs whose business it is to beat drums at his door and call aloud remarks like this: "It is half-past four o'clock and His Majesty is not up! He is neglecting his duty!"

As soon as possible after rising the Emperor receives the

members of the Grand Council and officials who require an audience. Those of the latter who are high enough in rank kneel on cushions when in his presence, the others kneel upon the bare floor. Any particular remarks or directions which the Emperor may make are added to State Papers in red, commonly called "the vermilion pencil." When the retinue of an official is met in the streets the rank of the man escorted can be ascertained by observing the colour and number of flounces on the umbrellas which are carried before him. Only a Viceroy, Provincial Governor, Tartar General, and two or three others are allowed as many as eight bearers of the chair in which the great man sits "like an idol," motionless, grave, and dignified. The chairs of these high officials are covered with blue cloth, those of lower ones with green. On leaving their Yamens and returning to them high officials are saluted with three cannon. Preceding them are two men wearing very wide ceremonial hats; they strike gongs at intervals a number of times according to the rank of their master. Other men and boys carry red boards, on which are inscribed the official's titles or commands to the people to keep silence and not to get in the way. Two men also carry a trunk containing changes of clothing for the great man. The lictors who clear the way wear tall black or red hats made of bamboo splits, ornamented with grey feathers. They carry chains, rods, or whips, to remind people of the punishments which their master inflicts. In the capital of the Empire the rank of officials is shown by the build and colour of their Peking carts, and by the number of heavy, brass-headed nails that are in the wheels.

When an inferior mandarin meets a superior he is bound to go down a side street or by some other means efface himself. Should this be impossible, the bearers of his large fans hasten and hold them between the inferior and the superior, so that with Chinese make-believe the latter may not appear to know that the former dares to be in the same world with him.

AN AUDIENCE HALL, PEKING,

To face page 271.

a drum or gong, and persons suffering from injustice or oppression may strike it till the magistrate comes out and give an informal audience to the suppliant. And yet one common proverb says, "If you have right on your side and no money, don't go to the Yamen gate though it stand wide open," and another advises the dead to keep out of hell, and the living out of Yamens. It is reported that the Board of Punishments at Peking are, with the advice of German and Japanese jurists, about to frame new penal laws. This is much wanted, for the existing ones, though much better than those of most ancient nations, are so vague that the Chinese may well say that it is "difficult to escape from the net of the law." The following enactment is a specimen: "Whoever is guilty of *improper conduct*, and such as is contrary to the *spirit* of the laws, though not a breach of any specific article, shall be punished at the least with forty blows." It is said that in the new code, which we hope will be more than a dead letter, lingchi, or death by a thousand cuttings, and other inhuman punishments will have no place.

In China there are no juries, and in theory there are no lawyers but in practice there are a species of lawyers called "searchers." These aid the judge by looking for a similar previous case, and if sufficiently paid by the defendant they can generally discover a precedent which enables his Lordship to come to the desired decision. The judge or magistrate begins with the assumption that the accused is guilty, which saves trouble. He abuses the unfortunate person, asks unfair and leading questions, and, in short, does all in his power to realise the ideal of an emperor who said, "I wish my people to dread the inside of Yamens as much as possible, so that they may learn to settle their quarrels amongst themselves"

A Chinese court of justice is literally a court; or rather a courtyard, partly or entirely roofed over. The judge sits at a large red table on which are black and red ink slabs, a sort

A Chinese Court.

To face page 230.

五月

of hammer, and a hollow cylinder. This last is full of tallies or slips of wood, and according to the nature of the offence he throws a certain number on the floor of the court. These are taken up by the attendants, and five blows nominally, but in reality only four, inflicted for each. This mitigation is an "imperial favour" in conformity with the Chinese maxim, that "in enacting laws, rigour is necessary; in executing them, mercy." Prisoners find by painful experience that it is the opposite of this maxim that is practised. In a stand behind are spears, swords, and other insignia of justice. Every one addressing the court, except official persons, must kneel.

The inducements which are used to make prisoners confess guilt or disclose confederates are as terrible as those we used three hundred years ago. One is called "Monkey grasping peach." The man is suspended by one arm over a horizontal bar, his other arm is passed down under one or both his legs, and his hands tied by the thumbs under his knees. We will not disgust our readers with details of such tortures as smoking the prisoner's head in a tube, cutting his flesh when made to protrude through the interstices of a wire shirt, whipping him with a scourge of small hooks. After a flagellation sometimes the culprit is obliged to go down on his knees and thank the magistrate for the trouble he has taken to correct his morals.

But ordinary kneeling is in many cases thought to be a too comfortable exercise, and so the prisoner is forced to kneel upon chains. The Chinese will cut off a man's eyelids and chain him facing the sun, or pour boiling oil into his eyes. At Peking one who was not a criminal, but only politically disliked, was buried in earth up to his chin, then loathsome, venomous creatures were inserted in an enclosure made round his face and head.

In Canton and elsewhere in China attempt is made to supply the deficiencies of police by inflicting terribly severe punishments upon those who are caught breaking the law. A man who.had bullied and annoyed some native Christians was complained about to a magistrate by a missionary. Little did the reverend gentleman know what h⁹ was doing. The magistrate had iron rings driven over the knees of the man's doubled up legs, thus maiming him for life. The missionary who told me this did not know why the magistrate was so apparently pro-Christian. No doubt it was in order that he might be troubled with no more complaints. Lately a Hong Kong newspaper reported that at a certain city two robbers were crucified and carried around on the crosses.

Sometimes a woman, as punishment for adultery, is made to stand in a cage, her head projecting through a hole in the top, till death by exhaustion or strangulation ensues, or until some one, seeking to obtain merit in heaven, puts into her mouth sufficient opium to end her struggles. If the sentence is less severe, the supports are gradually withdrawn from under the criminal's feet, and he or she is choked more quickly.

A friend told me that in Nanking he passed a man who had been in this sort of receptacle for four days and nights. The bricks upon which it rested had all been put aside so that strangulation could finish its hitherto prevented work. "Was the man unconscious?" I inquired. "So little so," was the reply, "that he said to my interpreter, 'Will the foreign devil not give me some opium?'" The tenacity of life which the Chinese have is often a doubtful advantage. I heard a man say that he saw three men who had endured the half strangulation and whole starvation of these cages for three days and nights, and that life was "still strong in them." A native Christian near Swatow was given fifteen hundred strokes of bamboo canes to make him confess a murder which he did not commit. A week afterwards he got a thousand more strokes. The British Consul remonstrated when he heard

JAIL-BIRDS IN CAGES.

of the case, and the man was let alone and has now quite recovered.

Wandering one day through a magistracy in Canton I came upon a horrid sight. A man was stretched across a board, his two thumbs being fastened behind his back to his two big toes. A torturer stood beside him with two bamboo canes fastened together in his hand, with which he had beaten the front of the thighs of the tied-up man until they were blue and bloody. From the nose of this operator hung two cancer-ous appendices, which probably procured for him his post, as ugliness helps the tormentor's work. The judge or magistrate asked the prisoner, who moaned miserably, questions. They were beginning to bring in other inducements to confession, so I fled, and gladly paid the porter ten cents, which he demanded, to let me out. My squeamishness caused mirth amongst the Yamen runners, and they would show me some of the things that constitute the "plant" of the justice business in China. One implement was a piece of hard leather like the sole of a shoe. This is used for striking a prisoner suspected of lying upon the cheek and mouth, until sometimes the features are so obliterated that the sufferer is said to have a "pig face." This attention is paid much to women. We wonder if it was with a piece of leather like this that the high priest Ananias commanded St. Paul to be smitten on the mouth. Another thing which the attendants pointed out to me, with a grin all over their faces, was a short, hard stick. With a single blow of this they can break an ankle-bone. One little instrument seemed comparatively harmless, and yet it is sometimes deadly. It is a piece of thin, flat bamboo. With this innumerable taps are administered until the prisoner's flesh becomes pulpy and sometimes gangrenes. An English officer told me that he saw a man get three hundred blows. There was a pause after each twentieth blow, and the mandarin asked the prisoner jeeringly to confess. "Then," said my friend, "they brought in a beam to go across the man's legs and the guide whispered that four men would jump upon this until the man confessed or his legs broke. I got sick and left."

And yet there are globe-trotters who can take snapshots of such scenes, and I have even heard of a gaoler being bribed to have a prisoner executed a day or two before his time, that the dreadful spectacle might suit the tourist's travelling arrangements. The Chinese are obliging in these matters. A friend of mine sent in his name to a magistrate, and said that he wished to see a trial. The magistrate replied that there was none that morning, but that if he could wait until the afternoon he would get one up for him.

However easy it is for a tourist to see torture or an execution inflicted in a Chinese city, we advise him, or even her, not to do so. A man known to the writer saw nine pirates beheaded. "The sight haunted me for weeks," he said, "and the worst of the show was the way children four or five years old tossed decapitated heads from one to the other, and putting straws into the blood, blew bubbles!" He described the men who were to be beheaded as being carried to the execution ground in baskets or crates, much in the same way as one sees pigs carried in China. Indeed, after the tortures to which they are subjected, few criminals could walk. Their hands were pinioned, and they were made to kneel side by side in a row. One criminal, however, managed to spit in the executioner's face. A mandarin arrived, and sat down at a table covered with red cloth. At a signal from him the executioner commenced at one end of the waiting line, and with his sword mowed off the heads as a boy cuts off with a switch the heads of poppies in a meadow. Heads when cut off are put in a bamboo cage and exposed in a public place.

An aspirant to the office of headsman practises upon turnips. He puts a black line round the vegetable, and aims at cutting it in two there. Country practitioners bungle much, and often take several chops. The fee of an executioner is only fifty cents per head, but he does not do badly at that, for business is generally pretty brisk. In a provincial town, where a friend of mine lives, the gaol was becoming too full, so the mandarin visited it to see what could be done. He liberated the light offenders, and had the heads cut off all the rest, thus giving to the gaol a fresh start in usefulness.

So great is the inconsistency, as it seems to us, in things Chinese, that when the law is most cruel there shines out a gleam of hope. It is enacted, for instance, that the life of a criminal condemned to death is to be spared if he have parents over seventy years of age and no brother over sixteen to support them.

Almost the lightest punishment that is inflicted in China is to be made to wear a cangue. This is a heavy wooden collar, three feet wide, which prevents the wearer from lying down or putting his hands to his face to drive off flies and mosquitoes. It is locked on the neck of the culprit during the daytime, but is sometimes taken off during the night. The name, residence, and offence of the prisoner are written on strips of red paper, which are pasted on the front of the board, and he is placed in the daytime usually in the vicinity of the spot where he committed his offence. He begs his living, unless his friends feed him, during his term of punishment, which lasts from one to three months.

Then there is the double collar—a contrivance something like a heavy door with two holes cut in it, by means of which two criminals are bracketed together and are thus held fast, frequently day and night.

Attached to the Yamen of a magistrate are a species of constable, or runner, whose duty it is to bring in those who are wanted. If Sherlock Holmes fails to do this, his detective powers are sharpened by a bamboo beating. To escape this *à posteriori* argument, the constable is wont to seize a near relative of the suspected person, have him flogged, squeezed in the fingers, boarded down upon a wooden bed, or in some

other way persuaded to disclose the whereabouts of his erring
and straying younger brother. The officials about a Yamen
seem to be absolutely indifferent to the sufferings they inflict.
At Peking those sent out to arrest a suspected criminal on a
recent occasion brought no chain or rope to secure his hands,
so they nailed them to the end of the cart in which they drove
back.

Have all Chinese nerves? It would seem as if these
threads of pain and pleasure had been left out of some of
them. A friend told me that he saw a man coming out of a
Yamen holding his wrist, from which his hand had been
severed as a punishment for theft. He was smiling as if it
were a joke.

The Chinese call their gaols hells, just as the prison hulks
that were used in Great Britain less than a century ago
were called "floating hells." They are infested with vermin
and maggots that get into the wounds of the bound
prisoners.

Chinese gaolers purchase their appointments, as they did
in England in the time of Howard; and, as was the case
there then, they receive no other pay but what they can
squeeze from the prisoners or from the prisoners' friends.
This is why the prisoners are from time to time taken away
from their fellows and return with bleeding limbs and so weak
as to be scarce able to crawl.

The gaolers will do anything for money, and nothing
without it. If you are sentenced to lose your head, and bribe
him, your gaoler can get some wretch under his charge to
offer himself as a substitute. Hearing that the gaoler wants
a head, a man who has no money and no friends to get him
out of prison, and who is almost starved in it, will say to his
custodian, "Give me a few good feeds, some samshu, and a
little money to gamble with, and then you can have my head."

In the north of China, in places not affected by foreign
criticism, a gaoler will exhibit four or five prisoners tied

together by their queues in a bamboo cage no larger than that provided for a tiger in a mean menagerie. "Any clothes on them?" I asked one who saw this. "Only loin cloths." "Any sanitary arrangements?" "None whatever." The absence of the last lately caused plague to break out in a prison in Peking, so the authorities may do something now. Indeed, I have heard that an edict has gone forth that the prisons throughout the Empire are to be purified morally and physically. We hope that it will be obeyed.

Less than a hundred years ago soldiers and sailors in Great Britain were occasionally flogged to death, or so severely that they died. The Empress-Dowager is in the same state of civilisation now. Before I left China she ordered a man who confessed that he was a would-be reformer to be beaten to death with bamboos. A Hong Kong paper said that he was beaten from four o'clock in the day until six. Then the flesh was hanging off his bones, but as life had not left they finished him by strangulation.

If attempting to poison her son, actually causing his favourite concubine to be drowned, cutting off the heads of coolies who had hidden treasure for her because dead men tell no tales—if half of these and other stories one hears at Peking are true, Tse-hsi must be a female Nero.

Every three years a mandarin has to make a report of the faults he has committed during that period. This task he might be suspected of performing in a very lenient manner, but he knows that a similar account is being prepared in less partial quarters, and that the discovery of any omission would convert a venial offence into one of dark dye. If the man is guilty, and also wise, he anticipates the order from Peking for his arrest. Resigning his office, and providing himself with a light wooden or paper cangue for his neck, with a small chain for his hands, and, above all, with money to bribe, he hastens to Peking. There he delivers himself in chains to the proper tribunal, and begs of the Emepror the favour of examination and punishment. If the accused cannot buy off capital punishment, the Emperor may be good enough to send him a silk cord, which means, " Strangle yourself." This is very kind and polite of His Majesty, because strangulation is more honourable than beheading by the executioner, as the body is not mutilated. So important is it considered to obey the command of Confucius to keep the body whole that the relatives of a beheaded man will sometimes buy his head and sew it upon his body. They believe that if he appeared in the other world without a head his case would be prejudiced. "You lost your head, did you? Oh, then you must have been behaving badly upon earth ! "

It is probably for this reason more than for its painfulness that lingchi, or the punishment of being cut into a thousand pieces, is so dreaded. As the victim, at least when it is paid for, is drugged with opium, and dispatched with about the third cut, though the other cuts are inflicted afterwards, this death is not so bad as being starved and choked in a cage. But how disreputable to appear in the other world with a body in pieces ! What standing could a man take in the world to come if he had lost his feet in the present one?

Even the Son of Heaven blames himself. It is no unusual thing for the Emperor in published edicts to ask Heaven's forgiveness for droughts, torrents, famines, and for other things which he could not have prevented.

Swallowing gold-leaf is another way in which a mandarin who has got into serious trouble commits suicide. It is considered to be in almost as good taste as using the silk cord.

Seeing in the local papers that lingchi, or the lingering death, was to be inflicted upon a woman in the execution ground at Canton, a man well known in Hong Kong went up to feast his eyes on the sight. Being a mere man without the nerves of a female globe-trotter, it greatly disagreed with him, and he was ill for days after. He is one who, even if he wished to lie, has not enough imagination to do so, therefore what he told us on his return may be considered substantially true. I could not listen to the narrative, much less repeat it, but this is how the man who had "supped" or breakfasted "on horrors" said the proceedings began. The woman was bound to a cross, and the executioner "cut from her two steaks and threw them amongst the crowd." The human wolves fought for them and eat them up between them. The narrator did not know whether this cannibalism was because of hunger (there are always at least a million people in China in a chronic state of starvation) or because the mob thought that to eat the flesh of a criminal would add to their strength or bring to them good luck.

It is only fair to remark before concluding this chapter that the punishments we hear of in China are seldom inflicted, some of them only in time of rebellion, and that very often they are not ordered by a magistrate, but perpetrated by leading villagers on their own account or by a gaoler in prison to extract money.

The Chinese are not a people to be ruled by sentimentalism. Some of the land and sea robbers are very desperate, while for cool impudence a Celestial thief is unsurpassed. Here is an example of the last quality. Several years ago, while the Supreme Court of Hong Kong was in session, a man entered with a ladder, which he placed upon a bench near the judge. The judge asked him what he wanted. He said that he had been sent to fetch the clock to be cleaned. In a rash moment the judge said that, as he was upon the ladder, he might as well take the clock. That clock never came back. Some of the punishments mentioned are inflicted for kidnapping children, and parents will always think that for that crime, which is a very common one in China, the penalty ought to be severe.

CHAPTER XXIV

CHINESE SOLDIERS

Extract from the *Ping Fa*—The army in a transition state—"Braves"—Pay
of soldiers—Tricks and tactics—Qualities of a good soldier—A military
reform board—Coal-dust for gunpowder—The army awakening—Visit
to a barrack—The weak part of the army—A military renaissance.

IT would appear from the history and literature of China
that the Chinese were once a fighting people. The
following is an extract from the *Ping Fa*, or "Art of War,"
written in the sixth century B.C. "If soldiers are not carefully chosen and well drilled to obey, their movements will be
irregular. They will not act in concert. They will miss
success for want of unanimity. Their retreat will be dis-
orderly (nothing about their advance!), one half fighting while
the other is running away. They will not respond to the
call of the gong and the drum. One hundred such as
these will not hold their own against ten well-drilled men.
A soldier must be well equipped. If the cuirass is not close
set, the breast might as well be bare. Bows that will not
carry are no more use at long distances than swords and
spears. Bad marksmen might as well have no arrows. Even
good marksmen, unless able to make their arrows pierce,
might as well shoot with headless shafts."

At the present time, so wide of the mark do the old style
of Chinese soldiers shoot that they might as well have no
rifles. Scandalously bad shots are, I believe, beaten with

CHINESE SOLDIERS—OLD STYLE.

To face page 240.

bambooes, but even this does not improve their aim. People live quite near the targets on the practice ground at Woochow on the West River; probably they think that the safest place. Compare with the above, orders which long ago a viceroy at Canton issued: " The soldier who runs away or shrinks, or whispers to a comrade when the enemy advances shall suffer death. Powder, shot, and arrows must not be thrown away at a distance, but reserved for closer action, as the want of them when needed is like waiting to be slain with the hands tied. The soldier who bravely kills an enemy shall be rewarded, but he who lies concerning his own merits, or usurps those of others, shall be decapitated."

When Sun Tzŭ, who wrote the "Art of War," was discours-ing one day with Prince Ho-lu of the Wu State, the latter said, " I have read your book, and want to know if you could apply its principles to women." Sun Tzŭ replied in the affirmative, whereupon the Prince took 180 girls out of his harem and bade Sun Tzŭ drill them. He divided them into two companies, and at the head of each placed a favourite concubine of the Prince. When the drums sounded for drill to begin, all the girls burst out laughing. Thereupon Sun Tzŭ, without a moment's delay, caused the two concubines in command to be beheaded. This restored order, and ultimately the corps was raised to a state of great efficiency.

So many kinds of soldiers are there in China that it is difficult to characterise the army as a whole. There are regulars and irregulars, foreign-drilled troops and local militia. These last are not trained at all, or in a way that is far behind the times. They only attend upon mandarins, or act as police.

An attempt has been made to improve these police soldiers, but though the new style wear a less stagy dress they know very little more of police duties than did their predecessors. I have seen them sleeping hours together in the daytime in their shelter boxes. One of them will drive away beggars by

16

a zealous application of bamboo to their shoulders, and then hold out his hand for the " cumsha " that you had denied to your tormentors.

The armies of China (each viceroy and provincial governor has one) are now in a transition state. While I have seen Chinese soldiers who had no other weapons than spears and blunderbusses, and no better clothes than beggars, I have seen others with Mauser rifles, and even with waterproof coats which, when a sprinkle of rain came, they put on proudly over rather smart uniforms. In one place I saw soldiers being drilled who were a great contrast to the ordinary dirty, untaught " braves," only the instructors need not have kicked the awkward ones upon the shins. The viceroy at Canton has now got quite a respectable guard, with bugle band and all complete. I have heard this band, and do not think that it could have been organised in order to follow the injunction of an old Chinese military writer : " Spread in the camp of the enemy voluptuous musical airs so as to soften his heart."

The Imperial Guard at Peking consists of four thousand Manchu troops that are not as worthless as the rest. There are banners or corps of Manchu soldiers under Tartar generals at important provincial centres, such as Canton, Foochow, &c. The majority of these bannermen are flabby opium-smokers, who are neither strengthened by exercise nor disciplined by drill.

Then there is the " Green Banner," or Chinese army, supposed to number 650,000 troops. So little confidence was placed in these soldiers, that when rebels in China had to be put down and foreign robbers checked, peasants were engaged at a much higher rate of pay and complimented by the title of " braves." The " soldiers " were left to do garrison and police duty and the " braves " faced the enemy. In fact the Chinese Government treated her regular army as the British Government did hers in the South African troubles, only that the Chinese soldiers were not required to fight. Chinese peasant "volunteers" got more wages and the title of "braves," as our "volunteers" got four shillings a day more than their fellow combatants of the regulars, and were called "gallant" *ad nauseam.*

If the ordinary Chinése soldier, as distinguished from the occasionally enlisted and comparatively well-paid "brave," had no stomach to fight, it is no wonder considering how little used to go into that member. A soldier's ration of rice was, until recent army reforms took place, so reduced between its departure from the public granaries and its arrival at his mouth that it scarcely kept him alive. His pay was from twenty to thirty cents a day nominally, but he did not touch more than half that amount. The general took what he considered to be his due out of the money provided for paying troops, and passed it on to the next in command, and so on. Very little was left for Tommy Atkins. The people who got up the rebellions that were so common in remote districts were generally soldiers dissatisfied because they were cheated of pay. One reason why good rifles were not supplied to the infantry or good horses to the cavalry is because the men used to desert and sell them.

Not long ago the soldiers who took the field against insurgents in the province of Kwangsi exchanged ammunition with the enemy for opium, and both sides firing their rifles in the air, engaged in sham battles. When other regiments were sent to reinforce these worthless ones the names of the regiments selected had to be kept a secret, as otherwise the men would all have deserted. Indeed, a rebellion used sometimes to be got up by a military mandarin. That worthy obtained money from the Government to enable him to provide more soldiers and war material. Part of this he gave to the leader of the rising to induce him to make peace, and the rest he put into his own coffers. Neither did the clothing of their troops trouble viceroys and provincial governors. Fans and umbrellas were occasionally supplied to soldiers, but, as a rule, only parti-coloured jackets which could be easily slipped on and off. On the back of the jacket the word "ping," or soldier, was inscribed. Without this label one might easily have made a mistake. Should courage fail the warrior, he threw off his jacket and retired into the comparative safety of private life. Was there to be an inspection? Coolies were hired for the occasion and put into blue and red jackets and conical hats. Falstaff said that he could get linen for his soldiers on any hedge; a military mandarin reversed this and got men for his linen in every village. A general inspected a regiment and lunched. When he was at the meal the jackets of the inspected men were sent to another place and put on coolies, who were then inspected.

Not long ago the people of Peking petitioned that a certain regiment might be sent away and another brought in its stead. The authorities were obliging. They ordered the regiment to march out to a place about fifteen miles away, change into jackets of another corps that were in readiness for them, and then march back.

In several of the provinces the army was literally one of dry bones. The names of men long dead were kept upon the rolls, drawing pay and rations by proxy. The fewer soldiers a provincial governor had the better were they supplied with noisy musical instruments and unmeaning flags. Their tactics seemed to have been to beat so many gongs and exhibit such large colours that their foes might be too frightened to attack. This was not so scientific, but it was quite as brave as modern Western warfare, which consists in finding the enemy and then hiding from him.

There have been for some years quite up-to-date forts and guns in China, but there was always something wrong, and perhaps the ammunition provided did not suit the gun. On one occasion during the war between China and Japan Chinese artillery had the enemy covered, but the guns would not go off because coal-dust had been supplied instead of gunpowder. Out of two barrels of European powder, a mandarin would make twelve. Only the outside ones of the shells in his store would be real, and so on through everything.

Quis custodiet ipsos custodes? The unreformed Chinese soldiers are as a class deservedly hated, for they rob and maltreat in every way those whom they are hired to guard and benefit. The advice of John the Baptist to the soldiers of ancient Rome was to do no violence to any man, and to be content with their wages. The warning is needed by the warrior in the backward parts of China, only in many cases he gets no wages to be content with. He does violence either to live or to fill his pipe with opium. In one town of which I heard, there was a row between Protestant and Roman Catholic native Christians—a sort of North of Ireland Orange riot. Soldiers were sent not exactly to settle theological differences but to keep the peace. The first day they demanded rice from the inhabitants, but cooked it themselves with their own charcoal, the second day they commandeered both rice and charcoal, and the third day they forced people to cook for them.

A Chinaman thrives in every climate. He seldom needs a physician and can bear pain patiently. He can live upon nothing and has little or no objection to dying. He is active, sober, docile, and what he learns he never forgets. These are the qualities of a good soldier. Given confidence in their leaders and sure pay, Chinese soldiers would be first rate. If England had taken all China in 1841 (considering her opportunities her moderation is wonderful!) instead of only Hong Kong, she could have made a Chinese army that would have held the world at bay.

I have seen the regiment we organised at Wei-Hai-Wei, and no soldiers could drill better. They fought too in a way that did them credit at Tientsin. As the persecutions of 1900 showed that the Chinese had souls and could be more than rice Christians, so the fighting of the same period proved that they had in them the stuff of which good soldiers are made.

The painful lesson which China learned when her soldiers were knocked sky high by Japan, and the "insults" inflicted by foreigners, have induced her to more or less put her military house in order. There is now at Peking a Military Reform Board which is collecting money and promising great things. A territorial system is to be introduced into the province of Pechili, which is calculated to give a force of a hundred and eighty battalions for three years' service. Each battalion will consist of men from one *hein*, or prefecture. Next year schools are to be opened in the same province for non-commissioned officers, and a higher one at Peking for officers. More attention is to be given to rifle practice, and a special tax levied to buy arms and ammunition. Attempts to organise commissariat transport and medical services have been made. The newly formed corps of the Chinese army carry on their ambulance material the Geneva Cross, so as to place their wounded under the protection accorded by that international convention. A college has been established for training medical officers for the army. This adoption of medical ministration will probably make the Chinese soldier fight better, for what he used to dread more than death was being left to die of his wounds. The Chinaman fears also that he will be unburied, and that no one will make the ritual offerings over a corpse abandoned on the field of battle. Quite a number of Chinese youths are now being trained in the German and Japanese armies for service in their own country. Surely the fact that she sent two colonels to see the last military manoeuvres in France shows that China is awakening.

Formerly there was no cohesion in the Chinese army, and each commander acted with irresponsible light-heartedness for himself. Now they are beginning to work together, but even if the widely separated provincial armies of China were good, in the absence of railways they are of little use, as they cannot be concentrated and sent quickly to where they are wanted. The general introduction of railways will change for the better the Chinese army, as it will so many other things in the country. Not so many years ago there were in the British army abuses and absurdities nearly as many and as great as there are now in the Chinese. These have for the most part disappeared, and China too, now that she has wakened up, will purge her military system.

At Woochang, on the Yang-tze, there is a Military College where foreign instructors, all or nearly all of whom are now Japanese, teach embryo military mandarins. At Han Yang, on the other side of the river, there is an arsenal where, as at Foochow, Tientsin, and other places, the latest guns are turned out.

It would appear, indeed, from a recent memorial in the *Peking Gazette*, that it is never considered too late for a Chinese military officer to learn. The memorial was from Viceroy Yuen Shih Kai, asking that a certain general should be pardoned for deserting in action during the Kwangtung insurrection, because when he was, after ceasing to be a general, put as a student into a lately established military academy, he was "humble and thorough with good results." The memorial was acceded to and a pardon granted.

Soon after the outbreak of the war between Japan and Russia, I saw Chinese soldiers being manufactured by the thousand at Nanking, Woochang, and Ichang. They were instructed by officers who had themselves been trained by foreigners, chiefly Japanese. They were to go to the North when sufficiently taught, and no doubt, if called upon to fight, they would do credit to their teachers.

When the guards of honour that met the Viceroy, who returned to Hankow during our visit to that place, presented arms to his Excellency, they did not do so kneeling as used

to be done by Chinese soldiers, but in the most correct
European fashion. It is said that there are at present as
many as 90,000 soldiers in China properly equipped and
trained by foreigners.

The Commissioner of Customs with whom I stayed at
Ichang, directed his Chinese secretary to make out a permit
for me to visit the barracks. I had to wait two and a half
hours until the secretary couched the large red paper, if not
red tape, document in language flowery enough to suit the
taste of a flowery land and a dilatory officialdom. I was
described as a "universal instructor" in the British army.
A servant was sent to carry these credentials before me,
which he did raised to a level with his head. I was received
by some officers, and then tea and material for smoking were
served. After this we made a tour of the barracks, beginning
with the school, for all these up-to-date soldiers must read
and write. On the walls of the school were many maps and
portraits of the world's great men. The only Britisher thus
honoured was Ruskin. There were also cardboards upon
which were shown every decoration and uniform of the
Japanese army. Pains seem to have been taken to impress
the Chinese recruit that Japan was the only enlightened
nation on earth.

The soldiers did their physical drill and athletic exercises
well, and evidently liked them. The barrack rooms were
small, but not crowded. I was told upon good authority that
these high-class soldiers were paid fair and regular wages.
They certainly looked well fed. They showed to me with
pride their arms and accoutrements, and these were in good
condition.

In winter the men wear a sort of tunic made of cheap black
material, trimmed with red. It is lined with khaki, so that
it may be turned inside out in summer, which seems to be a
warm and wasteful combination. Even the officers who
command these new soldiers have given up the flowing silk

garments, horseshoe cuffs, embroidered breastplates, and amber necklaces in which military mandarins rejoice, or did rejoice, and are dressed in more Western military style. Probably they are not subjected to corporal punishment as are their brothers in the unreformed parts of the military system. The officers, however, are the weak part of the army. They are not as good as our non-commissioned officers, nor will they improve until the Chinese cease to despise the profession of arms. At present an ordinary coolie may become an officer. When the soldiers of one captain fled on the approach of the allied armies into Tientsin, in 1900, he doffed his uniform, and earned money by taking care of the horses of foreign officers. A Chinese saying with regard to the military profession is, " You don't use good iron to make a nail, or a decent man to make a soldier." Well ! it used to be said of the British army that it was manned by the dregs of society, and officered by the froth.

From what I saw of the new army of China I would say that it is almost entirely under the influence of Japan. So great is the admiration for the fighting achievements of that country, that a veritable military renaissance is beginning in China, and Japan has only to say to the army Do this, and it will do it. It is not impossible that before very long the Chinese army or armies may be organised in accordance with the military system of Japan, and then if the officers can and will lead, China will no longer be robbed and bullied by the European Powers.

CHAPTER XXV

THE RELIGIONS OF CHINA

NO nation has so many moral maxims as the Chinese, but the Chinese do not pay as much attention to them as they do to their stomachs and money-bags. The Chinese care little for logic, so they give intellectual hospitality to Confucianism, Buddhism, and Taoism—three systems that are in many respects contradictory. They consider it safest, in the uncertainty as to the best way of reaching the regions of the blest, to take passage by all three of these religious routes. Confucianism supplies the Chinese with morals, Buddhism appeals to their spiritual nature, and Taoism to their gambling interest in chance and luck. So polite are they to possibilities that they admit any divinity at all likely to be useful into their pantheon.

Confucius was born 551 B.C., dragons and goddesses assisting at the event. His father was either a military officer or a district magistrate, and was over seventy years old

THE ALTAR OF HEAVEN, PEKING.

To face page 250.

when the future sage saw the light. Confucius inherited his father's great strength, and when he grew up his arms were so long that they touched his knees. It was, however, his mother who formed his character, for he was left fatherless before he had passed out of his boyhood. At fifteen his "mind was set on learning."

His marriage, which took place when he was nineteen, was not a success; he divorced his wife. Did the poor lady win a golf championship, exhibit her picture, write a book, or try in any other way to win publicity? If so, Confucius would never have pardoned her, for he laid it down that a woman should not be heard of outside her own home. His wandering life and uncompromising temper may have made him hard to live with. After filling for a short time the offices of Keeper of the Government grain-stores and Commissioner for the imperial lands in his native State of Lu, he became public teacher.

One of his pupils presented him with a cart and a pair of ponies, and in this springless conveyance he set out to visit some of the neighbouring petty States. Suggested reforms not being attended to, Confucius returned to Lu, and after some years became chief adviser to its ruler. Asked one day by this person what kind of crown was worn by the Emperor Shun, Confucius replied, "I do not know what kind of garments Shun wore; but I do know the principles on which he ruled his people. Why should not Your Highness inquire about them?" On another occasion, the Duke said to Confucius: "I have heard of a man, who, on removing to a new house, forgot to take his wife. Was there ever a case of greater forgetfulness?" "Yes," answered Confucius; "it is that of the man who forgets himself."

Miracles of good government are said to have been effected during the Prime Ministership of the sage. Then precious things might be dropped in the street without risk of misappropriation, and shepherds would not give water to their beasts before driving them to market lest they should weigh more than their real weight. Righteousness like this exalted the State so much that neighbouring rulers became jealous, and one of them sent to the Duke a present of fair women to corrupt him. This stratagem proving only too successful, Confucius left Lu and went, amongst other places, to Wei. The Duke of this principality had married a licentious woman called Nan-tsz. One day he drove through the street of his capital with Nan-tsz, and made Confucius follow in another carriage. Perhaps the Duke intended to honour the philosopher, but the people saw the incongruity, and cried out, "Lust in front and virtue behind!" Wei was no place for Confucius; he left it and went to K'wang. Here he was assailed by a mob. His companions were alarmed, but he calmly said, "After the death of King Wan was not the cause of letters and truth lodged in me? While Heaven does not let the cause of truth perish, what can the men of K'wang do to me?"

On another occasion when he was attacked by the band of a certain Hwan Tui, Confucius observed, "Heaven has produced the virtue that is in me; what can Hwan Tui do to me?" "Heaven" was much to the philosopher in all his troubles. "He who offends against Heaven," he said, "has none to whom he can pray"; and, again, "Alas! there is no one that knows me!" to which he immediately subjoined, "But there is Heaven; It knows me! I do not murmur against Heaven." By "Heaven," however, he may have meant only abstract right. One of the princes through whose territory Confucius and his disciples passed asked who he was. Confucius heard of this and said, "Tell him I am a man who in the eager pursuit of knowledge forgets his food, who in the joy of its attainment forgets his sorrows, and who does not perceive that old age is coming on."

Confucius compared himself to a dog driven from his home. He said, "I have the fidelity of that animal, and I am treated like it, but what matters the ingratitude of men? They cannot hinder me from doing all the good that has been appointed me. If my precepts are disregarded, I have the consolation of knowing in my own breast that I have faithfully performed my duty." The philosopher paid much attention to the details of life, though his own life was very simple. He ate little, but he always took care to have the proper sauce. His love of order was shown by his never sitting on his mat unless it were placed square. He drank little wine, wore plain clothes, and spoke cautiously. On one occasion he drew the attention of his disciples to the metal statue of a man with a triple clasp upon his mouth, which stood in the ancestral temple at Lu. On the back of the statue were inscribed these words: "The ancients were guarded in their speech, and, like them, we should avoid loquacity. Many words invite many defeats. Avoid also engaging in many businesses, for many businesses create many difficulties." "Observe this, my children," said he, pointing to the inscription. "These words are true, and commend themselves to our reason." But Confucius did more than caution people about words. He advised them to guard their secret thoughts, as from these spring not only words, but actions. He said that the superior man aims at nine objects: Clearness in seeing, distinctness in hearing, kindness in his countenance, respectfulness in his demeanour, sincerity in his words, a reverent carefulness in his work, search for information in doubts, consideration of the consequences in anger, righteousness in the aspect of gain.

Confucius laid no claim to originality. He was, he said, only an editor and compiler of the works of the ancients. However, he no doubt learned maxims from personal experience, such as the following: "Reading without thought is fruitless, and thought without reading is dangerous." "Where there is no permanency, there is no rest; where there is no rest, there is no meditation; where there is no meditation, there is no success." "To know what we know, and what we do not know is knowledge." "Have no friend who is inferior to yourself in virtue." "Virtue is the mean between two vices."

Confucius never tired of speaking of the beauty and necessity of truth, and his ear was an obedient organ for its reception. Cautious and conscientious, he would not commit himself to theories of the supernatural. He taught that men know nothing about the gods, but that they should live as if in their presence. His definition of wisdom was, "To give one's self to the duties due to man, and, while respecting spiritual beings, to keep away from them." When sick he declined to be prayed for, saying that his praying had been for a long time—by which he implied that a life well lived was the best prayer.

When asked about a future life, Confucius answered, "While you do not know this life, how can you know about a future one?" A disciple desired to be instructed how to die, and was told to learn to live well and then he would know how to die. Asked if there were one word which would serve as a rule of conduct for all life, Confucius replied, "Is not reciprocity such a word?"

In Confucianism all virtues branch and blossom from the instinct of filial love. It is the keystone of the system. Let the best in the heart of a child go out towards its parents, and that will pass by instinctive transitions into love within the family, which again will pass into rectitude towards mankind at large. Asked in what government consisted, Confucius answered, "When the prince is prince, the minister minister, the father father, and the son son, that is government." After thirteen years of continued wanderings the would-be reformer came home to die at the age of threescore years and ten. He had suffered much, once being even at the point of starvation. The sense of failure, however, was what was hardest to bear. "The kings," said he on his deathbed, "will not hearken to my doctrines; I am no longer, therefore, of service upon earth, and it is time for me to quit it."

If Confucius was irrationally despised before his death, since it he has been senselessly overestimated. When he did or did not do the most ordinary things they are noted as extraordinary. "When in bed" he did not speak, but, at the same time, "he did not lie like a corpse." "He did not eat rice which had been injured, nor fish which was stale."

The regard which the Chinese have for the "uncrowned monarch" may be estimated from the following, which has been translated from the Sacrificial Ritual :—

> "Confucius! Confucius! How great is Confucius!
> Before Confucius there never was a Confucius:
> Since Confucius there never has been a Confucius.
> Confucius! Confucius! How great is Confucius!"

His great influence may be accounted for by the fact that his writings were used as text-books in schools and for competitive examinations. From his childhood Confucius showed ritualistic tendencies, playing with sacrificial vessels and making ceremonial postures. When he grew up he was scarcely less attached to forms and ceremonies. In fact, he was a Chinese Lord Chesterfield. He taught the Chinese to observe distinctions of rank and to be orderly and gentle. He was "content to live in decencies for ever." When in the presence of Royalty he held in his breath as if he dared not breathe. It is more to his credit that when he met a blind person he saluted.

The writings of Confucius, in common with all Chinese classics, are free from anything debasing. If they do not ascend to heaven, they do not descend to hell. Confucius has given to the world the Chinese version of "the religion of a gentleman." The agnosticism of Confucius was, perhaps, a recoil from the extravagant metaphysics of Laoutsze, the founder of Taoism, whom he characterised as an "ignorant good man." This judgment may have been formed because Laoutsze acted on the principle that a sage knows how to pass for a fool. The name Laoutsze may be translated "Old child." The philosopher was born with white hair, and no wonder, for the event is said not to have occurred until his mother had carried him in her womb seventy-two, or some say eighty-one, years. His complexion was, according to tradition, white and yellow; his ears were of extraordinary size, and were each pierced with three passages. On each foot he had ten toes, and each hand was ornamented with ten lines. Taoism signifies the way of living, the method of best developing human nature. Some say that Tao was Reason, and compare it with the Logos, or Word of St. John's Gospel; but in reference to its meaning Laoutsze himself said, "Those who know do not tell; those who tell do not know." The book called "Tao Teh King" which Laoutsze left behind him, and which is the Bible of his religion, contains only five thousand words. Along with much rubbish, there is in it not a little that is good about the virtues of humility and unselfishness, culminating in the precept which even Confucius could not receive—to return good for evil. "To the not good," he said, "I would be good in order to make them good."

Instead of asserting themselves, Laoutsze urged his disciples to strive after self-emptiness. His favourite illustration was that of water, which seeks the lowliest places, but which, at the same time, permeates everything, and by its constant dropping pierces even the hardest substances. Emptiness, by which he means freedom from preoccupation and all selfish motives, is indispensable for the reception of truth. The Taoists taught that people become spirits, and are happy in a future world. On one occasion they fought well for an Emperor. Instead of giving to them the earthly rewards for which they had contended, he told them that they were spirits, and would be rewarded in the spiritual world.

Those, however, who were content with their portion in this life had only to take a dose of the elixir of life which the Taoists professed to have discovered, and they might defy death. The last enemy was powerless against their "pills of immortality." Laoutsze was as great a believer in non-interference by the State as was Herbert Spencer, and when we think of the fussy, must-do-something people who annoy their neighbours in the Western world, and of the mischievous philanthropists who demand that everything should be regulated by Government—when we think of these faddists, Laoutsze's doctrine of inaction is very attractive. He enunciated it as follows : "Do nothing, and all things will be done. I do nothing, and the people become good of their own accord." Using a wheel as an illustration, Laoutsze taught that "activity pivots itself upon a centre of rest." When a man can put to rest every desire and become one with the principle of quiescence that animates the universe, he is able to enter into its secrets and to emulate its wonders.

The following extract shows that Laoutsze held with Solomon that "the day of death is better than the day of birth," and with Shakespeare that we are "such stuff as dreams are made of": "Before death comes we shrink from it, as the maiden betrothed to the prince of a neighbouring State once shed tears at the thought of leaving her native soil and going to dwell amongst strangers. But when she found herself in a palace and surrounded by beautiful things, she laughed at the folly of her past tears. When death has taken place, who knows but that we may laugh at the ignorance which made us dread it? There is no certainty in knowledge, and the love of life, as well as the fear of death, may both alike have been mistaken. The man who dreams in the night that he is at a banquet wakes up in the morning to disappointment, and the man who dreams in his slumbers that he shed tears,

17

wakes up to find that a day of festive hunting is before him. Till the morning breaks there is no test to which a dream can be submitted. A great awakening is before us, and then we may know how much of a dream the present life has been."

But though Laoutsze did not value life or fear death, he was averse from war, considering that the least glorious peace is preferable to the most brilliant successes of war, and that the most brilliant victory is but the light from a conflagration.

So much has Taoism degenerated that it is now little better than a system of fortune-telling and an emporium of incantations against evil spirits.

In 250 B.C. eighteen Buddhist missionaries came to China, and they are now commemorated by having their images placed in most large temples. However, inquirers into the missionary problem of that time would have called the Buddhist propaganda in China a decided failure, for it made scarcely any way for three hundred years. Then it was introduced at Court, and adopted by the Imperial Government. By means of this State aid it grew and spread. Buddhism was a beautiful religion when it came to China, but it was soon debased by being mixed with Taoism and with an idolatry, like itself, also imported largely from India. The men who handled it were poor representatives of its founder. The Buddhist Scriptures have suffered even more than the Christian from superficial expositors. Unable to discover the truths underneath myths, symbols, and parables, they have mistaken the outer form for the substance, the shell for the kernel. It is said, for instance, that out of water rose a lotus lily, and out of this the universe; but this was only a simile conveying the idea that as the lotus grows from a seed beneath the water, so each single universe is evolved out of a primitive germ, the first origin of which is veiled in mystery. Everything rises into existence and ebbs away again, is evolved and disappears in an eternal circle. Darwin was anticipated by more than two thousand years. When asked how the first world began, and whence came that eternal law of ceaseless reproduction, Shakya Muni said that the solution of the mystery was beyond the understanding of the finite mind.

Buddhism accounts for the inequalities of earth by its doctrines of heaven, purgatory, transmigration, and nirvana. Instead of a fixed heaven and hell for which no one is good enough or bad enough, it proclaims a heaven and hell of many mansions. Each person goes to his own place—to the place which he has prepared for himself.

> "Our deeds still travel with us from afar,
> And what we have been makes us what we are."

He that is holy will be holy still, and he that is filthy will be filthy still. A good man will be born again better and higher; a bad one will be transmigrated into, say, a hard-worked ass or an unclean cur, or perhaps will vegetate only as a plant. He who is without desire, dead to himself, he alone truly lives. The path of deliverance lies in the renunciation of self, in the extirpation even of the desire to live. Until this is effected we must be born again. Shakya Muni was a spirit in prison 550 times—that is to say, he went through this number of incarnations before he escaped from the dizzy round of birth and death and attained to nirvana, or exemption from birth.

The "Three Precious Ones"—that is, Intelligence, Law, and Church personified in Buddha, or, as they are described by the ignorant, Buddha Past, Buddha Present, and Buddha Future—are three images placed side by side, which are nearly always found in Buddhist shrines, as the "Three Pure Ones" are in Taoist temples. You know Shakya Muni (Intelligence) by the curled hair and curious bump on the top of his head. The second statue (Dharma, i.e., Law) has four hands, two of which are folded in prayer; the third hand holds a rosary, and the fourth a book. The third statue (Samgha, *i.e.*, Church) is two-handed, one hand resting on its knee, the other holding a lotus flower.

The birthday of Shakya Muni—the day upon which he left the house of his parents and the day upon which he became Buddha the enlightened and entered into nirvana—are the three great festivals of Buddhism. Then there is the greatest amount of chanting, of prostrating, and of marching back and forward and round and round on the part of priests in the temples.

Of the five commandments of Buddha, "Thou shalt not kill any living thing; thou shalt not steal; thou shalt not commit any unchaste act; thou shalt not lie; thou shalt not drink any intoxicating liquor," the ordinary Chinese Buddhist obeys whichever suits him, just as those who profess and call themselves Christians do in reference to their Ten Commandments.

At the present time Buddhism is simultaneously derided and advocated, neglected and espoused by the Chinese. Its many inventions are decried by the learned and laughed at by the profligate, but more or less patronised by all. Its mystical atheism cannot satisfy the soul that thirsts for the living God.

Europeans who find it easier to worship from afar than to attend a place of worship near them, are now coquetting with Buddhism as with a fashionable beauty. They notice practices in later Buddhism which resemble Christian institutions, and they say that the latter were copied from the former. This borrowing theory can be disproved by one well-ascertained fact, which Dr. Eitel states in these words: "The whole canon of Buddhist scriptures was compiled and fixed in writing between the years A.D. 412 and 432, or at least seven hundred years after Buddha's death. There is not a single Buddhist manuscript existing which can vie in antiquity and undoubted authenticity with the oldest codices of the Gospels." As to the beauty of holiness, there is little of this in the degenerate Buddhism which those who live in China see.

The Chinese say that Confucianism, Taoism, and Buddhism are one, and certainly there is not much to choose between the last two. Both are thieves, like so many of their votaries. Taoism stole the worst features of Buddhism, and Buddhism stole the best features of Taoism. All three religions agree in this : that they give no light as to the character and intentions of the Ruler of the Universe.

Perhaps we ought to say, before concluding, that there are some 20,000,000 Mahommedans in China, and that these, with the native Christians, are the only Chinese who believe in and worship God in our sense of the word. If it be difficult to discover the number of real Christians in Great Britain, as is proved by the "Do we believe?" correspondence in the *Daily Telegraph*, how much more difficult is it to ascertain how many are in China? It is said that the Roman Catholic Church has about 500,000, and that there are something like 150,000 Protestants.

In the next four chapters we shall describe the state of religion, or rather of superstition, as it actually is : its practice, and not merely its theory.

CHAPTER XXVI

FENGSHUI AND OTHER SUPERSTITIONS

Hard to grasp—The two currents—Geomantic superstitions no longer cope with financial considerations—A missionary's answer—From a fengshui point of view—The green dragon and the white tiger—What are pagodas ?—The geomancer—The almanack—Sellers of lies—Palmists, spirit-mediums, and other humbugs—Planchettes—The phrenologist's answer—Superstitions connected with birth, marriage, and death—Looked to life.

NO superstition has had a more cramping effect upon the mind and life of a people than that which is known in China as Feng- or Fungshui. The word means, literally, wind and water, and certainly the system is as hard to grasp as are wind and water. Fengshui may have been nothing more before the geomancer impostors, the "wind and water doctors," got hold of it than an instinctive groping after sanitary science, and the attention which the Chinese pay to soils, aspects, water, and other potent natural influences is wiser than the neglect of them which is shown by many who consider themselves more scientific. Fengshui is terrestrial astrology. What astrology is to the student of stars feng-shui is to the observer of the surface of our planet. The features of the globe, say its professors, are the reflex of the starry heaven and foretell the fortunes of men no less than does the latter. They also teach that these fortunes are influenced by two currents that run through the surface of the earth. One is the male principle of nature known as the

" Azure Dragon "; the other the " White Tiger," or female principle. To obtain, for instance, a fortunate site for a building or for a grave these two currents should be in conjunction, forming, as it were, a bent arm with their juncture at the elbow.

For a city a place used to be chosen where there was a conjunction of the dragon and the tortoise, an amphitheatre of mountains, perhaps, representing the former and some lower hill the latter. The resemblance had sometimes to be eked out by, say, a temple on the tortoise's head or a pagoda
agon's tail.

a building be put up or a tree cut down in the hood the fengshui may be destroyed, and floods, , and famine may result. This is the argument iaking railways. Railway lines are straight, and straight is thought to be unlucky. However, superstitions cannot cope with financial considera- l when John Chinaman realises that railways, tele- d mines pay, he shames the devil and prefers dollars ii.

Jingpo the elders of the neighbourhood in which a ouse stood assembled to protest against the erection it built with the hope of catching a little fresh air close atmosphere of the unsavoury town. " Our be ruined by the tower," they said. The chief of on met them in solemn conclave. " What is feng- he asked. " Is it not wind and water ? Well, now, ange an amicable compromise. I will give you the you will leave me the air." The Chinese have a se of humour, and this answer prevented what might n a serious riot. Looked at from a fengshui point the Roman Catholic Cathedral, which is the most ous building in the city of Canton, must, when it was t, have been as distasteful to the citizens as was the at least sharp practice, by which its site was obtained.

" Why," they must have asked themselves, " should the French joss-house be so much higher than the uniform level which feng-shui requires ? "

When the United States consul at Nantai put up a flag-staff at his consulate, a demand was made for its removal on fengshui grounds ; as he did not comply, the people contented themselves with making an image of a little devil firing at the flagstaff.

Some Hong Kong and Canton Chinese, when about to erect a factory for making paper by foreign machinery, to save future fengshui trouble consulted the elders of the place near Canton where the building was to be put up about the plans, which were to be of foreign design. These wiseacres passed everything except a tall chimney. Here was a difficulty, for a factory must have a chimney. Some knowing one, however, suggested to try them with two chimneys, and, upon this change being made, the factory was sanctioned. Two of the local students soon afterwards won degrees, which was thought a proof of the wisdom of the decision.

I saw at Wuchow, upon the West River, a telegraph line that is said to have cost at least a hundred heads. When the poles were first put down the people kept on destroying them until they were intimidated by the number of executions mentioned. An individual, or collection of individuals, who erect a pawnshop in a street higher than the other houses must compensate every owner of a house that has been over-topped.

When two buildings are beside one another, the one on the left is said to be built on the green dragon, and the one on the right on the white tiger. The tiger must not be taller than the dragon, or bad luck will result. When it was proposed to construct a telegraph between Canton and Hong Kong the ground of the opposition against it was as follows : Canton means the city of rams or sheep, the mouth of the river is known as the " tiger's mouth " ; the district opposite

A PAGODA

Hong Kong is the " Nine Dragons " (Kau Lung). What more unfortunate combination could be found—a telegraph line to lead the sheep right into the tiger's mouth and among the nine dragons?

To dispel evil influences, or to collect good ones, pagodas which somewhat resemble our coast lighthouses have been built, the number of their stories being always uneven—three, five, seven, nine, eleven. Some say that pagodas are gigantic official umbrellas in stone, the stories being the flounces. Others say that the stories represent the stages through which mortals pass on their way to Nirvana. One theory is that pagodas were for the accommodation of evil spirits so that these gentry might not trouble the houses in the neighbourhood. The fact is, that we know as little about these singular erections as we do about the round towers in Ireland.

The geomancer is the interpreter of the feng-shui superstition. By looking at the wind, the water, the nature of the earth, the conformation of the hills, and so forth, he selects lucky sites for graves. He is a sort of fortune-teller, for the fortunes of the living are supposed to depend upon the burial-place they select for their dead relatives.

It is only natural that in a country like China, so full of water-ways, good feng-shui or good " wind and water," or, in other words, good luck on a journey, should have come to signify good luck in every event of life. The Chinese are in constant fear of saying or doing things in an unlucky time, place, or way, or in the presence of unlucky people. No man thinks of beginning a journey, of laying a foundation-stone, of burying a parent, or of doing anything at all important without consulting an almanack, generally the official one published at Peking. A young man, hearing a cry of distress, ran to the rescue, and found his father buried under the ruins of a fallen wall. " Be patient, my father," he said ; "you have always taught me to do nothing without consulting the almanack. Just wait a little until I see whether this is a suitable day for moving bricks."

There are many kinds of luck-expounders or fortune-tellers. Observe that "seller of lies" who will not look you in the face. He wears large glasses and looks wiser than any man could be. He is sitting in a retired part of the street with a table in front of him, on which are almanacks and other "books," probably not unlike those books of "curious arts" which the converts burned long ago at Ephesus. He resembles a spider waiting for a fly, and he has not long to wait, for his advice is continually asked about the name that should be given to a boy, the day on which he should be sent to school, what trade he should learn, and indeed about almost every detail in life. As to the fee, it is regulated by the paying capacity of the consultant, questions concerning the life of a rich fool being, of course, more difficult to solve than those relating to one who has no cash to throw away.

The following command which was given to the people of Israel must be a great difficulty to the people of China. "There shall not be found with thee one that useth divination, one that practiseth augury, or an enchanter, or a sorcerer, or a charmer, or a consulter with a familiar spirit, or a wizard, or a necromancer" (Deut. xviii. 10, 11). All these are found with the Chinese.

The commonest way in which a fortune-teller consults fate is by means of bamboo or paper slips inscribed with characters. The applicant comes to the table and selects a slip, the diviner dissects the character upon it into its radical and primitive, or in some other way, and writes the parts upon a board lying before him. From these he educes a sentence which contains the required answer. The man receives it as confidently as if he had entered Sybil's cave and heard her voice, pays his fee, and goes away. Other fortune-tellers refer to books, in which the required answer is contained in a sort of equivocal Delphian distich.

Many Chinese may say "A little bird told me," for they consult fortune-tellers who have trained the birds of the air to declare the matter. When the fortune-teller is consulted he takes from its cage a feathered soothsayer that ought to be singing in the air instead of telling lies, and puts it on a table upon which are arranged a number (generally sixty-four) of folded pieces of paper. The bird takes up one in its beak and gives it to its master, who opens it and explains the enigmatical verses that are written inside. The last time I was at Canton I saw one of these fortune-tellers surrounded by a large crowd of bird-witted people.

A Taoist priest takes a plate and places over it a piece of carefully wetted paper. After making mysterious gestures, he gently rubs the paper until figures and scenes appear, and from these he predicts the future.

Another way of fortune-telling is by means of a tortoise-shell and three ancient cash. The fortune-teller puts the cash into the tortoise-shell three times and empties them out before an image of the deity who presides over divination. He observes the relative positions in which they fall, and after comparing them with diagrams that belong to his stock-in-trade pronounces judgment on the matter that is inquired about.

I saw a planchette in a temple near Nanking, and these instruments are not at all uncommon. A large dish is filled with sand, and the two ends of a curved stick are moved over it. The points, guided by a god or devil, answer questions on the sand. The faces and figures of individuals whom clients desire to see are shown in mirrors with the readiness with which the witch of Endor brought up Saul for inspection.

Then there are palmists, hypnotists, and blind men who travel about telling fortunes. The last mentioned are led by boys, and give notice of their approach by means of a ball striking a drum. They are believed to see into the future better than those do who have the use of bodily eyes. Blind slave damsels, who are accredited with the spirit of divination, bring to their masters no small gain by soothsaying. Men and women who in Western lands would be described as spirit-mediums abound. Some calamity befalls a family. A medium is sent for, and is respectfully welcomed. Incense is offered to idols, for the medium always plays into the hands of the priests. She sits down, usually in the seat of honour in the guest-room, and falls into a trance. Suddenly there is a cry, " The spirit has come ! " and the medium slowly begins to speak in an unnatural voice. With an air of great authority she declares what the trouble is and how it may be remedied. Then more paper money and incense are burned, and more prostrations made before the idols. Gradually, with horrible contortions, the medium empties herself, as it were, of the influence.

The observations of Chinese phrenologists are very similar to those of their European confrères, and quite as clever, or more so. The governor of a province sent for a phrenologist and asked him to select among a number of ladies, who were all dressed in the same way, which was his wife. The phrenologist looked at them for a long time without being able to answer. At last he cried out, " It is she out of whose forehead a yellow cloud has just issued forth." Of course, everybody turned round to look at the lady, and the phrenologist equally, of course, guessed at once which was the governor's wife, and pointed her out with a gesture of wisdom.

In China, as elsewhere, many superstitions surround birth, marriage, and death. The day and hour of a child's birth are believed to influence all his after-life, so the fortune-teller makes it his business to cast horoscopes. One fortune-teller acquired a great reputation in a way that was almost accidental. A man who did not quite believe in him came to get his fortune told, but, instead of giving the day and hour when he was born himself, he gave the day and hour of his cat's birth. It so happened that the astrologer, at the time he was consulted, was thinking whether he had put some fish he had bought out of reach of his cat. He therefore murmured, when given the day and the hour, "That cat," and the man who had played the trick, thinking that it was discovered, hurried away and spread abroad the fame of the fortune-teller.

Immediately after a child is born a pair of its father's trousers are put upon the frame of the bedstead, in such a way that the waist shall hang downwards. On the garment is stuck a piece of red paper, having four words written upon it, intimating that *all unfavourable influences are to go into the trousers* instead of afflicting the babe.

One often sees a silver chain or hoop locked round the neck of a small Chinese boy. The father has collected a single cash or small copper coin from a hundred different families. Adding to this money himself he buys a lock for the purpose of locking his son to life, and making a hundred families concerned in his attaining to old age.

The Chinese believe that an eclipse of the sun or of the moon is caused by a dragon trying to eat up that luminary. It is the duty of mandarins to rescue it by frightening away the dragon. They summon Taoist priests to their Yamens, and these burn candles, recite formulæ, and tell the mandarins the number of times they should kneel and knock their heads on the ground. This ceremony is accompanied by a general beating of gongs and drums, and the result is viewed with much complacency, for the people observe that although, perhaps, half of the sun or moon seemed to have been swallowed by the dragon, the attack was beaten off and the injury was not permanent.

This superstition about eclipses has been used to flatter the Emperor of China. Clouds on a certain occasion having prevented the eclipse from being seen, the courtiers repaired to the emperor and felicitated him that the heavens, touched by his virtues, had spared him the pain of witnessing the eating of the sun.

When the writer was at Hong Kong a junk was run down by a steamer just outside of the harbour and many Chinamen were drowned. Several baskets of snakes were sent by the men's friends and released where the junk sank. They thought that the snakes would swallow the souls of the drowned and take them ashore.

It is considered a proof that a man is an exceptionally bad one when he is killed by lightning, or, as the Chinese say, "thunder-struck." On his back it is believed that characters recording his crime may be sometimes discovered.

CHAPTER XXVII

Fly only in straight lines—A haunted house—A service of exorcism—Fight-
ing fiends with fire-crackers—Foolish fears—Suicide—Prophylactics—
Charms—Timidity of spirit—A cash sword—Propitiating evil spirits—
In the hour of death—Three souls—Punishment of dishonest priests—
"The Universal Rescue" feast—View of the intellectual capacity of
spirits.

IT may be doubted whether the Chinese believe in a god,
but there can be no doubt that they believe in devils.
A Chinaman passes the time of his sojourn here in fear of
them. He thinks that evil spirits may assume the form of
snakes and foxes, and that they can enter into human beings.
He fancies that he hears their eerie sound when at night
they come to his house to inflict sickness and other kinds of
bad luck.

Malevolent spirits are supposed to fly only in straight lines,
so city gates must not be opposite one another, or, if they
are, some obstruction must intervene. For the same reason
opposite a window may often be observed an apparently
meaningless wall. A long, straight canal is seldom seen. A
turn is given to it, as is the case with streets, or an island
is formed to break the continuity, and so puzzle the spiritual
influences. On the wall of a house opposite the end of a
street there is nearly always a caution to evil spirits, sometimes cut on a stone brought from a sacred mountain and

let into the wall, to pass on and not trouble the inmates of the house.

A friend of mine in Hong Kong could not let an empty house belonging to him because, on account of a mark on the hall door, it was said to be haunted. He had all the wood-work, and especially the door, repainted. The mark came back. Again the door was painted and again the mark made its appearance. My friend was advised to get a Taoist priest to exorcise the devil. The priest said that if he were successful in the first attempt his fee would be only five dollars. My friend told him that if he did not get the devil out in his first attempt he would get no pay. The priest went with a bottle and searched round each room. After get-ting to the top room and hunting about for a while he called out, " I have caught the devil and have him corked up in my bottle." The mark, which we may suspect the priest himself used to make, appeared no more, and the house was soon let. West of the Suez Canal you seldom meet a man who has seen a ghost; east of it you seldom find a man who has not seen one.

In the reception-hall of a house at Canton I once saw a service of exorcism. It was thought that the master of the house, who had lately died, being offended by something, was inflicting sickness upon his son. A Taoist priest was called in. He arranged six wide bamboo tubes upon the floor, and on each he placed a saucer. Then he fastened to the sick boy's chest a card, or board, like that which Chinese criminals are made to wear describing their crimes. Having dressed himself in a dirty yellow official robe, and taken in his hand a sword, he, in company with the son who was being afflicted, marched round the bamboos six times, each time dashing a saucer to pieces with the point of his sword. Then more saucers were put on, and the operation was going to be repeated when I left. It was done to drive down the mischievous ghost to his own place.

The amount of money spent upon fire-crackers to frighten away evil spirits from weddings and funerals, and when people start upon journeys, is enormous.

The habit of fighting fiends with fire-crackers once emphasised a sermon I was preaching. A parade service was being held at a fort near Hong Kong, in a verandah that overlooked a Chinese village. Suddenly a roar of crackers, intended to drive away evil spirits from a wedding, came up and made me almost inaudible. I pointed to where the fusilade came from and said, "It would be well if we Christians would take as much trouble to fight the devils of drink, gambling, impurity, and such-like, as do those heathen below there to drive away the evil spirits which they ignorantly dread."

Chinese parents will inflict terrible burns upon their children to exorcise the evil spirits with which they fancy the children have become possessed. They have been known also to crush the body of a deceased infant into an indistinguishable mass, in order to prevent the devil which inhabited it from returning to vex the family.

A mother is sometimes tormented with the fear that her child may be only a spirit, come to stay for a little while. Should a child grow sick unto death, it may be put outside the door of the house to die. This is because the parents believe that in falling ill and dying their child has proved to be only an evil spirit. It may be done, too, to prevent the spirit of the dead from finding its way back and haunting the house.

More people kill themselves in China in proportion to the population than in any other country. In a large number of cases the motive is revenge, for the spirit of the dead is believed to haunt and injure the living person who has been the cause of the suicide. I heard of one coolie who attempted to kill himself because he received ten cash (about a farthing) less than he expected, and of another who sat at the door of

somebody who had cheated him and starved to death. A
certain Mrs. Feng had words with a Mrs. Wang about a pig.
The former threatened to take her own life, but was anticipated by the latter jumping into a canal.

Curious are the prophylactics which are used against evil
spirits. To cure or guard against ague, for instance, a man
should write the names of the eight demons of ague on paper,
and then eat the paper with a cake.

Most Chinese babies are the unconscious owners of "lucky
cash" attached to them by a red string. On their caps are
lucky characters or an image of the "old man" who
especially looks after children. We wear on our watch chains
coins and other things, and call them charms. The Chinese
wear charms too, but they believe what we have ceased to
believe, their power to influence events.

Wicked men flee when no man pursueth, and evil spirits,
according to the Chinese, are not less timid. They run away
from a house over the door of which long, narrow leaves are
nailed, because they mistake them for swords. They are
afraid of their own shadows when seen in a mirror, therefore
a small utensil of this kind is often put upon or near a bed
to scare them. So also is a knife with which a person has
been killed, when a charm so valuable against evil spirits
can be procured. Evil spirits are also very nervous about
nails which have been used in fastening up a coffin. Sometimes such a nail is beaten out into a wire, encased in silver,
and put on the wrist or ankle of a boy. Doors are often
made circular because then, being emblematic of the sun,
they are sacred, and evil spirits cannot go through them.
A tiger's head painted on a square board is put up to
frighten evil spirits, who are supposed to be much afraid
of this animal. One reason why cow-hide leather is never
put into the soles of the shoes provided for the dead is,
because a ruling spirit of the other world is believed to have
a head resembling that of a cow.

It has occasionally happened that in different localities men lost their queues as if by some mysterious conspiracy. An invasion of cholera could not have frightened the people more. It was decided that it was the work of evil spirits, and there was a run upon charm manufactories. It was thought that four Chinese characters, mysteriously woven together and wrapped up in the queue, would ward off the spirits.

What is called a cash sword is considered to be efficacious in keeping away evil spirits. This sword, which is generally two feet long, is made of about a hundred of the coins called cash, fastened on iron rods. The sword is often hung up above beds.

Those stone lions, which resemble the late Lord Salisbury more than the lions for which they are intended, on the roofs of important Chinese buildings, are probably charms against diabolical agency. May it not be symbolical of the fact that the devil " goes about like a roaring lion " ?

When a man becomes ill or loses money, it is sometimes thought that these misfortunes come from the enmity of the spirit of a dead person who was offended, either in the present or in a former state of being. In view of such suspicions, the family prepare suits of paper clothing, paper money, hats, shoes, umbrellas, even paper steamers, and an offering of meat and drink. Then Taoist priests are invited to burn the paper offerings and present the eatables according to established method of propitiating inimical spirits.

The Chinese when dying are generally terrified by the evil spirits they fancy they hear and see. A miserly merchant on his death-bed shouted out: " Don't you see the evil spirits? They are calling for money. Get them money or they will have me ! " His wife had to unlock the box and bring out strings of cash with which to appease the evil spirits. Contrast this with the death of a Chinese Christian child of which I have heard. She surprised the neighbours by saying she had not seen any evil spirits. She said: " There are no evil spirits near me; Christ is with me, waiting to take me, and why should I be afraid? "

The Chinese believe that they have three souls. At death one soul remains with the corpse, another is transferred to a tablet which a mandarin or literary person attending the funeral touches with a vermilion pencil; the third goes to purgatory. They vividly realise punishment after death. In the North, for instance, when water is scarce it is considered a great sin to waste it, and people believe that in the future world they will have to drink exactly as much dirty water as they have unnecessarily fouled in the world here. To save himself from this, a man who is conscious of spoiling water burns a paper representation of a cow. In this way he sends into the spirit world the cow to drink the dirty water for him. For each species of crime a special purgatorial punishment has been devised, modelled upon the tortures of earthly Chinese prisons and courts of injustice. Of these one of the quaintest is for dishonest priests who have taken money for saying prayers and have not done so. They have to read continually, in the spirit world, litanies from books badly printed, with only dim lamps to give them light.

How very similar the Chinese think the world beyond is to the one here may be seen by a feast called " The Universal Rescue," which is given from time to time to the hungry and destitute spirits who have no near male relatives surviving to make offerings of food. For the entertainment a spirits' house is roughly built, twenty feet long, eight high, and six broad. It is usually divided into five apartments, one a living room for ladies, and another for gentlemen, with a bathroom off each where they can wash after their journey. The fifth, or middle room, is for the " King of the Spirits," whose business it is to prevent his subjects from quarrelling over the good things provided. On the spirits' house a notice is placed, inviting the "good gentlemen" and "faithful ladies" in the spirit world to occupy it and "behave with propriety" while doing so. Amongst the many kinds of food provided for the feast there is one which shows great thoughtfulness. This is a species of gruel or salted paste, and is intended for spirits who may have left this world by having their heads cut off. They have no teeth or mouth to eat the rest of the menu, but it is supposed they can get this paste or gruel into their throats.

Sometimes no house is built for the spirits from the other world when they get a day out to visit their old earthly haunts. Economical hospitality, however, is provided in this way. On the top of a cone-shaped bamboo frame are placed thin slices of pork and fish. The sides are covered with more slices, so that there appears to be a solid mass of sliced fish, flesh or fowl. Again the spirits experience the hollowness of this world, for instead of the pile of food that they require after their journey, on removing the fish and pork coating there is nothing but bamboozling bamboo! The Chinese are deceivers ever; when not deceiving men they keep their hand in by practising on ghosts.

The Chinese have a low opinion of the intellectual capacity of evil spirits, and think that they can be easily deceived. If a man announce the death of a parent or brother he will probably laugh much. This is not heartlessness, but is done in order that the spirits may not have the satisfaction of knowing that they have caused sorrow. If parents have only one boy they will sometimes call him by a girl's name, and put earrings into his ears, so that evil spirits may think that he is a girl and not take him away. Sometimes they get him adopted into another family, and allow him to spend some of his time in it. In this way they think that they prevent the spirits from knowing which family owns the boy.

A funeral procession generally proceeds by some unusual

circuitous route. This is to puzzle the spirit of the departed and prevent him coming back to haunt the house.

If the spirit who is responsible for rain does not send it, he is sometimes put in strong sunlight for a while to let him see how he enjoys it. Occasionally even stronger measures are taken with him. A year ago a correspondent from Canton wrote thus in a newspaper, "Magistrate Fung, of the district of Hing Ning, having prayed without result for rain, dealt with the Demon of Drought in the following manner. He had an effigy made of paper and bamboo to represent this demon. Then he ordered policemen to arrest the effigy, bring it chained into his court and make it kneel down before him. On its arrival the magistrate banged on the table, scolded the effigy in a loud voice for causing the drought, and ordered him to be taken out and beheaded. Upon this some gentry of the place came forward, and begged the magistrate to give the demon three days' grace. If after this he did not bring rain let his head be cut off; they would be security for him. The magistrate nodded assent, the effigy was taken out of the court and placed on the top of the city wall. Not quite three days after there were thunder and rain."

After relating a similar occurrence, Abbé Huc asks: "Les Chinois de nos jours croient-ils à ces pratiques ridicules, à ces extravagances? Pas le moins du monde. On ne doit voir en tout cela qu'une manifestation extérieure, purement mensongère. Les habitants du céleste empire observent les superstitions antiques, sans y ajouter foi. Ce qui a été fait dans les temps passés, on le pratique encore aujourd'hui, par la seule raison qu'il ne faut pas changer ce que les ancêtres ont établ'."

M to U

A TEMPLE.

To face page 270.

CHAPTER XXVIII

OUTSIDE AND INSIDE A TEMPLE

The buildings of a temple—A holy show—A confused idea—The dust of
ages—A mixture of fear and fun—The soul of an idol—"Silks,
porcelains, and fancy gods"—Use of a temple—The first thing done—
What is prayed for—Opium given—Tears of blood—Patrons of vice—
Animals worshipped, also stocks and stones—What meant by worship—
Few services in temples—Not an easy chair—Religious processions—
Dragon Boat and other festivals—Trying to cheat God.

THE buildings of an important temple in China are
usually ranged one behind another on terraces, and
reached by granite steps. The centre of the stairs is often
levelled down and carved, an arrangement intended for spirits
flying in and out. Passing through the entrance gate you
get a general impression of elaborately sculptured pillars,
of tiled roofs turned up at the corners, of bronze and stone
lions and dragons, of frolicsome dolphins in bright green
crockery. Is it a house of merchandise? you ask, when
you see in the courtyards stalls for the sale of incense-
sticks, gaily coloured candles, faith-healing medicines, fortune-telling writings, and of everything upon which an
ecclesiastical if not an honest penny may be turned.

There is a market outside most temples, and there are
many restaurants and portable kitchens. In the neighbourhood medicine-men, conjurers, exhibitors of monstrosities,
and many other people of that kind establish themselves.

If the temple be at all important there is a permanent stage in front of it, upon which plays are acted for the diversion of gods and men. In the same way the dramatic performances of ancient Athens were connected with the worship of Dionysius.

To entertain a local god and his attendants on his birthday, and have a good time themselves, an association of workmen made a large temporary theatre of bamboo and matting at Kowloon, opposite Hong Kong. As the temple was some distance from this edifice, the gods were brought from their home and placed in a small shrine. We saw the transportation. Each divinity was borne on the shoulders of twelve bearers dressed in yellow silk robes. After these other men, gorgeous in red and gold embroidered clothes, carried highly ornamented glass receptacles containing food for the gods, should their divinity-ships require refreshment during the outing. In front and in rear of the procession were the usual umbrella-bearers, lantern-bearers, and tablet-bearers, having on their heads much-decorated hats, and on their shoulders official scarves. It was hot work supporting their dignity, so they had large white-feather fans stuck in their girdles. There was much noise caused by the inevitable pipes, drums, and cymbals, by the masters of the ceremonies shouting orders, and by the laughter even of those who took prominent parts in the heavenly pic-nic. Salvoes of crackers greeted the holy show as it passed the corners of streets.

When no one will go to the expense of giving a regular theatrical entertainment on the birthday of a god, poor parishioners sometimes supply a make-shift substitute. They erect a small mat shed opposite the entrance to the temple, and in this they place cases like book-cases, having in them small figures representing scenes from celebrated plays. Shrubs and flowers adorn the sides of the edifice, and glass chandeliers with lustres hang from the roof. In galleries there are those who make a noise called music.

A Temple.

At the main door of temples are grated receptacles for crackers to be exploded, and in front the poles and tablets which mark the Yamens of mandarins. In fact a temple is a copy of a great man's house. When a festival is in progress a visitor has to pass through lines of decrepit, decaying beggars who have reduced the display of abjectness and sickening sores to a fine art.

In addition to the idol or other curio which he may have bought from a dishonest priest, the only thing which the ordinary " Christian " globe-trotter gets from the inside of a heathen temple is a confused idea of ugly images, altar vases, candlesticks, lanterns, draperies, artificial flowers, zinc incense burners, and tinsel offerings. He understands as little of what he sees as did that Persian visitor to London who wandered into Westminster Abbey, and then related to his countrymen the horror which overwhelmed him when, as he approached a huge idol, it opened its mouth and roared loudly. And yet we think that organ music is soothing !

The dust of ages is in Chinese temples, and cleanliness is very far from their godliness. Some idols are washed once a year, but the majority never seem to change their clothes or to take a bath. This, however, is not for want of the means of washing, for a basin of water and a paper towel are often placed amongst the offerings to the gods.

Though afraid to disregard them, the Chinese freely laugh at the objects and ceremonies of their worship. The religion of most of them is a mixture of fear and fun. If a missionary is sarcastic about the idols after the manner of Elijah and the writer of the 115th Psalm, their worshippers are not offended, but rather pleased, because they do not love the idols but only fear them.

I have often observed idols being repaired and painted up for a temple, and have thought of Isaiah's graphic description of the manufacture of graven images. Inside, or it may be outside, shops which deal in this kind of goods they are to be seen lying in what looks like old lumber heaps. "No image-maker worships the gods," says a proverb. "He knows what stuff they are made of." As a matter of fact an idol is considered of no importance until a soul is put into it. This is done in the following way. Several small thin plates of silver are joined together by silver chains or wire and placed on a piece of cotton wool. Then a fly is put into the wool, and wool, fly, and silver plates are placed in the hollow between the idol's shoulders and a small door shut upon them. The fly dies and its life goes into the silver plates that represent the soul. The soul thus vivified makes the idol, which before was nothing, a divine person, deified by a fly! I see that a shopman in Shanghai is advertising "silks, porcelains, and fancy gods."

A Chinese temple is used for many of the purposes which hotels and public-houses serve in Great Britain. It is not a drinking-place, certainly, but people smoke opium in it and it is as much a lounge for idlers as are some of our free libraries. Dirty people, apparently in the last stage of decay, lie about. Barbers and pedlars do their business within temple precincts. Farm produce and utensils, boats and coffins are stored in temples. A court of a temple is frequently hired for a dinner party or other entertainment. For a consideration you can lay your bed amongst the gods and sleep the night. On the door of a court may be seen the blue and red curtain that indicates that gambling goes on within. The cocks and hens of the temple-keeper walk about as if the building belonged to them. Why not? They are far more innocent than are the astrologers, geomancers, and physiognomists who make the place a den of thieves.

The first thing worshippers in Chinese temples do, after kow-towing and knocking the ground with their foreheads, is to take from the altar two pieces of bamboo root having a concave and a convex surface. These they pass through incense flame and throw as dice would be thrown. If the round surface of both turn up it is a sign that the god is unwilling to hear and grant the petition; if one surface is round and the other flat he is engaged, or cannot be bothered, or will not do what he is requested to do. However, worshippers generally go on throwing the wood until it fall as they want it to fall. Having discovered in this way that the god is propitious, the votary makes his petition, and a priest or the temple-keeper strikes the large bell and drum that stand alongside the principal altar in every temple. This is to call the god to attention, for, as it was explained to me, he has so much to attend to that if called by word of mouth only he might be too busy or too tired to listen. Another way of ascertaining the divine will is to take from an altar, where there is always at least one ready, a receptacle made of a joint of bamboo in which are sticks about eight inches long, having numbers upon them. The tube is shaken and the number on the stick that falls first out is noted. It is then given to the temple-keeper, and he supplies one or two strips of paper or parchment, having on them a corresponding number. The papers contain writing about the matter prayed for, so oracular that it cannot be understood, or else something that is no better than a truism.

By this or similar means people try to get from the gods tips for betting or enlightenment that may enable them to guess correctly in the lotteries where so many seek fortune.

In religion, as it now is in China, there is very little that uplifts morally, much less spiritually. The prayers people pray in the temples nearly all involve the principle of a bargain, or betoken slavish fear, or are for directing dreams and other things that may help on mundane matters. A woman of Ningpo, who used to spend all the money she could get on incense-sticks, candles, and other offerings, was asked what advantage she expected from doing so. She replied that she hoped to induce the god to allow her, when born again, to be a man, which would be great promotion.

Paper images of women may sometimes be seen fixed in an inverted position to the rails of an altar. It is thought by their daughters-in-law, husbands, or whoever the sufferers may be, that the women whom the images represent will be changed in their lives, and especially in their tempers, by the action of the god. Paper figures of men are also affixed by mothers, wives, or concubines for the same reason.

In the lower apartments and courts of a temple at Faatee, opposite Canton, I saw on a festival in the first month quite a thousand women kow-towing and manipulating lighted materials in different ways in order to get a good husband, manage a bad one, or be blessed with male offspring. In upper rooms of the temple men were doing the same in reference to wives and sons.

When a woman has been blessed with offspring she goes to a temple to offer incense on the thirtieth day after the birth of a boy, and on the fortieth after that of a girl.

Seeing on one occasion the mouth of an idol smeared over with what looked like tar, I asked for an explanation, and was told that women afflicted with opium-using husbands pray that these self-indulgent ones may be induced to smoke less of the family income. When a wife thinks that the prayer is answered, she puts opium on the mouth of the god to reward him.

A less dissipated god is the god of wealth, as represented by images which I have sometimes seen. In these he was dressed in sackcloth, and red paint figuring tears of blood was under his eyes. He was weeping because his father had died and he could not share with him a fortune that had just come to him. Would this grieve you as much, young men of Britain?

Beside the altar in most temples there is a box covered

with silk or cloth standing upon a pedestal. This contains the seal of the god, and it is stamped upon paper charms or clothes, for the healing of the sick or the exorcising of devils.

People take a vow to keep a lamp burning before some idol in his temple for a month, a year, or some specified time. They usually pay the temple-keeper to buy the oil and trim the lamp.

Some of the divinities are patrons of vice, as Tu Chiêng Kui, the god of gamblers, and Ngú Hieng Kui, the god of thieves. The latter, when on earth, once stole a kettle for cooking rice. His mother scolded him for depriving people of the means of cooking their food, and advised him to bring it back to the place from which he took it. He said that the light of morning would soon appear and that he would be detected. The kind-hearted woman replied that if he would make the attempt, the heavens would be darkened so that he could return it in safety. He started off with the kettle and took it back unseen with the assistance of supernatural darkness. To the god of thieves people burn incense-sticks before going on a robbing expedition, as Sicilian bandits say prayers to a saint.

Some Chinese worship different kinds of animals. The monkey, when an idol, is represented as a man sitting, the face only being like a monkey. "His Excellency the Holy King" is the title under which this creature is worshipped. His image may be seen at the temple of The Five Genii in Canton. Often his name is written upon a slip of paper and used instead of an image. The monkey is believed to have control over hobgoblins, witches, and elves, and to be able to give success to human endeavours. A black monkey is regarded as the servant of the god of prostitutes, and so is a white rabbit. The fox has the seals belonging to high offices of government in his keeping, and is therefore worshipped by mandarins.

(An image of a winged tiger standing on its hind legs, and holding a coin in its mouth or paws, is worshipped by gamblers. Many gambling dens have this sign over the door.)

A dog, the dragon, a white cock, and other animals, real and imaginary, are also objects of worship. There is, too, the worship of large trees and of curiously-shaped stones which has prevailed amongst nearly all nations of antiquity. These stocks and stones often represent the gods of land and grain, and may be seen on altars in the country and at the corners of streets with sticks of incense burning before them.

When Confucianism was the only religion of China there was no idolatry in the empire, but when Buddhism and Taoism were recognised by the Government, State gods were invented. Of these the three principal are Fû-hsî, the god of medicine, Kwan Yü, the god of war, and Wan-ch'ang, the god of literature.

High officials are obliged at certain times to do acts of worship before these and other gods, and literary and military sages. In spring and autumn ceremonies are performed by mandarins in honour of the god of war and of Confucius, and incense is burned to Heaven and Earth, to the Mountains and the Streams, to the Wind, to Thunder and Rain. These last are not considered to be gods, but servants of Heaven who are able to benefit or injure mankind. The objects which the Emperor yearly or half-yearly worships at Peking, the mandarins in the provinces, as his representatives, have also to worship, and on the Emperor's birthday, or in mourning for his death, they must rejoice or lament with three kneelings and nine knockings in the temple which is dedicated to him in each provincial city.

Before a Chinese general goes to war he officially worships, kneeling down and pouring wine on the ground. When he has finished, a cup of wine is thrown upon his flag and the master of ceremonies cries out, "Unfurling the flag, victory is obtained; the cavalry advancing merit is perfected."

I do not know what a sea-general or admiral does, but this is, in some places, the worship which is offered to the god of the sea by the number one man of a Chinese junk before starting on a voyage. He spreads at the bow a sheet of paper, and on this places some simple altar furniture. Then he sacrifices a cock by cutting its throat and lets it bleed on the paper. When the blood dries, the paper is burnt.

It is, however, difficult always to discover what the Chinese mean by worship. Very often no more is meant than reverencing and paying respect. The mandarins are too intelligent and well-educated not to know that, for instance, the fox has nothing to do with their seals of office, but because the ignorant people think that it has they pretend to reverence this animal.

There are few services as we understand them in temples. When they do take place the so-called music is furnished for the most part by drums, horns, gongs and pipes. The birthday of the god is the time when the postures and impostures of priests may best be seen.

The only thing that at all resembles a sermon is the occasional reading aloud of the Sacred Edict. This is a collection of moral essays, if not written at least published by the Emperor Yung Ching at the close of the seventeenth century.

I saw a procession to and service in a temple in the native city of Shanghai in order to pray off plague. How much more efficacious it would be, I thought, if those numerous priests, divesting themselves of gorgeous ecclesiastical clothes and putting aside deafening bells and cymbals, would clean the streets.

The Rev. Dr. Norman M'Leod, who was a big, burly man, was once in a boat with a thin, little, frail-looking brother minister. As they were crossing the Highland loch, one of those fierce, quick mountain storms came down, and the boat was in danger. "Brother," said the little minister, "let us pray together." "Na! na!" said the Highland boatman; "the wee one can pray, but the big one maun tak' an oar!" That is sound theology, but it would not suit the purpose of any kind of Chinese priest.

In a few temples in China I have seen a chair which certainly was not an easy one. It was a sedan, intended to be carried by means of poles on men's shoulders. On the seat, back, and arms of the chair knives with their edges upwards were fixed. When the god is prayed to for rain and none comes, the head-man of the village orders a religious procession, sits in the chair on the knives without clothes (he is a sort of ex-officio chairman), and is carried a certain number of times round the temple or village. It is thought that this should soften the god's heart even more than the prohibition of pork, which is often made with the same end in view under similar circumstances. Sir Henry Blake, when Governor of Hong Kong, bought one of these knife chairs at a village temple as a curio, and his A.D.C. told me that the head-man said that he was glad the chair was gone, as he had experienced one ride on its knives and did not hanker after another.

It would take too much space to describe even the most important of the religious festivals that are held from time to time. The one, however, that most attracts the attention of foreigners is the feast of lanterns, which begins upon the fifteenth day of the first month. Parents who have been blessed with children in the past year, or who wish an addition to their family, present lanterns at a temple devoted to a goddess called "Mother." The relations of a bride often send to her a lantern representing a god holding a child by the hand. If in the second year she has not had a child a lantern representing an orange is sent. The characters for an orange and for "make haste" being similar, the lantern is a punning reminder of her duty.

DRAGON FESTIVAL.

To face page 280

Lanterns of every conceivable form are sold. They resemble elephants, dragons, horses, lions, crabs, shrimps, beetles, butterflies, flowers, fruits, and so on. Human faces are caricatured, and in some lanterns figures are made to move round and round by heated air.

There are at the beginning of spring various kinds of religious processions by day and night. In one a life-sized buffalo made of bamboo and paper is carried about by certain officials and then burnt. Believing that to get a fragment of it brings good luck, the crowd rush at the blazing quadruped. In another procession a dragon is represented, but it resembles more a monstrous centipede, the legs of the men who move it being plainly visible. The passage of the dragon through the streets is thought to dispel evil influences, especially plague and other kinds of sickness.

In these processions boys and girls, dressed as heroes and heroines of past ages, ride on horseback or seated under gaily decorated pavilions of wood, are borne on the shoulders of men.

In religious processions the idols walk by men getting inside of them, or else they are carried on chairs.

A Chinese serving with the Hong Kong company of the Royal Engineers knew enough English to ask if he might go to church for three days. As he was not a Christian the request seemed extraordinary until he explained that he wished to attend the Dragon Boat Festival.

This festival is held on the fifth day of the fifth moon in memory of Wat Yuen, a minister of state who drowned himself because he could not get his reforms carried out. It is a sort of serio-comic Oxford and Cambridge boatrace. The boats, which are supposed to be searching for the body of the patriot, are from fifty to a hundred feet in length, and three or four feet wide. Some of them at Canton carry as many as one hundred and fifty men. The men sit two abreast, and rapidly propel the boat by means of short paddles, to the accompaniment of drums and gongs placed at intervals along the centre of the boat. A man with a fan or a flag in each hand regulates the movements of the scullers. The boat has a dragon's head with open mouth and long whiskers in the bow, and a dragon's tail over the stern. It is decorated with red flags and umbrellas. At the last festival at Canton there was in one boat a man dressed as a mandarin with an opium pipe and money bag to caricature an unpopular official. Small parcels of boiled rice packed in leaves, representing the offerings fishermen threw into the river when seeking for the body, are eaten during this festival.

Dragon-boats are thought to drive away plague. This notion is derived from the fact that from about the date of the festival onwards the virulence of the plague begins to abate.

Very picturesque were the thousands of decorated real boats and miniature paper ones that we saw during the festival in the harbour of Aberdeen, which is a considerable village in Hong Kong. And the enormous crowds of spectators that lined the shore were so good-humoured and well behaved. "Why," said a British police inspector to us, "if you were in a mob like that in England you would be lucky if you kept your shirt."

On the tenth night of the eighth month the moon is thought to be largest, and then a festival in her honour is held. "Moon cakes" are offered to the luminary, and afterwards eaten by the worshippers. Friends exchange all sorts of moon-shaped presents.

The Chinese have yet to learn the truth which St. Paul insisted on, probably thinking of heathen superstition, that God is not mocked. Miss Gordon Cumming tells us, in her "Wanderings in China," that in one temple which she entered she noticed that little strips of red paper were pasted over the eyes of the idols. On inquiring why this was done, the priest explained that these were prayers to the several gods, telling them that repairs were necessary, and beseeching them kindly to retire from the temple till it were again made fit for their presence.

Chinamen are as convinced that they can mock God as are perhaps the majority of Englishmen. Under the pretence that the gods are content with the spirit of things, sacrifices of no value are offered to them, such as a smear of blood, a tuft of feathers, a decoction made of pig-skin instead of opium, while the real thing goes to the crafty priests.

"Do the idols really partake of the sacrifices?" asked a missionary.

"No," was the prompt and cynical reply of a hearer. "Nobody would offer oblations if they weighed an ounce the less for the family feast."

Oranges, which look better than they taste, are kept for giving in the temple, just as a doubtful coin is reserved for the offertory in "Christian" England.

A Chinese, in order to insure for the future, subscribes two or three hundred dollars to a temple. He has it registered as a thousand dollars, hoping that the god will be deceived in this simple way. When storm-signals are put up at Hong Kong, dozens of little paper junks are thrown by the Chinese into the sea. They do this to fool the god into thinking that the paper presentment is the original, so that he may wreak his wrath upon the former and spare the latter.

An association is formed for visiting a sacred mountain and worshipping at the temples to be found there. Then perhaps it occurs to the members that it would be easier and cheaper to bring the mountain to Mahomet. This is done by worshipping after a feast an image of the mountain god at a paper "mountain." The worshippers think that the divinity will not distinguish between the mock and the real mountain!

The Chinese do not even think that the gods can take care of themselves. When the Taiping rebels captured the city of Ningpo, an old priest fled to the house of the missionaries

for safety. They gave him asylum, but could not help askin
him why the gods did not protect their priest. The poo
man replied that they had all returned to heaven in grea
alarm.

The people go to a particular temple in Ningpo on one da
in the year to pray for the preservation of their homes fror
lightning, regardless of the fact that the temple has bee
struck more than once.

CHAPTER XXIX

MONKS AND PRIESTS

A contemptuous toleration—Good beggars—Roast duck for supper—A
"purgatory pick-purse" traffic—A bank for the spirit world—A hint to
Western clergymen—Ecclesiastical vestments—"Bald-headed asses"—
"Buddha is such a kind god"—Vain repetitions—Praying-wheels and
circulating libraries—No thought relaxations—"Need not buy rice"—
"Let-live societies"—A monastery described—Nunneries.

THE first monks of Buddhism in China were not priests,
and they were even more despised than are their
successors, for their abandonment of father, mother, brothers
and sisters, and their renunciation of marriage and the hopes
of offspring, seemed a giving up of the highest conception of
duty that a Chinese forms. In self-defence they became
priests and received a contemptuous toleration, as their official
work was considered to be of use in the affairs of life and
especially in those of death.

Many of the monasteries in China are endowed either with
land or with money, or with a tribute of rice, but usually with
not enough to defray expenses. This being the case, the
grey-robed monks come down into the thoroughfares of men,
and calling attention to their wants by a gong, ply the craft of
mendicancy. Both Buddhist and Taoist priests are adepts at
tricking money out of simpletons. Two of the former, seeing
some fat ducks in front of a house, began to weep. A woman
came out and inquired what was the matter. "We know,"

they answered, " that the souls of our fathers have passed into
the bodies of these creatures, and the fear we feel of your killing
them will certainly make us die of grief." The birds were
at length handed over to the safe keeping of the " bonzes,"
and that night there was roast duck for supper in the
presbytery.

When people mourn their dead, priests ply a " purgatory
pick-purse " traffic. They tell the wife and the mother of a
dead man it has been revealed to them that he is in great
misery in purgatory, and that the only thing to be done for
his release is to hold a three days' service. The family
anxiously inquire for what sum they can obtain such a service.
After careful calculation the priests submit an estimate, and
the money is got somehow. Perhaps on the third day the
principal priest will discover that though the poor man has
been nearly liberated from the pit, a little more money is
required to get him quite over the brink. This is easily
believed, because the priests teach that the "spirits in prison "
are subject to the same doorkeepers, gaolers, and executioners
as torment people in earthly Chinese gaols, and that these
have all to be bribed. During the three days' service, too,
the priests must be entertained well, and also the anxious
friends who come to inquire how the work of liberation
progresses.

The less unselfish object of Taoist religious services is to
appease the spirits of the dead and prevent them from injuring
the living.

The priests conduct these services in a sing-song mechanical
way. They talk and laugh and smoke in the midst of them.
This may not be irreverence in the eyes of a broad-minded
Deity, but it looks so to those of us who are not habituated to
it. Then the priests have organised a bank for the spirit
world, and periodically announce their intention of remitting
money on a certain day. In this bank the provident make
deposits, and believe that they can draw upon them after

death. "Keep your certificates," say the spiritual bankers, "and give them to some trustworthy friend to burn after your death, and in this way they will reach you in the world beyond."

About twenty years ago a priest erected a sort of wooden sentry-box in a street in Peking. Long and sharp nails were driven into the box on all sides. In it his Reverence took his stand, and declared his intention of remaining there until the sum required for building the temple for which he pleaded was collected. The points of the nails prevented him from sitting down or even leaning in any position. For two years he stood his sufferings, which were mitigated as time went on by the withdrawal of the nails one by one, as the money which each was held to represent was collected from the passers-by. We mention this case as a hint to Western clergymen who are raising money to build churches.

There are gradations of monks, and according to his reputation for sanctity, length of service, and other claims, one may rise from being a servitor who performs menial offices to officiating priest, or even to abbot.

No monk is allowed more than one set of garments, and these he wears both day and night. When officiating, Buddhist priests are usually vested in yellow cloaks made of many pieces patched together to represent the rags of poverty. The cloaks are fastened across the left breast, leaving the right arm bare. Their heads are clean shaven twice a month, hence the appellations, "bald-headed asses" and "bald-headed turnips," which are sometimes given to them. On their heads three, six, or nine scars are made, by allowing as many pastilles soaked in oil to burn out on them. This is done at their ordination to insure that the vows which they take with the burning shall make an impression upon them. The nails on the fingers of the higher clergy are allowed to grow to a great length, and cleanliness is considered by them to be worldly and irreligious.

Taoist divines do not shave their heads, but fasten the hair on the top of the head with a pin or skewer.

Some monks never leave their cells, receiving food through a hole in the door. This food is, for those who are true to their vows always, vegetable; meat, fish, eggs, milk, and butter being considered sinful to eat. There are monks, however, who will eat and drink like other mortals. One of these, being remonstrated with for doing so, smiled and said, "Buddha is such a kind god that he pays no attention to these minor details."

Even his identity, as symbolised by his name, a monk has to give up, and take in exchange a so-called religious appellation.

In their desire to show contempt for the things of sense many monks voluntarily go beyond the routine of slavish obedience that is required of them. Not content with starving, flogging, and burning themselves, they invent for their private use tortures that would not discredit a Chinese executioner.

The expression on the features of most monks is one of blank abstraction, which is probably largely due to their repeating Pali or Sanskrit words, the meaning of which they do not understand. The repetitions are marked by beads, and at services by an acolyte ringing a bell or striking a wooden, pot-bellied fish that has a large eye, signifying watchfulness. As if this devotion were not mechanical enough, praying-wheels are sometimes used. I have heard of one revolving by means of steam from a tea-kettle, so that tea and prayers can be made at the same time.

Many monks being too ignorant or too lazy to read, put some of the one hundred and twenty-eight sacred books into cylinders and turn them round. This is an easy way of getting through a circulating library, which we commend to novel-readers.

Buddhists believe that they approach Nirvana when they abstract themselves from earthly desires, even from thought itself. One monk passed nine years with his eyes fixed upon a wall. In most monasteries there is a "Hall of Contemplation," where, in nooks curtained off, "holy men" spend weeks and months on their knees contemplating.

The relaxations of more mundane monks are, for the most part, opium-smoking and cricket-fighting. The latter mild sport is apparently considered one of the legitimate clerical amusements of China, as the angler's art is in Britain.

In China the moral character of priests is thought a matter of indifference. They are represented as villains in popular dramas and novels. Criminals, in order to avoid arrest and punishment, sometimes shave their heads and enter monasteries. Another way priests are obtained is by the purchase of boys, who are brought up to the business. Priests receive money for exorcising with charms and liturgies evil spirits, and for engaging in worship in private houses. Some get so much outdoor relief in this way that it is said they need not buy any rice.

Taoist priests eat meat and do not shave their heads. The priests of Confucianism are rather professors of ceremony than priests in the ordinary sense of the word.

Members of "let-live" societies, believing in the sacredness of life are in the habit of buying captured birds and fish, even big valuable turtles, in order to give them liberty. At the monasteries are places where these people support sheep, goats, and other animals, also big and little fishes, until they die, never allowing them to be killed for food. If fowls thus kept lay eggs, the eggs are buried. No ecclesiastical bodies could be fatter or more lazy than the pigs which I saw luxuriating in their comfortable styes the first time I visited the Ocean Banner monastery at Honam, opposite where the steamers land at Canton. The last time I was there the fat livings were vacant, as the incumbents had died—not by a butcher's knife, but perhaps from boredom and repletion.

As we entered the front door of this establishment two

martial idols, with sword in hand, confronted us. Pa
through the first courtyard and coming to a porch-like l
ing, our eyes fell upon four colossal images that coml
the grotesque and the hideous in equal proportions.
guard for Buddha the four quarters of the universe.
face of one is painted white, the faces of the others red, g
and blue respectively. The first idol holds an umbrella
second a stringed instrument, the third a sword, and
fourth a serpent. All four kings of heaven, as they are c
have many strips of red paper pasted upon them. T
contain either a record of vows to be performed if pray
answered, or thanks for favours already bestowed.

Going through this porch we came to the great shri
the monastery. Upon the central altar rests, in additio
the usual furniture, an imperial tablet upon which is inscr
"May the sovereign reign ten thousand years, ten thou
times ten thousand years." From the roof hang four ban
or streamers, and upon each of them in velvet letters is
name of O-mi-to-fat.

We saw the monks taking a meagre meal of rice in t
refectory. On boards suspended from the walls are inscr
quotations from the classics. As the brethren are not all
to speak when dining, it is supposed that they will inwa
digest the words of wisdom which in this way are set b
them, as well as their rice. In the kitchens we were at
huge boilers in which the rice is cooked.

Every monastery prides itself upon the possession
tooth (what a number of teeth he must have had !), a hai
some other relic of Buddha. This heirloom is preserved
bell-shaped dagoba made of white marble. In the mon
garden there is a pond containing sacred fish.

The last thing we were shown was a brick cremato
where, after death, the remains of the priests are burr
accordance with a rule that holds in reference to all Chi
Buddhist priests.

Nunneries in China are common, the inmates being for the most part girls, who preferred to be nuns than wives, or children of parents too poor to keep them. There may be virtuous nuns, but an adage runs—

> " Ten Buddhist nuns, and nine are bad,
> The odd one left is doubtless mad."

CHAPTER XXX

NEW YEAR'S DAY IN CHINA

A capon's destiny—Kites—The opening of the seals—New Year's wishes—
Frightened by their faces—Decorations—The birthday of every one—
Official and other devotions—No one has an empty mouth—Cathedral
music—Gifts—Ladies break away from the monotony of their lives—
Resolutions made—Words of good omen.

NEW Year's day and the few days following are, with the
Dragon and Moon festivals, the only time when the
Chinese cease from their exaggerated activity. Like our
Easter, the date upon which New Year's day falls is regulated
by the moon. It is generally about the end of February.

At the approach of the festival, street stalls are put up, as
at an English fair, for the sale of all kinds of things. The
owners are said sometimes to sell at a loss in order to realise
money to meet their liabilities, for New Year's day is the
greatest of the four annual settling-up times of the Chinese.
He who cannot pay his debts then is said to have a capon's
destiny, in allusion to the number of fowls killed at the
festival. The doors of his shop may be carried away and
evil spirits allowed to enter his premises. In these circumstances many commit suicide.

It is not considered good form to dun any one for debt on
such a joyful festival as New Year's day, so the creditor looks
about for his debtor with a lantern in the broad light of New
Year's day. By a social fiction the sun is not supposed to

have risen, for there is the lantern; it is still yesterday and the debt can be claimed.

But though the Chinese pretend to great honesty in paying their debts on New Year's day, some of them are not above robbing houses and otherwise behaving dishonestly in order to get money to do so. Many are like that coloured resident of Georgia, who complained that he was obliged "to work hard all day and steal all night in order to make an honest living."

Before Chinese New Year's time the gods, or at least some of them, leave the idols and go up to the other world to report to "the Pearly Emperor Supreme Ruler" how people have been behaving themselves during the year here below. "When the cat's away the rats climb over the bamboo fence," and when these gods are away men do what they like.

Though the great day for flying kites—a pastime in which the Chinese delight—is the ninth day of the ninth moon, they also indulge in it considerably as the new year approaches. The "wind chickens" or "paper eagles" are sometimes so large that it takes at least three strong boys to manipulate them. I once tried to pull one down to earth, and it nearly pulled me into the sky. They are of all shapes, resembling dragons, tigers, bats, centipedes, mosquitoes, and many kinds of birds. The hovering of a kestrel and the quick dive of a sparrow-hawk are beautifully imitated by expert guidance of the string. Sometimes strings attached to the kite are so arranged that as it passes through the air it sounds like an Æolian harp. At night lighted paper lanterns fastened to kites show up well.

As a sign that holidays are going to be held the seals in Government offices are deposited in a box and sealed up on the twentieth day of the twelfth month. "The opening of the seals" on the twentieth day of the first month is an occasion of much ceremony at some yamens.

What was commanded to the Israelites, "Thou shalt write

them upon the posts of thy house, and on thy gates " (Deut. vi. 9), is done by the Chinese when, before New Year's day, they paste red paper inscriptions on doorposts, junks, farm implements, and upon almost everything. There is nearly always a prayer for the " five blessings "—riches, health, love of virtue, longevity, and a natural death. A literary man's hall door would have on it such a wish as this :—

" May I be so learned as to secrete in my mind three myriad volumes,
   May I know the affairs of the world for six thousand years ! "

One pony's saddle had a red New Year's strip on it bearing this legend :—

" May this be a prosperous year, and everything be as I want it."

A shopkeeper would adorn his door with such mottoes as these:—

" May profits be like the morning sun rising on the clouds ! "
" May wealth increase like the morning tide which brings the rain ! "
" Manage your business according to truth and loyalty."
" Hold on to benevolence and rectitude in all your trading."

The inscriptions are generally made and sold at tables in the streets by literary men. On the doors themselves are put gold-speckled paper and new pictures of the " door gods."

Across the windows are pasted strips of paper bearing the notice " Chieh, the Supreme Duke, is here ; bad spirits, get you gone." Some two thousand years ago Chieh gained great power over evil spirits, and to-day, though they have wit enough to read writing they have not sense enough to know that they are being deceived, and therefore sneak away when they find that their old comrade is within. Another way of making a spirit think that he has been anticipated, is placing a little mirror over the front door. Seeing his own ugly face reflected, he will think that another spirit is in possession and will fear the consequences of poaching.

We may say here that the bit of glass which is often fastened on the front of a boy's cap is also intended to frighten evil spirits. Seeing themselves in the glass they run away and leave the child unharmed.

Just before New Year's day houses and temples are cleaned, and Chinamen themselves will venture to bathe in warm water in which are infused certain aromatic leaves.

The signboards of shops are festooned with red cloth, and over doors are placed highly coloured paper lanterns, artificial flowers and ornaments made of red and gilt paper with peacocks' feathers stuck into them. Strips of blue paper on doors indicate houses into which death has entered during the year. At the door of every house or in the reception-room are placed a branch of the New Year tree, a large citron called "Buddha's fingers," and a plant of narcissus, the last growing in pots containing no earth but only water and pebbles. Servants and children receive presents and acquaintances use such greetings as "I congratulate you on the New Year!" "May your wealth increase!" "May your hands obtain what your heart desires!"

New Year's day is considered the birthday of every Chinese person, and a child, even if only born the previous day, enters his second year upon it. On each succeeding New Year's day the Emperor is re-enthroned, and afterwards receives the congratulations of his ministers and the members of his household.

Tsao, the god of the hearth or kitchen, represented either by an image or by an inscription on paper placed over the oven, may be seen in all houses in China. This deity watches the everyday proceedings of the family, especially noting the talk of the women while they work. On the twenty-third of the twelfth moon the god is supposed to ascend to the world above, with a report of the family under whose roof he has spent the year. On this night offerings are presented to induce him to give as favourable a report as may be consistent with his notions of veracity. Barley-sugar will make his mouth sticky and prevent him from wagging his tongue too freely, so that is a common offering. On the last day of the old year the picture of the old kitchen god is taken down and a new one pasted up in its place. To the new god cakes, fruit, and other offerings are made next day.

At the dawn of New Year's day the head of each household gives thanks at a temporary altar in the reception-room to Heaven and Earth for past protection, and asks for its continuance during the year just begun. At the same time and place he offers the following gifts : five or ten small cups of tea, the same of samshu, different kinds of vegetables, five bowls of rice, ten pairs of chopsticks, an almanack of the New Year tied with red string for luck, two or more ornamental candles, and a pile of loose-skinned oranges. After this paterfamilias, in the name of the assembled family, worships and makes similar offerings to the ancestral tablets. A great *feu de joie* of crackers ensues, and then the men dress in handsome silk clothes and pay complimentary visits to the different branches of their family and to others. On the long red visiting-cards which they use are stamped, besides their names, pictures emblematic of offspring, official employment, and longevity, the three things most desired by a Chinaman. After handing in visiting-cards, they shake their own hands and not those of the people who are waiting to receive callers. Social inferiors pay their respects to superiors, pupils salute teachers, and children, who are beautifully dressed in clothes of many colours, prostrate themselves before their parents. Even the last baby of the family will take part in the ceremonies, and will wear a cap ornamented with eighteen gold, silver, or copper figures of the disciples of Buddha.

Relations coming to call are led to the domestic altar, where they do reverence to the ancestral tablets. Then tea, cakes, and sweetmeats are handed round and small packets of melon seeds, of loose-skinned oranges, and of sugar and flour made up into brown balls are given as presents. "During the first part of the first month," so runs a common saying, "no one has an empty mouth." This business of visiting and saluting goes by priority in the genealogical table, so a man in middle life may be heard to complain of the fatigues of New Year time, as he being of a "late generation" is obliged to kowtow to children two feet long as they are "older" than he!

And gods are visited as well as men. On Chinese New Year's day I have found the inside of a temple so interesting that I have remained there for a long time in spite of the choking smoke and deafening noise. The smoke came from the thousands of ornamental candles and incense-sticks that were lighted, each one by a worshipper, and by the mock or lie money which they set on fire and throw into two great bronze receptacles. The worst part of the noise, or perhaps we should say of the cathedral music, was caused by a man who, with a club in either hand, beat at the same time with all his might a huge drum and an equally large gong. All classes came to contribute to the burning and to make at least three chin-chins, from the elaborately dressed mandarin and his womankind to the little-dressed coolie with the one and only wife that he, poor fellow, could afford.

Rare fruits, fine tea, sweetmeats, silks, and ornaments are sent as New Year presents. A selection is made by the recipient, and the remainder returned with this note on the red ticket that accompanies them: "We dare not presume to accept such precious gifts." The compliment is returned up to the same value.

It is a tradition that when the people of Hang-Yang offered a pigeon as a New Year gift to a certain philosopher, he accepted the bird, but let it fly away and said, "All things should live happily on this day." This is the reason why many Chinese will not eat animal food upon New Year's day. All, however, partake of dumplings. These are to the Chinese New Year what plum-pudding is to our Christmas in England, and indeed the two days are celebrated much in the same way, only that the Chinese seldom get drunk. To eat cakes of ordinary grain on New Year's day instead of dumplings is considered like not having any festival. The food for the feasts is cooked before the first day of the year, as on that day no cooking is done.

Chinese New Year's holidays are spent for the most part in ingenious kinds of gambling, in the dreamy forgetfulness of opium, and in sitting well dressed, doing nothing, in erect blackwood chairs.

Great numbers of crackers, fastened together and suspended from the tops of houses to the bottom, are exploded on New Year's day, and the day before and after. These are meant to frighten away evil spirits. In places where there has been a particularly fierce fight with devils one walks knee-deep in the red paper *débris* of explosives. Drums, gongs, cymbals, and every article that will give forth a sound are banged indefatigably all day long and far into the night.

Ladies break away from the monotony of their lives at this season. From the fourth to the seventh day they worship at the shrine of the goddess who presides over marriage, and attend exhibitions of flowers in their best clothes and in the conspicuous disfigurement of paint and cosmetics. The fifteenth day of the first month, when the Feast of Lanterns is celebrated, is another ladies' day. They throng the streets at night to gaze at the illuminations and fireworks (the latter called the "letting off of flowers"), and to guess the riddles which are inscribed on lanterns hung at the doorways of houses.

The Chinese think that a new year brings to them a fresh

lease of life, and they make then as many fragile resolutions as we do.   On the last day of the year boys will shout out in the streets, *Mai saou* ("I will sell my idle ways"), with the laudable desire of being more diligent during the new year.

One must be very careful only to speak words of good omen on New Year's day.   The words that they write, too, on that day the Chinese think give a good or a bad character to the whole year, so they begin their letters with such words as "Happiness," "Wealth," "Long life."   Superstitious importance is also attached to the first person met on New Year's day.   To meet a fair woman on first going out is an omen of good luck, but to meet a woman is only one degree better than to meet a Buddhist priest, who is regarded as foreboding the worst possible fortune.

Of the many insults and acts of brutal, useless bullying that were inflicted upon the Chinese by the foreign armies after the Boxer trouble, none were more felt than the interruption and prohibition of New Year's festivities.   No one was allowed to explode fire-crackers.   Even formal bows on the streets were forbidden by the Japanese police.   It was not considered safe to perform the usual ceremonies even in the privacy of one's own courtyard.   Women were arrested for indulging in what they considered seasonable gambling.   Under these strange and bitter conditions many Chinese were heard to exclaim that it would have been better not to have any New Year at all!

CHAPTER XXXI

MISSIONARIES

I HAVE never been officially connected with foreign missions, and do not hold a brief for missionaries, but, being weary of ignorant abuse of people who, after all, are God's creatures, I would like to advance some extenuating circumstances from my experience in China why all the missionaries in that country should not be hanged.

Were missionaries cockroaches or black-beetles they could not have been more scorned than they were on board the ship that brought me across the Pacific on my way to Hong Kong. Even the captain, who seemed to be both a good and a sensible man, became mad when he spoke of them. I inquired why this was, and he answered, "One day when I was smoking a cigar a missionary walked up to me and said, 'Do you know, Captain, that you are committing the sin against the Holy Ghost by smoking?' This is why I am not in love with missionaries." "But why," I asked, "should you, on account of one, so furiously rage against all, especially as that one seems to have been a lunatic, or at least an idiot?

He may have been one of those persons who are not missionaries at all, because they have never been sent by proper authority, but have come into the mission-field for reasons of their own. It would be well-spent money were missionary societies to bribe idiots like the one you struck upon to stay at home lest they cause heathen Britishers, heathen Chinese, or any other heathen people to blaspheme." Unfortunately for the cause they have at heart some missionaries are without a saving sense of humour. One of these had "The Lord is my shepherd" painted on her trunk. This did not edify as she hoped it would when the notice "Not wanted on the voyage" was stuck on after it.

"I am going to send my boy to see the world," said the father of a not very presentable son. "Are you not afraid of the world seeing him?" asked a candid friend. Those who select missionaries cannot be too careful as to the specimens they allow the heathen to see. We should wash our soiled linen at home. I do not wish to defend certain untrained Americans who, coming out first as colporteurs, blossom into Reverend Doctors, and then trade in houses and land for the societies they represent, if not for themselves.

Before leaving Hong Kong I saw an annual consignment of female missionaries land in order to be distributed throughout China. Their physical appearance did not impress one. What waste of money to send out people whom a fever or two may sour and depress and necessitate their becoming returned empties! True, those who select female missionaries are on the horns of a dilemma. Well-favoured girls marry and leave the business. Anæmic, unladylike, partially deformed ones, who have no chance either at home or abroad in the matrimonial line, do not physically adorn the Gospel or make its message attractive to the heathen. If the beauty of holiness were always underneath an ugly exterior, we would not have made the above remark. And how much more attractive it is when it coexists with physical good looks and the ways of one who could not be mistaken for anything but a gentlewoman!

No people are more misunderstood or arouse more senseless prejudice than missionaries. They are frequently thought of as visionaries who imagine that a little street preaching will induce the Chinese or other heathen peoples to become Christians. In any case, it is asked, "Are not the heathen better left alone, and are not the religions they have the ones that are best suited to them?" These objectors I would answer by asking, "Have you gone with missionaries to their stations and seen them at work? Have you visited heathen temples and seen the people at worship?"

An English merchant who had come home was asked about a medical mission hospital in the Chinese town where he had resided. He replied that he had never heard of it, and did not believe that it was there. On his return to the Chinese town he found that the hospital was in the street in which he lived himself. The real work amongst natives is not seen by Europeans unless they go to look for it.

Not a few of those who scoff at missionary work are like the thief who, when convicted on the evidence of three witnesses of stealing a horse, complained that he could easily have produced a hundred witnesses who did *not* see him do so.

A missionary bishop in China related the following to me. He had at one time translated the New Testament into the Chinese that was understood in his district, and when doing so he used every now and then to call together natives, both Christian and heathen, and read to them his work as far as it had gone. When he had finished reading the first chapter of the Epistle to the Romans, in which St. Paul describes the condition of ancient heathen morality, one intelligent Chinese remarked, "The rest of your work you may have done in England, but what you have just now read so perfectly describes China, that it must have been written in the country." And the other hearers said the same. Even in the opinion of some of her own people, then, China does need a better religion and morality than she has.

And in proportion to the need in which China stands of the Gospel is the difficulty of making her comprehend and appreciate its message. To the Greeks of old the sublime self-sacrifice of the Cross of Christ seemed foolishness, and to the Chinese now it has, when first they hear it, the same appearance. To a missionary who had described the death of our Saviour, a Chinese remarked, "That Jesus Christ plenty big fool."

Those who know the crowd, the noise, the smells, and the heat in the narrow streets of a Chinese town, are aware that street preaching here at least, is, as a rule, impossible. What missionaries do is this. On first coming out they get teachers and work hard at the colloquial language of the district in which they are to be located. If the station be a well-established one, they will find in it a primary school, a high school, and what is proudly called a theological college. This last is composed of pupils from the two former who seem likely to become good catechists and native clergymen. "Suffer the little children to come unto Me," said our Lord, and the schools are intended to facilitate this result, and also as a means of getting hold of the grown-up relatives of the children.

We speak of the romance of war and of the romance of the mission-field, but on active service in both cases the arrangements are of a most practical nature.

But it may be asked, "Is not missionary effort like that of a blind fowl picking at random after worms?" to use a Chinese saying. It has been calculated that only the ninth part of a Chinaman falls per annum to the bag of each of the foreign and native Christian workers. Is the game worth the candle? The Lord Jesus Christ thought so when He gave His marching orders. Nor is the proportion between converts and workers much more satisfactory in the large cities of Great Britain.

It should be remembered by those who complain of the few converts made that mission influence extends far beyond the circle of actual adherents—that prejudices are modified, and confidence won from multitudes who as yet give no sign of any personal leaning to the foreign faith. Missionaries sow the seed, and though it may not fructify in their day, a glorious harvest may be reaped by their successors.

In her book "The Yangtze Valley" Mrs. Bishop states that a Chinese servant of hers said that he liked to serve missionaries because he never got boots thrown at his head "in the foreign teachers' houses." This quaintly alludes to the indirect and unconscious influence for good of missionaries. Control of temper amidst the trifling, perhaps, but continuous torments of the tropics, payment of wages agreed upon, kind treatment of servants—the fame of such things as these causes inquiry to be made about the "Jesus religion," and arouses a desire to learn what is the power making for righteousness which it contains. In this way is given a daily object-lesson of justice and unselfishness.

Those who have honestly tried to understand missionaries and their work know that, with few exceptions, their lives are a standing reproach to the self-indulgence of the average mandarin, not to speak of the European. What more natural than to sneer at missionaries and wish to get rid of the reproach?

Missionary work is humanising as well as proselytising, and every mission is a centre of light and leading. It is the only agency practicable for extending into the interior the influence of Western civilisation, for missionaries are the only foreigners who are in touch with Chinese native feeling. The official classes are aware of this, and hence their hostility to missionaries. They feel that the enlightenment of the millions means the extinction of their own authority over them.

European merchants in China, instead of abusing missionaries, ought to help them in every way, for while the purpose of missionaries is religious, they are unconsciously, perhaps, yet of necessity, unpaid commercial travellers. They speak the language of the people and penetrate into interior districts as merchants do not, and the contents of their houses, their clothing, their appliances of all kinds constitute at each mission station and as they travel a miniature exhibition of the superior conveniences which foreigners possess. In this way a market is made for the merchant by the much-abused missionary and his household.

Every one tries to use missionaries and no one shows any gratitude towards them. A British consul tells us that he has known mandarins, whose hostility to missionaries had brought on a riot, to send their valuables for safety to these same missionaries.

These two sayings are current amongst the Chinese: "Worship the gods as if they came, and if you don't it is all the same." "Worship the gods as if they were there, but if you worship not the gods don't care." People so indifferent to their own religion are not likely to be much prejudiced against another one.

On the subject of religion China is perfectly tolerant. Missionaries are not disliked because they preach Christianity, but because they are foreigners or suspected of being political agents. The people often say, "We have no objection to Jesus; doubtless He was good. Make an image of Him and put it by the side of our gods, and we will knock our heads before Him as well as before them. Some advantage may come from so doing." If missionaries are more frequently attacked by Chinese mobs than other foreigners, it is simply because they live in districts remote from naval or military protection. They are in direct contact with the natives, and are the first, because the handiest, victims to an anti-foreign rising. When urged to kill missionaries, Chinese

mobs do so with regret, and I have often observed that the
people, when let alone, seem to be fond of the "foreign
teachers." It is quite touching how even the poorest sometimes wish to give them presents.

Missionaries may not always have added the wisdom of a
serpent to the harmlessness of a dove, but as a class and
when they have been properly selected they are the greatest
force working in China for progress. They teach children in
their schools to be clean and to speak the truth. They have
done most of what has been done for female elevation. They
have led the way in establishing schools for Western education. Text-books of almost every class have been translated
by them.

As for medical missions, it is almost impossible to exag-
gerate the good they do. Yet even these last, though they
are the best advertisement of Christianity to those who have
benefited by them, are an offence or stumbling-block when
they are, as often happens, misunderstood. Medicine in
China is still largely looked upon as a black art akin to
sorcery, and, when one remembers of what loathsome ingredients the drugs of the Chinese medicine-man are often composed, one need not wonder at the readiness with which
the ignorant masses are made to believe that remedies so
efficacious as those administered by the "foreign devils" are
compounded of eyes and other parts of the human body.
Only a few years ago it was circulated that a missionary stood
upon the wall of the mission compound at Swatow hooking
the eyes out of people as they passed with a fishing-rod.

To raise persecution against Christians it was said, at the
time of the Boxer trouble in 1900, that they had poisoned the
wells and marked houses with a red substance in order that
those who dwelt in them might be stricken with sickness.

When the last sacrament is administered to a Roman
Catholic convert who is dying his friends have sometimes
been excluded from the room. One or more of these have

peeped in and seen the priest bending mysteriously over the sick man. This, coupled with the European custom of closing the eyes of the dead, may have given some colour to the horrible imputation that missionaries steal human eyes for medicine or photography.

Then for unmarried missionary girls to travel about, either alone or in charge of a male missionary, shocks at first Chinese notions of morality. Such conduct, it is thought by people who believe that the place for woman is the hearth, can have but one meaning, and to this conclusion they are assisted by the evil reputation of their own nunneries and monasteries.

However, the free and friendly intercourse of missionaries of both sexes only causes suspicion at first. Before long it becomes known that the single missionary ladies are not immoral, but very much the reverse, and that the married ones are not playthings and servants, but companions on an equality with their husbands, and intelligent advisers of them. Then the Chinese critics, changing their minds, begin to think that their own women should be raised to the same level, and that only foreign women working among them can bring about the desired change. " Your wife can teach as well as you," said a man to a missionary. " Our wives are wooden-headed ; they know nothing."

Certainly missionary ladies ought to receive a little training in business habits. One who had not this advantage over-drew by mistake her banking account. When informed of this by her bankers, she wrote back that they must be in error as there were still several cheques in her cheque-book.

The Chinese are very suspicious, and when they do not understand who people are or what is the nature of their work they will believe any explanation. That a missionary should come so far for no other reason than to teach a new religion is unintelligible to them. Surely, they think, behind what seems only a harmless craze there lurks a sinister design.

To many a Chinese a missionary appears an advance agent of the gunboat. Missionaries come, territory goes, and it is little wonder if the Cross has come to be thought of as the pioneer of the sword.

Abbé Huc tells how a mandarin asked him who the Lord of Heaven about whom he preached was, and suggested that he was the Emperor of the French. Even now the conviction is all too general that the propagation of Christianity is a political movement. Whatever may be said of Roman Catholic missionaries, this is certainly not true of Protestant ones. They object to be made political tools of their Governments at home, and do not want, if killed, to be avenged by executions enforced by gunboats. They know that if St. Paul and the other first apostles had been protected by gunboats we would not be Christians now.

The questions which are asked missionaries when they go for the first time to a remote place in China show the ignorance that prevails about them and the countries from which they come. If the missionary have a beard people "stare themselves full," and ask if he were born with it. Other questions will be such as these: "Why do not your people shave their heads, as we do?" "Why do you not have black eyes like we; have they faded?" "Why do foreign ladies wear coverings on their heads when they go out? it is just like men." "Is there a sun and a moon in your country?" "Are there hills and trees?" "Where is the country where the people have one leg, one arm, one eye, and where there are only women?" A difficult question to answer is the common one, "Why was Jesus Christ not born in China; how is it we did not hear of Him sooner?"

All classes in China are now giving Christianity a respectful hearing. The family bond is a help. They come over in families. A missionary friend of mine the other day baptized a grandfather aged fifty-seven, a son thirty-five, and a grandson eighteen. Even the bad and irreligious lives of nominal

Christians in the Far East cannot stop the progress of mission work.

Imitation is the sincerest flattery, and the preaching halls and medical dispensaries of Christian missions are being copied by the Chinese. Rooms are hired and lecturers paid to preach Confucianism, and well-to-do men subscribe to places where free Chinese medicines are given to the poor.

In order to allay prejudice a missionary should be a gentleman in heart. The civilities to be observed on entering or leaving a house, on welcoming guests or bidding them farewell, where and when to stand and sit, how to behave at table—these things must not be ignored by missionaries who would make their presence and their teaching acceptable.

A convert gets into trouble if he gives up subscribing to guilds and temple services, and the Christian Chinaman who refuses to perform ancestral worship is thought to receive the curses not of the living only, but of five previous generations of the dead. When proper missionaries are chosen they are large-minded enough to understand and sympathise with such difficulties. They teach positively and not negatively, and recognise what is good in those whom they try to convert— as, for instance, that the average Chinaman obeys the Fifth Commandment better than does the average Christian.

Missionaries in China who do not go about telling people that unless they believe this and that without doubt they shall perish everlastingly, but who desire to show a more excellent way than the way of Taoism, or even of Buddhism, these men should receive our sympathy and encouragement, for nowhere is missionary work as difficult as in China. Think, for instance, of the difficulty of explaining to an ancestor-worshipper such words as, "If any man come to Me and hate not his father, he cannot be My disciple. For I am come to set a man at variance against his father."

The divisions among Christians that are so perplexing to the heathen ought not to be put to the account of missionaries, as this much-maligned people did not make them. And certainly the missionaries whom I knew in China kept these sectarian distinctions as much as possible in the background, and each was careful not to build upon another man's foundation. A Chinese said to a friend of mine, "I am a Christian, a plopel (proper) Christian, a London Christian, all same as you." My friend explained that there was no superior brand of Christians in London, but the Chinese would persist in calling himself a "London Christian" because it was, under God, by means of the London mission that he was converted. Would it be just to accuse this mission of making a new sect called London Christians?

One of the "Problems of the Far East" that perplexes Lord Curzon is the missionary who, "taking with him a portmanteau full of Bibles, thinks that by dropping its contents here and there, he is winning recruits to the fold of Christ."

Had Lord Curzon globe-trotted a little longer in China he would have discovered that portmanteaus are quite unsuited to the climate, and that missionaries do not use them. Certainly missionaries have not much time for higher criticism, but few of them can be so ill-instructed as to think that all the Bible is of equal value or that it can be given with safety to heathen people without note or comment. "What is the educated Chinaman likely to think," asks Lord Curzon, "of Samuel hewing Agag in pieces before the Lord?" I fear that familiarity with the punishment of lingchi, or death by many cuts, in China would prevent people being troubled because a sort of lingchi was inflicted upon Agag. Much more in need of softening and explanation would an educated Chinaman consider the injunction that a man should leave father and mother and cleave to his wife.

Of course, there are people who have no power of adaptation and never should be missionaries. One such, before he had learned Chinese, was asked to give an address. " Say something," said an old missionary, "and I will interpret." The novice began, "My friends, truth is relative and absolute." "He says," interpreted the man of experience, "that he is very glad to see you."

Some Chinese who were meditating conversion are reported to have said, "If the foreign teacher will take care of our bodies, we will do him the favour to seek the salvation of our souls." It is often asserted that all Chinese Christians are like this—that they are only "rice Christians," who pretend to be converted in order to get rice, money, or the influence and protection which is supposed to be attached, and often is attached, even by Chinese officials, to Church membership.

There are hypocrites in China as well as in Britain, but that all converts are of this kind is proved to be untrue by the way Chinese Christians suffered torture and death rather than deny their faith during the Boxer persecutions of 1900. I have only known one missionary who, having considerable private means, helped to support his converts, and that was during the Boxer trouble, when they could not get employment. Missionaries are not such fools as they look.

A tea-grower near Foochow asked an Englishman known to the writer to buy his tea. "No," he replied, "I get as much tea as I require from my old customers." "What! Not buy my tea! I Christian all same as you." "I do not see any connection between your tea and your Christianity. I only buy unmixed tea."

I have had named to me many Christian Chinese merchants who lost much money because they would not keep open their places of business on Sunday. At Swatow a man used to go on board ships every Sunday to shave and cut hair. After he was baptized he ceased to do this. Hearing of his scruples, the captain of a ship laughed and said that a Chinaman would do anything for dollars. He sent and offered him twelve dollars if he would come and cut his hair on Sunday. The barber refused this, and also an offer of twenty dollars

from a passenger who had made a bet that the barber could
be bought.   Indeed, Chinese Christians give more than
they get.   In many parts of China, even very poor people
support their Churches, and Chinese who have emigrated to
Australia, the Straits Settlements, and elsewhere, pay missionaries to evangelise their countrymen at home, notably at
Canton.

The commonest criticism that is made about missionaries
is that their charity should begin at home, and that they
should not abandon the perishing British heathen.   This
generally comes from those who have gone abroad themselves
or from those who are asked to subscribe to home missions.
In great Britain we hear of people being so much preached to
that they are gospel-hardened, and certainly there are enough
evangelists there to give every one a chance of hearing of
Christ's kingdom.

As a matter of fact, however, nothing does the Church at
home so much good as thinking of and working for the Church
abroad.   It is the old story of the Russian traveller.   On the
point of perishing from cold he stumbled upon a man buried
in the snow.   He set to work to pull him out and rub him,
and the exercise kept in circulation his own blood.,   That
Church does most for the heathen at home that does most for
the heathen abroad.

Money lent to the Lord in obedience to His command to
evangelise the world is well invested.   America and Great
Britain may one day become not only almost but altogether
heathen, and we shall get a good return for the money
advanced if Chinese and Indian Christians are sent to
reconvert us.

CHAPTER XXXII

AS THE CHINESE SEE US

"Foreign devils are very singular"—"Just like monkeys"—"That's the
devil's house"—A foreigner is always suspected—A bare skin as a
mark of respect—Our European odour—Foreign smoke and foreign
dirt—The want of religion of foreigners—"Exceeding strange"—The
Platonic intermingling of sexes not understood — "And she has
manners too"—Morbid unrest—Curious rather than useful.

THE theory of Chinese sovereignty is that the Emperor,
or Son of Heaven, is monarch of the whole earth, and
that all other nations are his subjects and tributaries. Thinking that it would be a diplomatic thing to do, Lord Macartney,
when he went to Peking as Ambassador, took with him a
carriage and presented it to the Emperor Kienlung. This
was a mistake, for the gift was considered tribute.

Even in the treaty ports there are natives who have not
learned to discriminate between the various nationalities
represented there. In his "Chinamen at Home" Rev.
T. G. Selby thus writes: "Travelling on a boat crowded
with native passengers, I was amused at overhearing the
conversation of two simple countrymen. 'How much whiter
his skin is than ours!' 'Yes,' said the passenger addressed, 'foreign devils are very singular. They are born
entirely white or entirely black.' The man's impression
obviously was that colour was as uncertain as in a litter of
puppies, and that Sikh, Negro, and Englishman all came

from the same stock. The ignorance was perhaps a trifle uncommon, but the prejudice it represented is all but universal."

The Chinese call themselves the black-haired race, and all foreigners red-headed devils. It is related by Miss Gordon Cumming that one of her friends with bright red hair was travelling in a remote district of China with a companion whose hair was a nut-brown colour. Finding that they could not escape from the curiosity of the crowd, who struggled for a sight of them, they suggested that if the people must see them they should pay for the privilege. " Yes," they cried, "we will pay so many cash for a good look at you, but we can only pay half that sum for looking at the other foreign devil, as his hair is not nearly so red." The travellers, taking them at their word, collected a large quantity of cash, which they subsequently scattered for a general scramble, to the great delight of all present.

Not knowing or forgetting the origin of their queue, the Chinese think that it is unnatural for us not to have this appendage. In the interior of the country they will peep under a missionary's hat to be sure that there is not one coiled up inside.

A Chinese friend, who had not the smallest idea of being deficient in politeness, confided to the author of " Chinese Characteristics," that when he first saw foreigners it seemed most extraordinary that they should have beards all round their faces *just like monkeys*, but he added, reassuringly, "I am quite used to it now." This reminds us of what the people in another place said of a certain missionary, " He speaks our language; if his whiskers were shaven off he would be nearly as good looking as we are."

Chinese children often scream with fright when they see a European for the first time, especially if he have a red beard like the bogey-man depicted in their picture-books. The children thought that these were mythical personages—but no !

there is one of them in the flesh. They run to their mothers. Mother seizes the tearful little one and carries him into the house, putting at the same time her hand before his mouth to keep out the evil that is supposed to emanate from foreign devils. Not long ago at Tientsin a little girl got convulsions and literally died of dread when a German soldier harmlessly, as he thought, chucked her under the chin.

In the lately acquired British territory opposite Hong Kong, I heard a boy, when asked whose was a particular house, reply, "That's the devil's house." He meant nothing more than that the only European in the neighbourhood lived there.

A mandarin, after visiting a missionary known to me, questioned the missionary's house-boy about his master's habits, as though he were a wild beast. "What does he eat?" "How is it cooked?" "When does he go out?" and so on.

In the interior of China a foreigner is always suspected. He is supposed to be able to see into the earth and discover precious metals. If he is a missionary, he is a political agent come to get himself killed, so that his death may be an excuse for land-grabbing on the part of some European Power. If he engage in famine relief, it is thought that his ultimate object is to carry off people to his own barbarous country. Should he offer any food or drink to visitors, they think that death is in the pot. Even the ink with which a book is printed by a foreigner will be suspected of being poisoned. Many Chinese women are afraid to enter a foreigner's house lest they should be bewitched.

The unceremonious way in which our officials go about their business seems undignified to the Chinese. If, in our eyes, mandarins make a poor show when carried through streets in the centre of a crowd of fantastically dressed street boys and beggars, to the Chinese our consuls and people in authority cannot seem of much account when they walk about with pipe or cigar in mouth, and with, perhaps, no other retinue than a wife or a dog.

Chinese ladies dress, and do not undress, for evening parties, so they are greatly shocked when they hear that Western women do the reverse. One of the things that astonished the author of "Those Foreign Devils" was that when female foreign devils go to Court they regard "a bare skin as a mark of respect." Chinese ladies are also concerned because their European sisters do not wear visible trousers, and they cannot understand how they eat when their waists are girt in. For a woman to show her shape is considered in China most immodest. Even upon a man tight clothes can only be explained if the poor fellow have not enough cloth to cover himself properly. How, they ask, for pity's sake, can Europeans, with their closely fitting garments, catch vermin? A Chinese will feel the board-like shirt-front of a Westerner with wonder, and ask if his collar does not cut the wearer's throat.

I saw one day, at the Peak tramway station at Hong Kong, half a dozen Chinese ladies, apparently visitors to the island, dressed in the height of their fashion. Some British ladies stepped out of the cars wearing gowns that showed their figures and hats stuck over with artificial flowers and bits of birds. When they had passed, the Chinese ladies, pointing at their compressed waists and inartistic headgear, laughed in a way that should stagger European complacency.

Western women can see themselves as the Chinese see them by looking at a collection of wax or paper dolls on a street stall at China New Year's time. They will probably find some, as I have, dressed in European women's fashion, as understood, or caricatured by, the Chinese.

As for the clothes of Western men, they are thought to be melancholy, undignified, and generally absurd. "What," they ask, "can be worse for the health than to have the waistcoat of evening dress open in front, thus exposing the chest, a most vulnerable part?"

A friend told the writer that the first time he gave a swallow-tail coat to a new Chinese servant to brush he saw the boy round the corner holding the garment up to the light and shaking with mirth. "Why was it cut so in front and at the tails, what were the two buttons behind for; how did the thing go on?"

The Chinese think it strange that we should wear a hat in summer out of doors when it is warm, and take it off indoors in the depth of winter. They hold a fan before that part of the bare head or face where the sun would strike, which is surely more sensible than our plan of wearing a headdress in warm weather.

But, indeed, we have to consider not only how the Chinese see us, but how they smell us, for what they call our European odour is quite as nauseous to them as their yellow smell is to us. Think of that, ye well-tubbed Britishers! A missionary friend, who is a very clean man, told me that he has often been pained by seeing Chinese hold their noses when talking to him. They say that we smell rank because we eat beef.

Celestial dislike and prejudice, however, is more than skin deep. China is economically independent, and can produce what she wants herself. For this reason foreigners are regarded as intruders who bring hurtful things and set bad examples.

Dr. Legge, who laboured for forty years in China, had the following conversation with Kwo Sung-tâo after his arrival in London as Chinese ambassador in 1877. "You know," said the Chinaman, "both England and China; which country do you say is the better of the two?" Dr. Legge replied, "England." The ambassador was disappointed, and added, "I mean looking at them from a moral stand-point—from the standpoint of righteousness and benevolence." "After some demur and fencing," writes Dr. Legge, "I replied again, 'England.' I never saw a man more surprised. He pushed his chair back, got on his feet, took a turn across the room, and cried out, 'Then how is it that England insists on our taking her opium?'" It is significant that the Chinese call opium foreign smoke and foreign dirt.

In a memorial which was addressed to the Emperor of China in 1884 by the High Commissioner Pêng Yu-lin, it was stated that "since the treaties have permitted foreigners from the West to spread their doctrines, the morals of the people have been greatly injured."

A Chinaman defined a Christian as one who "eats beef" (thought a wrong thing to do in the south of China) and says "God damn!" It is to be feared that this is not an uncommon impression of the religion, or want of religion, of foreigners that is formed, at least in the treaty ports. The Chinese say that while we profess Christianity, its spirit influences our actions far less than do economic considerations, that Christianity is even less to us than is Confucianism to them, and that it is like our impertinence to send missionaries to China.

The Chinese think that we neglect and ignore the five great relationships which are taught to them in their classics —the relationship of sovereign to subject, of father to son, of husband to wife, of younger brother to older, and of friend to friend.

Celestials observe that in Western countries when a son comes of age he goes where he likes, does what he chooses, and has no necessary connection with his parents nor they with him, and they think this the behaviour of a grown calf or colt to the cow or mare, proper for brutes but not for human beings. By the Chinese, trees are raised for shade and children for old age.

Writing of the things which astonished him most in Europe, a Chinaman said, "When sons and daughters are grown up, the parents need no longer look after them, but may let them be altogether their own masters. Children then regard their parents as strangers, and merely show them courtesy when they see them. The most respectful form of this courtesy is to apply their mouths to the right and left lips (*sic*) of the elder with a smacking sound." The kissing in which foreign devils indulge seemed to their critic " exceedingly strange " ("Those Foreign Devils," p. 81). He tries in the words quoted to make intelligible that which in China is an unknown practice. Even a mother does not kiss her baby, though she will press it to her cheek.

The Chinese are of opinion that our marriage laws are very foolish. " Only fancy," they say, " a European cannot legally have a concubine, even when he has no son, and his wife is old or no longer pleasing to him." The Platonic intermingling of sexes in Western society the Chinese do not understand ; they are sure that our treatment of women is a mixture of imbecility, ill-breeding. and buffoonery.

A Chinese opponent of railways lately wrote that they would be useless in China as far as women are concerned. "The wives and daughters of a European (*sic*) take no pleasure in staying at home ; but, in the case of our womankind, gadding about is held in great disrepute."

The author of a native work called "The Sights of Shanghai " complains that foreigners and their wives stroll about in the public gardens arm-in-arm, and shoulder to shoulder, without any bashfulness whatever." For men and women to talk together in public is, in the opinion of the Chinese, bad, but for them to shake hands or take each other's arm is barefaced immorality. Etiquette in the Flowery Land requires that men and women passing things to each other should lay them upon a table instead of handing them directly. So far is this carried that one of the classic books raises the question whether, if a woman is drowning, it is permitted even to her brother-in-law to take her by the hand to save her life. This being so, we may imagine what the Chinese think of Western ladies who dance with the arms of unrelated men about their waists. The amah (or nurse) of a friend of mine, when told by her mistress that this was really done, exclaimed, "Vely same!" ("Very shameful").

A Chinese critic of "foreign devils" thus describes a European dancing party. "Invitations are sent to an equal number of men and women, and after they are all assembled, tea and sugar, milk and bread, and the like, are set out as aids to conversation. Then the host decides what man is to be the partner of what woman, and what woman of what man. This being settled, with both arms grasping each other, they leave the table in pairs, and leap, skip, posture and prance, for their mutual gratification. A man and a woman previously unknown to one another may skip together."

When the Chinese hear of the Christian precept that a man should leave his father and mother and cleave to his wife, they are, if good Confucianists, horror-stricken; for Confucianism requires a man to cleave to his father and mother, and to compel his wife to do the same.

We say that the Chinese worship their ancestors, and they retort that Western nations worship their wives. They hear of men amongst us adoring and being devoted to their wives, and if any of them get hold of the Prayer-book of the English Church they see that when a man is being married he says to the woman, "With my body I thee worship." Is not this proof positive?

Some of the manners that do us credit astonish the Chinese. They think, for instance, that it is very strange we should hand chairs to women, make way for them in the streets, carry things for them, condescend to eat with them, or to use the same basin that they have used, and that we should treat them generally as equals, if not superiors.

Two Chinese, handsomely dressed in the native style of

gentlemen, sat down to dinner in the saloon of a steamer plying between Canton and Hong Kong. They both understood English, and one was an Oxford graduate. "Are Chinese allowed to travel first-class, Captain?" called out an American lady. "Oh, yes," replied the skipper, "we take Chinese, Americans, and all nations." Then the very lady-like Yankee, turning to the Oxford graduate, asked, "And how do you like our food, and our knives and forks, John?" The Chinaman answered politely that he was becoming almost as expert with knife and fork as with chopsticks. After a little while, turning to the captain at whose side he sat, he softly asked, "Do you wonder now that we Chinese are not in love with foreigners?" I had this from the captain himself.

The Chinese think that our manners are those of barbarians. It is not necessary or possible for Europeans living in China to learn the three hundred rules of ceremony or the three thousand precepts of behaviour that are laid down in Chinese classics, but we might put into practice a few of the elementary principles of Christianity, and then we would be thought to be almost as good as Confucianists. Certainly the foreigner who does not take the trouble to learn even the alphabet of Chinese politeness cannot avoid giving frequent offence unconsciously. For instance, if he wear spectacles and do not remove them when a visitor comes into his room, he will be thought very rude. The Chinese strongly object to be looked at through glasses.

When we show manners the Chinese are surprised. A lady told me that on a recent occasion, when she went into a shop at Canton, the door was soon blocked up by a crowd of idle gazers. My friend, who speaks Cantonese well, said to the crowd in that dialect, "I beg your pardon, would you allow me to go out?" They at once made room for her, and she heard them remarking, "She speaks our language, and she has manners too!"

The Chinese do not think that the subjects upon which we examine our students are as important as they seem to us. At the time of a recent examination for degrees at Peking the conversation of a Chinese official and of an English one turned on the examinations. The former remarked, "I understand that examinations in the West are all about clocks, watches, and such things — the mechanical arts."

Our idea of progress is to have railways and other means of motion, and to be always moving about. To the Chinese this seems to be morbid unrest. They say that we do not live, so intent are we in increasing the means of living, and that in consequence we are always discontented.

The Chinese highly approve of the tramway cars, lavatories, and fire-engines of the West, but many of our contrivances are, in the opinion of the educated, curious rather than useful, and in that of the ignorant connected with magic, and with magic Confucius warned them to have nothing to do. Whatever he may pretend for the sake of advantage, the most unprogressive yellow man despises the most inventive white man. The inventiveness of the latter is, in the eyes of the former, no more worthy of respect than is the cunning of a fox or the strength of an elephant.

Still, we never know what a Chinese is feeling under his cloak of stolidity. One did allow himself this expression of surprise when he saw for the first time a train on the new railway at Canton, "No pullee, no pushee, but go like hellee!" The huge steamers, too, that glide into Hong Kong, with apparently nothing to move them, seem very magical.

When we object to the smells in Chinese cities, the inhabitants say, "They are surface smells; they will evaporate," and rightly think that their system of drainage, or rather of no drainage, is far less dangerous than is our underground drainage.

Few Chinese visitors to England think as much of us

as we do of ourselves. Rather they are shocked at the foulness of our city slums, at the drunkenness and licentiousness upon the streets, at our murder and divorce records, at the figures of the national drink-bill.

Chinese who have travelled in Europe say that our system of having a different currency in each country, however near to each other, is very inconvenient. This is true, but it does not come well from those who have coins of which it takes about a thousand to make a dollar. In their opinion our prisons are absurdly comfortable, but they admire the school system by which we try to keep people out of prison.

The Viceroy of Canton once said to Sir Henry Blake, Governor of Hong Kong, from whom I heard it, "I cannot understand you English. You keep people more comfortable in prison than ever they were in their lives, and expect in this way to prevent crime. Just send some of those ruffians who go from us to Hong Kong back to me, and I'll cut off their heads. Why go to the expense of keeping alive those who will not work for a living?"

The Chinese say that Europeans do not know how to make tea. To put milk and sugar into it is as horrible, in their opinion, as it would be in ours to put them into old port wine. Either milk or sugar destroys bouquet and flavour.

The Chinese and our interpretation of things are so different! Here is an illustration. To bring me to conduct Divine Service at two forts at Hong Kong, a steam launch used to be hired by Government. Orders were given to the Chinese cockswain, and these he wrote in his own language on a piece of paper. A friend of mine finding one of these papers and knowing Chinese, thus translated it to me, "To fetch the old man who tells stories to the soldiers in fort——" The Chinese thought that my craft was the same as that of his countrymen, who earn a living by spinning yarns to the crowd at street corners. After all, the Gospel is "the old, old story."

The Chinese must misunderstand us as often as
understand them.   The regimental pet of the Roya
Regiment is a large white goat.   When a battalion
regiment was in Hong Kong the animal used to be le
the band by its silver-mounted head-collar every
when they marched to the parade service.   It was,
the most regular church-goer in Hong Kong.   A c
Chinese, many of them visitors to Hong Kong, wou
outside the Church to see the battalion march up.   (
the general's wife, observing these people looking at tl
remarked to the writer, " The Chinese must think
worship that goat!"   "Certainly," I answered;   "\
less to go upon, a Western globe-trotter would i
Chinese goat-worshippers."

Index

Lightning Source UK Ltd.
Milton Keynes UK
UKHW020652241218
334505UK00008B/630/P